THE CULT OF THE
VIRGIN MARY

THE CULT OF THE
VIRGIN
MARY

PSYCHOLOGICAL ORIGINS

MICHAEL P. CARROLL

PRINCETON UNIVERSITY PRESS

LIBRARY OF CONGRESS CATALOGING IN PUBLICATION DATA WILL BE
FOUND ON THE LAST PRINTED PAGE OF THIS BOOK

ISBN 0-691-09420-9
ISBN 0-691-02867-2 (PBK.)

THIS BOOK HAS BEEN COMPOSED IN LINOTRON BEMBO

FIRST PRINCETON PAPERBACK PRINTING, 1992

PRINCETON UNIVERSITY PRESS BOOKS ARE PRINTED ON ACID-FREE
PAPER AND MEET THE GUIDELINES FOR PERMANENCE AND
DURABILITY OF THE COMMITTEE ON PRODUCTION GUIDELINES FOR
BOOK LONGEVITY OF THE COUNCIL ON LIBRARY RESOURCES

PRINTED IN THE UNITED STATES OF AMERICA

7 6 5 4 3

For my parents,
WILLIAM CARROLL *and* OLGA CIARLANTI,
who provided the opportunity,
and for
HERBERT THURSTON, S.J. (1856-1939),
who pointed the way,
and to the memory of
KARI CONNIDIS BOYDELL (1984-1985),
whom I do and will miss.

CONTENTS

CONTENTS

LIST OF TABLES

There is an episode in Benjamin Disraeli's novel *Tancred* (1845) in which the young English hero of that name falls asleep in a quiet garden near Jerusalem, and awakens to find himself in the presence of a young woman. By her costume and manner, he recognizes immediately that she is a Palestinian Jew. On her part, she recognizes Tancred to be a European Christian, but is uncertain as to what sort of Christian he is. To find out she asks him, "Pray, are you of those Franks [European Christians] who worship a Jewess, or of those who revile her, break her images and blaspheme her pictures?" The woman's implication (and, by extension, Disraeli's as well) is that to the outsider there are really only two types of Christian: those who worship the Virgin Mary and those who do not. Tancred responds in the orthodox manner, by suggesting that he venerates the Virgin but does not worship her. The remainder of the conversation becomes a device to argue for the Jewish origins of all Christian religions, which is one of the major themes of Disraeli's book. Nevertheless, the conversation ends by emphasizing again the point on which it started: "We have some conclusions in common," says the young woman. "We agree that half Christendom worships a Jewess and the other half a Jew."

Most scholars interested in the study of religion might take issue with the bald assertion that intensity of Marian devotion is the only thing that differentiates the various Christian churches. But few, I suspect, would quarrel with the assertion that the Roman Catholic emphasis upon Mary is one of the things that most distinguishes the Roman Catholic Church from other Christian groups. All the more surprising, then, that scholarly studies of the Mary cult are so few. The general neglect of the Mary cult by sociologists of religion seems especially surprising, given their great concern over the past ten or fifteen years with the study of other religious cults.

One of the clearest definitions of the term "cult" has been given by Swatos (1981: 20), who defines a cult as a "collectivity centering around a real or imaginary figure whose followers believe that their lives are made better through activities which honor or are proscribed by the leader." This definition seems implicit in virtually all sociological studies of cults, and the Mary cult clearly falls within this definition. Yet if we survey the now vast sociological literature on the subject, we find dozens of articles and books on the general subject of cults, and more on particular cults such as Scientology, the Hare Krishnas, Christian Science, est, the Way, The Divine Light Mission, and, of course, the Unification Church of the Reverend Moon—but very few works on the Mary cult among Catholics.

What explains this general neglect? Does anyone doubt that over the centuries the Mary cult has attracted a far greater number of adherents than will ever be attracted by the Church of Scientology, the Hare Krishnas, and so on? Even today, when mainstream religion is supposed to be in decline, how many cults can boast anything approaching the twelve million pilgrims a year who go to the Shrine of Our Lady of Guadalupe, or the four and one-half million a year who go to the shrine at Lourdes? Possibly this neglect of the Mary cult reflects only a predilection for the exotic, or perhaps a lack of concern with history.

Quite apart from the Mary cult's intrinsic importance, there is a second and more practical reason that might have led to greater scholarly concern with the Mary cult: ecumenism. Simply put, the Mary cult is probably the single greatest obstacle to the eventual reunification of the Christian churches. John Henry Newman (1967 [1865]: 174-177), for instance, told us long ago that there were two great barriers to his conversion to Catholicism: the doctrine of transubstantiation, and the Catholic emphasis upon Mary. Newman's reservations about the Mary cult have been echoed time and time again by any number of Protestant theologians, and, at least since Vatican II, by an increasing number of Catholic theologians. Yet despite its obvious relevance to the ecumenical movement, the study of this cult has been neglected.

The Mary cult has not, of course, been ignored completely. Even if we overlook the obviously devotional material and those works concerned only with theology, there remain a number of scholarly works that do touch upon the Mary cult, if only briefly. Most of these, however, take that cult (or some aspect of it) as a given, and then relate it to other aspects of the social order. In her very popular book, for instance, Warner (1976) takes for granted the existence of the Mary cult and argues that it has served to lower the status of women over the centuries; there are any number of investigators (see, for instance, Wolf, 1958; Lafaye, 1976; Kurtz, 1982) who have assumed the cult of

Our Lady of Guadalupe in Mexico as a given, and have argued that this cult served to integrate Indians into the Spanish-dominated society of post-Conquest Mexico; the Turners (1982) took as their starting point the apparitions at LaSalette and at Lourdes, and went on to argue that these apparitions proved popular because the message associated with each addressed concerns typical of nineteenth-century Europe; and so on.

The approach taken in this book, however, is quite different. My concern is not with the effects of the Mary cult on society but rather with the question of origins. By this I mean the sociological, psychological, and historical processes that have given rise (and continue to give rise) to the Mary cult as we know it today. Why, for instance, is Mary both "Virgin" and "Mother," simultaneously? This juxtaposition of qualities was not typical of most earlier mother goddesses in the Mediterranean area. Why was the Mary cult absent in the first four centuries of the Christian era, only to appear relatively suddenly in the fifth? Why has the Mary cult always been stronger in certain areas of Europe than in others? Why do apparitions of the Virgin occur to certain people at certain times in certain places rather than to other people at other times in other places? These are all questions relating to the origins of the Mary cult, and these are the questions that this book is designed to answer. The answers will provide us, as well, with some novel explanations for many of the incidental features of the Mary cult—such as, for instance, why Marian scapulars have had (until recently, at least) to be made of wool, or why the Miraculous Medal, one of the most popular of all Marian cult objects, has on its obverse two pierced hearts surmounted by a large "M." Finally, the same arguments used to explain aspects of the Mary cult will provide us with answers to some questions that might seem to have nothing to do with the Mary cult, such as why the Roman cult of the Great Mother took hold in Italy in precisely the second century B.C., and why the earliest images of the crucifixion of Jesus Christ in Christian art appear in the early part of the fifth century, at the same time that the Mary cult first emerged.

In pursuing the question of origins, it will be convenient to divide this book into two parts. Part I will be concerned with the Mary cult as a whole. Chapter One will lay out a number of patterns that seem to be associated with this cult. Chapter Two will evaluate most of the hypotheses about the Mary cult that have been proposed, if only in passing, by earlier investigators. As we shall see, some of these are supported by the data, others clearly are not. None of these hypotheses, however, seems capable of explaining all the empirical patterns outlined in the first chapter. Chapter Three is the heart of the book, since it introduces the psychoanalytic interpretation that can be used to explain most aspects of the Mary cult, including those described in Chapter One. Chapter Four is a continuation of the argument in Chapter Three, and is specifically concerned with using the argument developed there to explain why the Mary cult emerged suddenly in the early part of the fifth century. Chapter Five is not concerned with the Mary cult at all, but rather with some observations about the nature of Roman religion that seem inescapable, given the explanation of the Mary cult that has so far been developed.

The second section of the book focuses specifically upon the study of Marian apparitions. This focus derives partly from the fact that these apparitions have always played a central role in the history of the Mary cult, and partly from the fact that the processes that give rise to these apparitions represent an intensification of those that generate support for the Mary cult in general. Chapter Six is, in effect, a general introduction to the study of Marian apparitions. After making an initial distinction between those apparitions likely to have been hallucinations and those likely to have been illusions, this chapter will focus upon Marian hallucinations and describe some of the general processes that give rise to such events. Chapter Seven will consider in detail three particular Marian apparitions, all of which occurred in France during the nineteenth century: at Paris (to Catherine Labouré) in 1830, at LaSalette in 1846, and at Lourdes in 1858. Chapter Eight will consider two more well-known apparitions: those that occurred at Fatima, Portugal, in 1917 and those at Tepeyac, near Mexico City, in 1531. In Chapter Nine we will consider three Marian apparitions that seem to have been illusions—those at Pontmain, France, in 1871; at Knock, Ireland, in 1879; and at Zeitoun, Egypt, in 1968.

The book will conclude with a brief chapter that speculates on the likely development of the Mary cult in the near future.

I want to thank the anonymous reviewers of my manuscript whose comments were insightful and helpful. I also want to thank both Gail Ullman, Social Science Editor for Princeton University Press, and Margaret Case, copyeditor for this book, for their patience, their hard work, and their encouragement. Finally, I must thank Veronica D'Souza, Grace McIntyre, and Denise Statham, whose typing skills made it much easier to write this book than would otherwise have been the case.

London, Ontario
September 1985

PART I
ORIGINS OF THE MARY CULT

SOME OBSERVATIONS AND PATTERNS

In the next few chapters we will be considering several theories and hypotheses about the Mary cult. Suppose, just for the sake of argument, that some of these were more correct than others. How would we know this? The problem is not trivial. There seems little point in considering various explanations of the Mary cult unless we first decide how to evaluate them. In a few cases, it will be possible to use a variant of the hypothetico-deductive procedure favored by philosophers of science and by social scientists attracted to that field. That is, in some cases it will be possible to derive a precise prediction from the hypothesis being considered and to then test that prediction using quantitative data. Generally, however, the nature of the question being considered will preclude such a procedure. How, then, to evaluate these hypotheses?

The only reasonable alternative would seem to be some type of criterion of intelligibility. We can, in other words, evaluate a theory by determining the degree to which the theory makes intelligible a wide range of seemingly disparate observations by allowing us to order those observations into a single coherent pattern. The pros and cons of using a criterion of this sort to evaluate scientific theories has been widely discussed in the philosophy of science and there seems little point in duplicating that effort here.[1]

But if we say that a good theory is one that brings a sense of order to a range of observations, then obviously our first task—before considering any particular theory or hypothesis about the Mary cult—is to delineate the more important patterns observed to be associated with that cult. The observations about the Mary cult established in

[1] For a good discussion on the use of an "intelligibility" criterion in evaluating scientific theories see Cheshire (1975).

this first chapter must become part of the yardstick against which all theories of that cult must be judged.

My own review of the scattered literature on the Mary cult suggests that there are three patterns in particular that must be accounted for by a good explanation. They have to do, respectively, with the historical development of the cult, the distinctiveness of Mary in contrast to the goddesses found in the Classical religions, and the geographical distribution of the cult.

HISTORICAL DEVELOPMENT

Protestant theologians have always had two strong objections to the Mary cult. The first is that there is little or no basis for such a cult in the New Testament. Mary, after all, is mentioned in only about a dozen passages, and usually only in passing. The Gospel of Mark, for instance, which is generally taken to be the earliest of the four Gospels, mentions her only once (Mark 6:3), and the Acts of the Apostles, our earliest record of the early Church, also mentions her only once (Acts 1:14).

The second objection is historical: there is little or no evidence that anything like the Mary cult existed during the first four centuries of the Christian Church. Hilda Graef (1963a; 1963b), who is perhaps the most well known of the modern Catholic apologists for the Mary cult, has responded to this criticism by arguing that the neglect of Mary in the early Church has been overemphasized. But she can point to only four bits of evidence that seem to indicate Marian devotion in the early Church: Mary is mentioned in some of the apocryphal works, notably including the *Protoevangelium of James*, there is a reference in the late fourth century to an apparition of the Virgin Mary to one Gregory the Wonderworker, who is supposed to have lived a century earlier; there is a papyrus fragment that dates from the early fourth century, which seems to record a prayer asking for Mary's intercession; and the Eastern Church (though not the Western) had introduced a single feast of the Virgin sometime before the beginning of the fifth century. I must emphasize that these four observations constitute the whole of Graef's evidence in support of the view that popular Marian devotion existed in the early Church.

But even Graef, along with most other Catholic commentators

(see, for instance, Hirn, 1957 [1912]: 188-189; Laurentin, 1965: 41; Greeley, 1977: 95) seems willing to admit that popular devotion to Mary did not become widespread until the latter part of the fifth century. Almost invariably, these Catholic commentators see this increase in Marian devotion as an aftermath of the Council of Ephesus (A.D. 431), at which Mary was proclaimed to be the *Theotokos*. Literally, this term means "God-bearer" but it is usually translated these days as "Mother of God."

Whatever the impetus, there is no doubt that popular devotion to Mary did increase in the fifth, sixth, and seventh centuries. The first church in the city of Rome dedicated to Mary, for instance, was dedicated to her within a few years after the Council of Ephesus (Denis-Boulet, 1960: 65-66). The earliest Marian shrine was apparently a sanctuary near Constantinople, where there is a record that the "veil of the Virgin" was venerated from about the middle of the sixth century onward (Graef, 1963a: 138). In the West, the earliest feast of the Virgin was the Purification, which was introduced in the latter part of the seventh century, and was quickly followed by the introduction of feasts commemorating the Assumption, the Annunciation, and the Nativity of Mary (ibid.; 142-143).

Generally, it appears that from the latter part of the fifth century onward there was a steady increase in the development of the Mary cult that reached its apogee, in the opinion of most commentators, in the eleventh and twelfth centuries. The relatively sudden appearance of a well documented Mary cult in the fifth century, then, is obviously one of the observations that must be accounted for.

MARY AS VIRGIN MOTHER

It is very tempting to see Mary as simply the latest in a long line of mother goddesses who have dominated Mediterranean religions over the past several millennia. This would be a mistake. Although there are similarities, Mary is quite different from almost all earlier mother goddesses in at least one very important way: she is completely disassociated from sexuality.

To understand exactly how Mary is disassociated from sexuality, we must remember that to Catholics Mary is simultaneously both mother *and* virgin. There is nothing problematic about the association

(5)

of Mary with the "mother" label: she is mother because she gave birth to Jesus Christ. On the other hand, the association of Mary with the "Virgin" is more complex, if only because the assertion that Mary was (or is) a virgin means three distinct things in Catholic tradition. First, it refers to a belief in the Virgin Birth, or more precisely, the Virginal Conception, that is, to the belief that Mary conceived Christ as the result of divine intervention and without aid of sexual intercourse. Second, it refers to what Catholic theologians term Mary's *in partu* virginity, which is the belief that Mary's maidenhead was never ruptured even though she gave birth. Finally, it refers to Mary's perpetual virginity, that is, to the belief that Mary abstained from sexual intercourse even after the birth of Christ.

Belief in the Virginal Conception is of course a belief common to almost all Christian sects, and is not uniquely associated with the Roman Catholic Mary cult. The motif of the virgin who is impregnated by a god and who gives birth to a hero was part of a great many myths and legends in the pre-Christian Greco-Roman world, as well. The most famous story incorporating this motif concerned Romulus (the legendary founder of Rome), and his twin brother Remus, who were supposedly born to a mother who had been impregnated by the god Mars.

The other two beliefs, however—Mary's *in partu* virginity and her perpetual virginity—are more closely associated with Roman Catholicism alone, and are generally rejected by Protestants. The basis for this rejection is the New Testament itself, since all four Gospels make explicit reference to the "mothers and brothers" of Jesus (Matt. 12:46-49; Mark 3:31-34; Luke 8:19-21; John 2:12). Likewise, in his Letter to the Galatians (1:19), St. Paul talks of having met "James, the Lord's brother." For most Protestants, these passages clearly suggest that Mary had other children after the birth of Christ, and thus that she was not a lifelong virgin. Catholics, however, have always sought to give these passages an interpretation that left their belief in Mary's *in partu* virginity and in her perpetual virginity intact. Over the centuries, for instance, a few Catholic commentators have suggested that the "brothers" in these passages were Joseph's children by a previous marriage. The prevailing view (especially among Catholic commentators today) has been that the term translated as "brothers" really refers to "kinsmen" of some sort and not to siblings.

I suspect that most non-Catholic readers will have little difficulty with the assertion that an emphasis upon Mary's perpetual virginity is a central element in the Catholic Mary cult. They may experience more difficulty, however, in accepting the assertion that Catholic doctrine could be so concerned with Mary's *in partu* virginity, that is, with whether or not the hymen of "the simple maid of Galilee" (to borrow Luther's phrase) remained intact throughout her life. Let me emphasize, therefore, that the issue of Mary's *in partu* virginity was a major concern of the early Church, and was an issue addressed by all the great theologians of the period. (For some indication of the Christological implications of Mary's *in partu* virginity, and thus why this was considered such an important issue in the early Church, see Graef, 1963a). In fact, a belief in Mary's *in partu* virginity is still very much a part of Catholic doctrine and still very much emphasized by Catholic theologians (see Smith, 1980; Hardon, 1975: 151; Owens, 1967: 693-695; Miegge, 1955: 36-52).

The issue of Mary's *in partu* virginity is worth stressing because it is only by focusing on this that we can justify the often-made and quite facile identification of Mary with the great virgin mother goddesses of the ancient Near East, such as the Canaanite goddesses Astarte and Asheroth, the Akkadian goddess Ishtar, and the Sumerian goddess Inanna. In what is still the best comparative study of these Near Eastern goddesses, Patai (1967) notes that they were invariably seen as *in partu* virgins, that is, as possessing intact maidenheads. But he also notes that all these goddesses were invariably associated with sexual promiscuity. All these goddesses, for example, were seen as taking on a wide range of human and divine lovers, and in some cases (all discussed at various points of Patai's book) we have exceedingly graphic descriptions of the couplings between these goddesses and their lovers. The modern rationalist, of course, might argue that it makes no sense to talk of a goddess who is sexually promiscuous and yet who preserves her maidenhead intact—to which the Sumerian rationalist would presumably respond by saying that it makes more sense than arguing that a woman like Mary could give birth and yet preserve *her* maidenhead intact.

In any event, given that these Near Eastern goddesses were, like the Virgin Mary, thought to have intact maidenheads, Mary's uniqueness lies only in the fact that she was, unlike them, a perpetual virgin. In other words, Mary is unique because she alone was completely disassociated from the act of sexual intercourse.

Mary's distinctiveness is even more clearly established when she is compared with the major goddesses of the Greco-Roman world. Many of these goddesses were clearly mothers, and many were clearly virgins, but few if any were virgin mothers. Mary, for instance, has often been compared to the goddess Demeter (called Ceres by the Romans), who was certainly a mother figure by virtue of her association with agricultural fertility. Demeter was not, however, a virgin in the sense of being disassociated from sexual intercourse. One of the oldest traditions surrounding her, for example, tells of her coupling with Iasion "in a field that had lain fallow and was thrice ploughed" (Rose, 1928: 94); and Iasion was by no means her only lover. Artemis (whom the Romans called Diana) and Athena (Minerva) were well known virgin goddesses, but there is little or no basis in Greco-Roman mythology for portraying either as a mother figure.

The case of the goddess Isis merits special consideration for two reasons: the Isis cult was one of the most popular and widespread of all the goddess cults in the Greco-Roman world, and Isis has been seen, perhaps more than any other goddess, as a precursor to the Virgin Mary. At first glance, Isis does seem very similar to Mary. Most of the myths involving her, for instance, portray her as a devoted wife to her husband Osiris and a devoted mother to her son Horus. There is certainly no report of Isis engaging in sexual intercourse with anyone apart from her husband. Moreover, quite apart from the figure of Isis herself, we know that there were periods during which the women who attended Isiac temples in Rome were supposed to refrain from sexual intercourse.[2]

Nevertheless, if you had said "Isis" to the average Roman during the period of the empire, he or she would almost certainly have thought "sexual promiscuity." The association of Isis with unsavoury sexuality would have been due in part to the fact that she and Osiris, though husband and wife, were also brother and sister. Although brother-sister marriage had been routinely practiced by the Greek-speaking Ptolemaic kings of Egypt (where the Isis cult originated) in the period prior to the Roman conquest, that type of marriage was strongly at variance with moral codes that prevailed within the Roman Empire as a whole. For the most part, however, the association of Isis with sexual promiscuity derived from the activities associated with Isiac temples. For instance, in his *Amores* (Book II, 2: 25-26) writ-

---

[2] For detailed discussions of the Isis cult in the Greco-Roman world see Witt (1971) and Heyob (1975).

ten at the end of the first century B.C., Ovid tells us that men often used these temples as a trysting place. Martial (*Epigrams*, Book XI, 47: 3-4), writing in the second half of the first century A.D., suggests that simply walking by a temple of Isis could provide a man with sexual temptation. A few decades later Juvenal (*Satires*, 6:488-489) suggests that wives routinely used these temples to carry on clandestine affairs.

Perhaps the most well known of the stories linking Isiac temples to illicit sex was a story reported by Josephus, according to whom a Roman aristocrat named Decius Mundus became enamored of a Roman matron named Paulina. Knowing that Paulina was a devotee of Isis, Decius Mundus secured the help of Isiac priests, who were to tell Paulina that she should come to the temple in order to experience "divine intercourse" with the god Anubis. Sure enough, Paulina met Anubis in the temple, and willingly submitted to his sexual advances. Needless to say, "Anubis" was Decius Mundus in disguise. When the Emperor Tiberius heard about the incident, he had Decius Mundus exiled, the temple of Isis destroyed, and several hundred Isiac priests crucified.

In her discussion of the Isis cult, Heyob makes the point that the association of this cult with sexual immorality was probably undeserved. She suggests (1975: 118-119), for instance, that the story related by Josephus was probably a fabrication, and given that it is similar to any number of legends, this is probably the case. Nevertheless, whether or not this particular story is correct, or even whether or not there really was an unusual amount of trysting at Isiac temples, the fact remains that Isiac temples had a reputation in the Roman world for being centers of promiscuity. In discussing the temple of Isis at Rome, Witt (1971: 138) says succinctly that for "the baser folk in the Italian capital . . . the temple could mean little else than a brothel." Given this association (deserved or not) between Isiac temples and sexual promiscuity, it becomes impossible to argue that Isis—like Mary—was in any clear way disassociated from sexuality. Moreover, the association of Isiac temples, and thus Isis herself, with sexual promiscuity suggests that Isis was very similar to the sexually promiscuous mother goddesses of the ancient Middle East, such as Inanna, Ishtar, and Astarte. This is hardly surprising, since there is an enormous amount of documentary evidence (reviewed in Witt, 1971) to indicate that the Isis cult did originate in Egypt, a Near Eastern society.

Were there, then, *any* Greco-Roman goddesses who were disassociated from sexuality? Lewis Farnell (1907: 305-306) specifically addresses the question of whether any Classical goddesses could legitimately be described as "virgin mothers." He concludes that the general answer would seem to be "no." He further suggests that the "virgin mother" motif exists in Classical mythology only to the extent that it has been projected back onto that mythology by Christian scholars familiar with the Virgin Mary. Only in the case of Cybele, the Phrygian goddess whom the Romans worshiped as the *Magna Mater* ("Great Mother") is Farnell willing to concede that there might be any evidence of a virgin mother. Cybele and her cult will become very important to the theoretical argument to be developed in Chapter Five, but here I only want to emphasize again that the association of Mary with motherhood and her complete disassociation from sexuality make her unique in relation to all earlier Mediterranean goddesses of any importance, save possibly Cybele.

GEOGRAPHICAL DISTRIBUTION OF THE MARY CULT WITHIN EUROPE

There are probably some individuals intensely devoted to Mary in every country in which there are significant numbers of Roman Catholics. Nevertheless, if we measure the strength of the Mary cult in a given region in terms of the number of religious rituals in an area that focus primarily upon Mary, and the degree to which the community at large participates in these rituals, then it is clear that the Mary cult is stronger in some areas of Europe than in others. Mediterranean scholars, for instance, have always noted that the Mary cult seems to be a distinctive feature of the Latin Catholic countries, primarily Italy and Spain, that border the northern edge of the Mediterranean (Wolf, 1969). Even Catholic commentators like Laurentin (1965: 159-161), more concerned with theology than with anthropology, have noted that Marian devotion in Italy and Spain seems especially intense—a phenomenon often mentioned in studies of local religion in these areas.[3] The ethnographic literature relating to local religion in Europe

[3] Christian (1972; 1981a; 1981b) has produced an excellent series of books dealing with local religion in Spain. There seem to be no comparably comprehensive descriptions of local religion in Italy, but see Maraspini (1968: 221-255), Gross (1973: 203-212), and Tentori (1982).

suggests that only Poland might come close to Italy and Spain in the intensity of its Marian devotion.[4] This seems congruent with Laurentin's (1965: 139-140) finding that when the Catholic hierarchies of Italy and Spain find an ally in their quest for a greater emphasis upon Marian devotion within the Church, it is usually the Polish Catholic hierarchy.

We must be careful not to assume that simply because Marian devotion today seems especially intense in Italy, Spain, and Poland, these areas have always been the centers of Marian devotion in Europe. The issue of regional variation with regard to the Mary cult has, unfortunately, not been of any great concern to historians of religion, who—when they talk of the Mary cult at all—usually prefer to discuss trends in Europe as a whole. One way to assess the intensity of Marian devotion in the various regions of Europe over the centuries, however, is to look at the nature and location of Catholic shrines. Jarrett (1911), for instance, lists ninety-four shrines that he feels have been particularly important in the history of Catholic devotion in Europe. Table 1-1 presents these by location and by nature of dedication, that is, whether the shrine was dedicated to the Virgin Mary exclusively, to one or more saints, to Jesus Christ, to some mixture of these individuals, or whether there was no specific dedication.

One finding that emerges immediately is that there have been more major Catholic shrines in France than in any other region of Europe; but we must be careful in interpreting such a figure. In his study of local religion in Spain, Christian (1981a) points out that the impetus for establishing a shrine in Spain during the Middle Ages and the Renaissance was usually a desire on the part of the rural clergy to gain a certain amount of autonomy relative to a Spanish hierarchy concentrated mainly in the large urban areas. For that very reason, however, the Spanish hierarchy usually resisted the establishment of shrines (a fact reflected in Table 1-1). The greater number of shrines in France than in, say, Spain, could therefore easily be due to a hierarchy more willing to tolerate local autonomy.

Far more relevant to our present concerns is the type of shrine that was erected in the various areas of Europe. As Table 1-1 makes clear, there is a dramatic difference between the Catholic shrines erected in the British Isles, most of which date from the pre–Reformation pe-

[4] Local religion in Poland is described in Benet (1951: 36-11), Zalecki (1976), Gieystor (1979: 253-256), and Davies (1981: 159-200).

TABLE I-I

The Most Important Catholic Shrines Erected in Europe

Location	Dedicated to Virgin Mary Exclusively	Dedicated to One or More Saints	Dedicated to Jesus Christ	Mixed Dedication	No Specific Dedication	Total
British Isles England, Scotland, Wales	1	17	—	1	—	19
Ireland	0	4	—	—	—	4
Total for Br. Isles	1 (4%)	21 (92%)	—	1 (4%)	—	23 (100%)
Continental Europe France	22	7	1	2	2	34
Italy*	11	1	1	1	—	14
Spain	6	1	—	—	—	7
All Other Areas Combined	12	1	2	1	—	16
Total for Cont. Europe	51 (72%)	10 (14%)	4 (6%)	4 (6%)	2 (3%)	71 (101%)

* Does not include any shrines in the city of Rome, since Jarrett (1911) simply reports "Rome" as being a single object of pilgrimage over the centuries.

SOURCE: Jarrett (1911).

riod, and those erected in Continental Europe both before and after the Reformation. In the British Isles virtually all Catholic shrines (21, or 92 percent, of 23) were dedicated to one or more saints. There was, in fact, only one important shrine in the British Isles dedicated to Mary, the shrine at Walsingham. The pattern on the Continent is just the reverse, and this seems to be true in every country there. The vast majority of shrines (51, or 72 percent, of the 71 shrines on Continental Europe) were dedicated to the Virgin Mary exclusively. The data in Table 1-1 thus provide some basis for saying that the association of the Mary cult with Continental Europe, as opposed to the British Isles, is longstanding.

I know of no other way to assess systematically regional variation over the centuries directly. It is possible to assess the intensity of Marian devotion indirectly, however, by considering the degree to which various anti-Marian religious movements have flourished in the various regions of Europe. For instance, most Protestant groups strongly reject the Catholic emphasis on Mary. But we tend to forget that, for a while at least, Protestantism made significant inroads into areas of Europe that are now considered Catholic. The experiences of France and Poland seem especially relevant here, since we have seen that there is some basis for associating each of these two countries with the Mary cult.

In the case of France, the rise of the Calvinistic Huguenots during the sixteenth century has been documented by any number of historians. Hillerbrand (1973: 162) has estimated that by 1598 (when the Edict of Nantes effectively limited their numbers), French Protestants probably composed about one-tenth of the population. In evaluating this figure, however, we must remember that the Huguenots were concentrated primarily in the south of France, and that in these regions they probably constituted far more than 10 percent of the local population.

Various Protestant movements (first Lutherans, then Calvinists and other groups) also made significant inroads into Poland during this same period. For instance, at one point, a majority of those in the upper house of the Polish Diet, and possibly a majority in the lower house as well, were professed Protestants (Hillerband, 1973: 171). Although the Diet was not representative of the general population, the predominance of Protestants there at least suggests that they formed a sizable minority in Poland during this period.

It is worth noting that the experiences of France and Poland in the Reformation contrast sharply with those of both Italy and Spain. Apart from the activities of a few highly visible individuals, the Reformation made no significant inroads into either Italy (except possibly Lombardy) or Spain (Braudel, 1973 [1949]: 763-768). Italy and Spain, then, are not only associated with the Mary cult in the modern era but have been disassociated from any anti-Marian movement since at least the time of the Reformation—which cannot be said of either Poland or France.

Furthermore, although Protestantism was clearly the most successful of all Christian movements with an anti-Marian emphasis, it was hardly the first. On the contrary, the rejection of Mary's ability to intervene in response to prayers directed to her was a doctrinal element associated with many of the great heresies of the medieval period. Table 1-2 lists those popular medieval heresies that challenged the Mary cult in some way, and gives for each both an indication of those regions of Europe in which it received its greatest support, and a summary of its position on Mary.

It is clear from Table 1-2 that even before the Reformation anti-Marian movements flourished both in areas (such as England) that would later adopt Protestantism and in those (such as southern France) where Protestantism would make significant inroads. But perhaps the most important information to be gleaned from the table concerns the areas not listed there. Given the concerns of this book, one of the most important of these areas would seem to be southern Italy. (Northern Italy, as Table 1-2 makes clear, was home to at least two anti-Marian movements in the medieval period, the Cathars and the Waldensians.)

This is not to say that medieval heresies never flourished in southern Italy. On the contrary, the Spiritual Franciscans and their more extreme successors, the Fraticelli, were especially popular there. These groups, however, challenged the Church over the issue of clerical poverty; they did not challenge the Mary cult. Similarly, the Flagellant movement, best known for encouraging processions of self-flagellating penitents, originated in Perugia and quickly spread throughout Italy and throughout Europe. But the Flagellants, far from being an anti-Marian movement, actively encouraged the veneration of Mary, and very specifically argued that God could be influenced by Mary's intercession (Leff, 1967: 486-489). Heresies, then, did take hold in

TABLE 1.2

Popular Medieval Heresies That Opposed the Mary Cult

Name of Heresy	Areas of Greatest Strength	Position on the Virgin Mary
Cathars (including the Albigensians)	southern France, northern Italy	some groups saw both Christ and Mary as only "angelic beings"; some groups saw both as only allegorical figures; all groups denied that prayers to Mary would be of any value
Heresy of the Free Spirit★	various regions of Germany	denied that Mary had power to intercede on behalf of human beings; further denigrated Mary by arguing that any human being could easily excel Mary in virtue
Waldensians	northern Italy, southern France, Austria	did encourage some veneration of Mary, but denied that prayers to Mary would be effective
Lollards	England	denied that there could be any intermediaries between human beings and God; singled out the veneration of Marian images and Marian pilgrimages for special denunciation
Hussites (including the Taborites)	Bohemia	though John Hus himself was somewhat sympathetic to the veneration of Mary, the Hussites generally, including more radical Taborites, denied that Mary had the power to intercede on behalf of human beings

★ More of a philosophical movement than an organized heresy, but almost always included in discussions of medieval heresy.

SOURCES: Lambert (1977); Leff (1967); Peters (1980); Russell (1971); Spinka (1966); Stacy (1964).

southern Italy during the Middle Ages; but they were not anti-Marian.

Table 1-2 might at first seem to suggest that the case of Spain is similar to that of southern Italy. The Spanish situation, however, is complicated by the fact that most of Spain was under Muslim domination from the eighth to the thirteenth centuries. The disassociation of Christian Spain from anti-Marian movements, then, should only be dated from the thirteenth century on.

If we look for areas of Europe that are today associated with the Mary cult and that both during the Reformation and the Middle Ages were never associated with a widespread anti-Marian Christian movement, then we are reduced to two cases: southern Italy and Spain.

EMPHASIS UPON MARY IN TWO FOLKLORIC TRADITIONS

There is some folkloric data which, though limited, bears upon the issue of regional variation with regard to the Mary cult. In Thompson's *Motif-Index of Folk Literature* (1955), motifs v200-v299 all involve sacred persons of one sort or another, and v250-v289 involve the Virgin Mary specifically. For any particular body of religious folklore, then, the degree to which the Virgin Mary is emphasized can be estimated by comparing the number of motifs involving the Virgin Mary with the number involving other supernatural mediators, such as saints (v220-v229) or angels (v230-v249).

Unfortunately, there appear to be only two cases in which a substantial amount of the religious folklore associated with a traditionally Catholic area of Europe has been classified using the Thompson scheme. The first of these involves Spain, where Keller (1949) has provided a *Motif-Index of Mediaeval Spanish Exempla*,[5] and the other is Ireland, where Cross (1952) has provided a *Motif-Index of Early Irish Literature*. On the other hand, these two cases are in some senses ideally suited for our purposes: although Catholicism has been established in both countries for a long time, we would expect that a Marian emphasis should be far more evident in Spanish than in Irish folklore.

Table 1-3 presents the number of motifs involving, respectively,

[5] "Exempla" were folktales included in medieval sermons, usually for the purpose of illustrating some principles of Catholic morality.

saints, angels, and the Virgin Mary, as listed in each of these two indexes. In evaluating the numbers, remember that what is being counted are *motifs*, not individual folktales. The entry 72 in the first row of Table 1-2, for example, indicates that in his survey of traditional Irish literature, Cross (1952) found 72 different motifs, each of which involved a saint. Many of these 72 were found in a number of different folktales. Motif v224.2 (food eaten by saint miraculously replaced), for example, was found in six different folktales; v229.4 (saint banishes snakes) was found in four; v229.8 (saints create magic concealing mist) was found in four; and so on.

Table 1-3 tells us, then, that Cross found 136 separate motifs that involved saints, angels, or the Virgin Mary; of these, only eight (or 6 percent of the total) involved the Virgin Mary specifically. By contrast, in his study of medieval Spanish exempla, Keller found 43 motifs involving saints, angels, or the Virgin Mary (here again, the number of folktales involved exceeds the number of motifs); of these, 29 (or 67 percent of the total) involved the Virgin Mary specifically. The data, in other words, confirm our expectation: compared to other supernatural mediators, such as saints and angels, the Virgin Mary is more emphasized in the Spanish material than in the Irish. Limited though such an analysis is, it provides another bit of evidence to strengthen the association between Spain and the Mary cult.

AN ORTHODOX DIGRESSION

It will have been evident to many readers that I have thus far ignored the Mary cult in those areas of Eastern Europe and the Near East dominated by the various Orthodox churches. This might seem to be a serious omission, since several Catholic commentators have implied that Marian devotion within the Orthodox tradition is just as strong as within the Roman Catholic tradition. Graef (1965: 130-133), for instance, suggests that a common emphasis upon Marian devotion is the factor that will most facilitate the eventual reunification of the Roman Catholic and Orthodox churches.

But the enthusiasm of Catholic commentators like Graef notwithstanding, there are at least two reasons for treating the Roman Catholic Mary cult separately from the Orthodox Mary cult. First, although it is true that Marian veneration is more intense in Orthodox than in

TABLE I-3

Emphasis upon the Virgin Mary, in Contrast to Saints and Angels, in the Religious Folklore of Ireland and Spain

	Number of Different Motifs in Which Central Character Is:			
Source	a saint (motifs v220–v229)	an angel (motifs v230–v249)	the Virgin Mary (motifs v250–v289)	Total
Motif-Index of Traditional Irish Literature (Cross, 1952)	68 (50%)	60 (44%)	8 (6%)	136 (100%)
Motif-Index of Mediaeval Spanish Exempla (Keller, 1949)	5 (12%)	9 (21%)	29 (67%)	43 (100%)

Protestant tradition, Mary does not enjoy in the Orthodox tradition the same exalted status that she does in Roman Catholicism. The Orthodox churches, for instance, tend to reject those Marian doctrines which imply that Mary had a "nature" superior to the "nature" of other human beings. Thus, the Orthodox churches reject the doctrine of the Immaculate Conception (which says that Mary was forever free from any taint of original sin) and the Assumption (which says that Mary's body was taken up into heaven). That the Roman Catholic Church in the modern era proclaimed these doctrines to be dogma is usually taken by Orthodox leaders as a major stumbling block to reunification.

Just as the Orthodox tradition does not credit Mary with a nature intrinsically different from that of other human beings, it also does not single out Mary as the most important of all supernatural beings apart from God himself, as does the Roman Catholic tradition. There is, for instance, a strong tendency in Orthodoxy to equate Mary and John the Baptist, and to imply that they are the female and male representatives, respectively, of the same personage (Bulgakov, 1935: 137-148). One historian (Benz, 1963: 60-64) has tried to contrast the Roman Catholic and the Orthodox views on Mary by arguing that the Orthodox tradition recognizes Mary in her role as *Theotokos* (or God-bearer), but distinguishes her from *Sophia*, or Heavenly Wisdom, the female personification of the divine principle, whereas the the Roman Catholic tradition has merged these two concepts and has in the process deified Mary.

Even if we focus less upon theology and more upon popular religion, we still come to the conclusion that the Mary cult in Orthodox areas is different from that in Roman Catholic ones. First, even in a Mediterranean country such as Greece, where (on the analogy with Italy and Spain) we might expect to find a strong Mary cult, commentators (Friedl, 1962: 99-103; Gearing, 1968) have noted that popular religion tends to be overwhelmingly Christocentric, that is, far more concerned with events from the life of Christ than anything else. In those Greek religious rituals that do involve Mary, she is not likely to be the exclusive or even the principal focus. Several investigators, for instance, have noted that the concept which most dominates religious rituals in many Greek communities is "the Holy Family," where this term sometimes refers to God the Father, God the Son, and Mary as *Theotokos* (Campbell, 1966), and sometimes to Christ in his dual role as Son and Savior, and Mary as *Theotokos* (du Boulay, 1974). In other words, we do not find in Orthodox communities large numbers of rituals emphasizing Mary to the exclusion (or near-exclusion) of Christ—which is precisely what we do find in Italy, Spain, and Poland.

Although it seems clear that the veneration of Mary is less intense within the Orthodox tradition, this in itself would not be sufficient grounds for treating the Orthodox Mary cult separately from the Roman Catholic Mary cult. We could, after all, think of Marian veneration as a continuum, and give the Orthodox tradition a position on this continuum that falls somewhere between the Roman Catholic and the Protestant tradition. "Degree of Marian veneration" would then become the dependent variable that we sought to explain.

But there is a second reason for considering the two Mary cults separately: the Mary venerated within the Orthodox traditions seems to be defined differently from the Mary venerated within the Roman Catholic tradition.

In the Roman Catholic tradition, Mary's distinctiveness as a goddess lies in the fact that she was seen to be Virgin and Mother simultaneously. On the other hand, although most Orthodox traditions accept Mary's *in partu* virginity and her perpetual virginity (and, of course, all accept the Virginal Conception), it also seems that the Orthodox Mary tends to be venerated primarily in her role as *Theotokos* (Mother of God) and hardly at all as Virgin. The only historian who seems to have commented specifically upon this deemphasis of Mary as Virgin is Fedotov (1966: 103), and he was talking only of the Russian Orthodox tradition. But the same impression comes through in accounts of Marian devotion in other Orthodox areas.[6] It seems clear, for instance, that prayers to Mary in such areas almost invariably invoke her only as "Mother of God." And "Mother of God" is usually the only title to appear on Marian icons in Orthodox regions (Gerhard, 1964: 8).

The fact that the Orthodox Mary is venerated almost exclusively in her role as the Mother of God reinforces the impression that the main thrust of Marian devotion in the Orthodox tradition is Christological. In other words, Mary is venerated primarily because of her close as-

---

[6] Apart from the references given in the text, additional information relating to Orthodox views on the Virgin Mary can be found in Iswolsky (1960: 144-149), Zernov (1961: 234), and Meyendorf (1962: 200).

sociation with Christ. Although many Roman Catholics might pay lip service to this valuation, the tremendous emphasis placed not only upon Mary as the Mother of God (a status that does derive from her relationship to Christ) but also upon Mary as Virgin (which derives from qualities intrinsic to Mary herself) suggests that the Roman Catholic Mary is more easily seen as an independent deity than the Orthodox Mary.

In any event, since it is the simultaneous juxtaposition of "mother" and "virgin" (in the sense of "completely disassociated from sexuality") that most distinguishes the Roman Catholic Mary from earlier goddesses, the fact that this juxtaposition is not present in the Orthodox tradition in the same degree as it is in Roman Catholicism makes it likely that the Roman Catholic Mary cult and the Orthodox Mary cult derive from different social-psychological processes. The rest of this book deals only with the processes that give rise to the Roman Catholic Mary cult.

PREVIOUS EXPLANATIONS OF
THE MARY CULT

In this chapter I shall review and evaluate hypotheses about the origins of the Mary cult offered by earlier investigators. Only in Geoffrey Ashe, however, will we encounter someone whose primary concern is with origins; otherwise, we will be dealing only with offhand remarks. This means that our first task will usually be to draw out and make explicit the theoretical argument that lies behind a relatively vague hypothesis. I have limited my enquiry to those hypotheses offered by scholars in sociology, psychology, and history whose works on religion are relatively well known and well respected. If such scholars have opinions regarding the historical or psychological origins of this cult, then I assume those opinions—however casually they are offered and however vague they might be—to be worth investigating.

SWANSON: TYPE OF POLITICAL REGIME

In his *Religion and Regime* (1967), a work that has become a classic in the sociology of religion, Guy Swanson sought to explain the Reformation by linking type of religious world-view (Catholic or Protestant) to type of political regime.[1] In that book, Swanson did not address the issue of the Mary cult, but as a result of the investigations reported there he came to realize (like the Palestinian Jewish girl in *Tancred*) that an emphasis upon Mary is one of the things that most distinguishes the Catholic tradition from the Protestant. In his own words:

[1] The discussion of Swanson's argument presented in this section is taken from Carroll (1979: 39-42).

As I finished that study [*Religion and Regime*] I found myself turning again and again to a fact that had had no place in my interpretation of these relationships: the place of honor given in Catholicism to the Virgin, to her mother, to the Church as the bride of Christ and the mother of the faithful, and to the women on the roll of saints; and, by contrast, to the absence of female figures among those held sacred by Protestants. (Swanson, 1974: 326)

Swanson considered the possibility that a differential emphasis on male and female supernatural beings might be attributable to the same variable that he had found to be crucial in predicting which European states had embraced Protestantism and which had remained Catholic: the type of political regime that characterized the society in question. His original typology of political regimes included five categories, but in his more recent work he has reduced these to two: on the one hand, those regimes in which "men gained important positions in the operations of the central state as a consequence of their constituting or representing somewhat autonomous special interest," and on the other, those regimes in which men gained such positions "only in their capacity as members of the commonalty" (Swanson, 1968: 108; see also the usage employed in Swanson, 1973). Adopting the terminology employed by Paige (1974) in his summary of Swanson's argument, the first type of regime will be called "factional" and the second type "communal."

Swanson (1968) expanded his original theory by noting that order in a society can be maintained in either of two ways: through socialization or social control. Socialization, he argues, requires that a set of values and goals be common to all or most of the subgroups in a society. When this does not occur—when a society is composed of several different and autonomous subgroups, as in a "factional" society—Swanson predicts that the society will give more normative emphasis to social control than to socialization. Conversely, when a society lacks such autonomous subgroups—as in a "communal" society—greater normative emphasis will be given to socialization.

His reasoning at this point takes a very ingenious turn. Borrowing from the literature on leadership patterns in the nuclear family, Swanson argues that since women are universally allocated the role of raising and socializing children, a normative emphasis on socialization will lead to a religious emphasis on females. Likewise, since men are universally allocated the role of "task leadership" (a part of which always involves exercising social control over group members), a normative emphasis on social control should lead to a religious emphasis on males.

Unfortunately, Swanson chose to test this bold argument in a very indirect manner. He started out with a sample of forty preindustrial cultures. But instead of coding those cultures for the relative emphasis that each gave to male as compared to female supernatural beings— which is the clear dependent variable in his argument—he coded them for the type of unilineal descent rule that they used. He simply assumed that a religious emphasis on females would lead to matrilineal descent (which he interpreted as a symbolic expression of the belief that children are closer to their mothers than to their fathers), whereas a religious emphasis on males would lead to patrilineal descent (a symbolic expression of the belief that children are closer to their fathers). The predicted association was discovered: matrilineal descent was associated with communal regimes, and patrilineal descent was associated with factional regimes.

Swanson's data, of course, drawn as they are from the non-Western societies, are not relevant to the Mary cult. The theory supported by these data, however, is. If Swanson's general theory is correct, we would expect an association between Catholicism and an emphasis upon the feminine in religion, because each derives from the presence of a "communal" regime. The Mary cult could then be seen as one expression of this greater emphasis on the feminine in Catholicism (a focus on female saints, the Church as the Bride of Christ, and so on, being other expressions of this same general emphasis). The advantage of this theory is that in linking Marian devotion to type of political regime, it offers the potential for explaining variation in such devotion from society to society.

But despite the undeniable elegance and appeal of Swanson's theory, it is very likely wrong. Consider a key link in the Swanson argument, namely, his assertion that matrilineal descent reflects a greater symbolic emphasis on the feminine. This is, at the very least, an unusual perspective. Most anthropologists see matrilineal descent as reflecting matrilocal residence, and see this in turn as deriving from a matridominant division of labor (that is, women contribute more to subsistence than men), or a relatively high societal status for females, or external warfare (for a discussion of these hypotheses, and some data relevant to each, see Ember and Ember, 1971). Still, the fact that Swanson's perspective on matrilineal descent is so out of step with mainstream anthropological thinking does not mean that he is incorrect, only that he is imaginative.

Data have become available, however, that allow us to evaluate the posited link between matrilineal descent and a symbolic emphasis upon the feminine fairly directly. Whyte (1978a, 1978b) coded every second society in the Standard Cross-Cultural Sample (hereafter SCCS) on a variety of variables relating to the status of women. One of those variables (column 1 in Whyte, 1978b) was "sex of supernatural beings." Whyte compared male and female supernatural beings in each society in terms of both numbers and relative power. Each society was then assigned to one of four categories:

1. supernatural beings exclusively male
2. supernatural beings of both sexes, but males more numerous or more powerful or both
3. supernatural beings of both sexes, but males more numerous with power equal, or males more powerful with numbers equal
4. supernatural beings of both sexes, and equal in number or power or both, or females either more numerous or more powerful than males.

Societies coded 3 and 4 can clearly be regarded as giving more emphasis to female supernatural beings than societies coded 1 or 2. Since Murdock and Wilson (1972: column 10) provide information on the descent rule used in most of the societies in Whyte's sample, it is relatively easy to test Swanson's argument. Limiting ourselves to societies using either a patrilineal or a matrilineal rule (since these are the only types of society that Swanson considers), the relationship between descent rule and emphasis upon female supernatural beings is given in Table 2-1.

As is clear from the table, the Swanson argument is contradicted; there is no relationship whatsoever between the use of matrilineal descent and an emphasis upon female supernatural beings (phi = .00, p = n.s.). If this is so, then Swanson's data, which turn up an association between type of regime and matrilineal descent, are not relevant to his analysis which posits a relationship between type of regime and a symbolic emphasis upon the feminine.

TABLE 2-1

Relationship between Type of Unilineal Descent Rule Used and Relative Emphasis upon Female Supernatural Beings, for sccs Societies

Descent Rule	Relative Emphasis upon Female Supernatural Beings	
	low	high
exclusively patrilineal	15	7
exclusively matrilineal	7	3

NOTE: phi = .00, p = n.s.

On the other hand, a test of Swanson's theory using data that do seem relevant to it can be constructed using the information on the political organization of sccs cultures provided by Tuden and Marshall (1972). In column 3 of their work, they code the highest level of effective sovereignty for each culture ("the highest level of indigenous political integration at which functionaries have and commonly exercise power to enforce important decisions"). The local community is the baseline, so that a society in which the local community is the highest level of effective sovereignty would be coded 0, one in which effective sovereignty is exercised only one level above the local community would be coded 1, and so on.

In column 4, they code the existence of any type of political organization above that specified in column 3 that lacks effective sovereignty but tries to coordinate the activities of the various politically autonomous subgroups that exist in the society. Such "higher levels of political organization" range from informal groups based on a common cult, common descent, and so on, to formal confederations.

Since for Swanson a "factional" regime is one in which relatively autonomous political groups jointly participate in a central government, it seems fair to say that a society in which politically autonomous subgroups come together in a common forum in order to influence each other—as in the sccs societies characterized by "higher levels of political organization"—is also practicing factional politics. If, as Swanson argues, factional politics lead to a greater symbolic emphasis upon the masculine than the feminine, then we would expect the following prediction to be true: Societies characterized by the presence of an organization that tries to coordinate politically autonomous subgroups will give greater emphasis to male supernatural beings than societies lacking such an organization. Since this prediction talks about an emphasis upon male supernatural beings, those societies coded 1 or 2 on Whyte's "sex of supernatural beings" variable would be relatively high on this dimension, whereas those coded 3 or 4 would be relatively low.

The data relevant to this prediction are presented in Table 2-2. Since Swanson (1968) limited his theory to unilineal societies, only such societies are included in this analysis. Unfortunately for the Swanson theory, the data do not support the prediction (phi = .09, p. = n.s., using Fisher's Exact Test, one-tailed). Even if we include nonunilineal societies in the analysis, the data—not shown—still fail to support the Swanson hypothesis.

Swanson, of course, might argue that this is not a proper test of his theory, and that it would be supported by a more appropriate test. He might be correct. Still, the fact that there is no link between matrilineal descent and an emphasis upon female supernatural beings, the fact that the prediction which I derived from his theory was not supported by the data, and the fact that Paige (1974) has presented an alternative explanation for the one association that Swanson did find (between type of unilineal descent rule and type of regime)—all suggest that al-

TABLE 2-2

Relationship between the Presence of a Political Organization That Tries to Coordinate Politically Autonomous Subgroups and Relative Emphasis upon Male Supernatural Beings, for sccs Societies

Political Organization that Tries to Coordinate Politically Autonomous Subgroups	Relative Emphasis upon Male Supernatural Beings	
	low	high
Absent	5	10
Present	4	12

NOTE: Includes unilineal societies only; phi = .09, p = n.s.

though Swanson's theory is bold and ingenious, it is nevertheless incorrect.

THE STRUCTURALIST HYPOTHESIS:
THE MARY CULT AND PATRONAGE

During the mid-1960s, French structuralism was just coming into vogue, and at that time one of the greatest popularizers of the structuralist method in the English-speaking world was Edmund Leach. One of his best known articles during this period was entitled "Virgin Birth" (Leach, 1969 [1966]). This title may be misleading, since Leach's primary concern in this article is not with Christian beliefs about the Virgin Mary, but with what he calls a "legendary" issue in social anthropology: the alleged ignorance on the part of some "primitive" peoples of the male role in reproduction.

In the first part of his essay, Leach establishes two points: first, there are some societies whose members say that women can conceive without aid of human fathers, and second, there are no societies in which the people are ignorant of the causal link between sexual intercourse and reproduction. These two observations might seem inconsistent. Not so, says Leach. A belief in the possibility of "virgin birth" is ideology, and is determined less by physiological knowledge than by the social organization of the society in question. A "virgin birth" ideology, in other words, develops as a structural reflection of the prevalent type of social organization in some societies. Although Leach claims to be using here the structuralist method developed by Lévi-Strauss, it seems obvious that his approach is equally influenced by Durkheim and Mauss (1963 [1903]).

Leach then illustrates his point by considering the Christian belief that Mary was a virgin when she conceived and bore Christ. From a structuralist point of view, what is the logic that underlies this belief? For Leach, the essential feature of this Christian belief is that it portrays an all-powerful male (God) who deigns to impregnate a mere human being (Mary). The immense gap between God and Mary, says Leach, is a structural reflection of a society in which power is concentrated in the hands of small group (usually all males) and in which the social distance between these rulers and those they rule is immense. Leach (1969: 99) offhandedly suggests that this type of social structure characterized "Byzantium and eighteenth-century Brazil," which explains for him why "the cult of the Virgin was exceptionally well developed" in those societies—an assertion he does not bother to document.

Leach's remarks on the Mary cult, however, are brief and only a prelude to what, for him, is clearly the most important part of his argument: the relationship between social milieu and the beliefs held by professional anthropologists. Why, asks Leach, if there is so little basis for believing that there has ever been a society truly ignorant of the causal link between sexual intercourse and reproduction, were so many nineteenth-century anthropologists willing to believe in such ignorance? For Leach the answer is obvious: their belief well reflected the social environment from which most nineteenth-century anthropologists were drawn. Leach argues that most nineteenth-century anthropologists held strongly patriarchal views, and this predisposed them toward a fantasy world in which men used women for sexual pleasure but did not assume responsibility for the resulting children. A society in which people are ignorant of the link between sex and reproduction is precisely that sort of Victorian fantasy world, and it was *this* that led so many nineteenth-century anthropologists to attribute ignorance of physiological paternity to so many "primitive" societies.

Leach's article provoked a lively debate in British social anthropological circles, and many of his critics were apparently stung by his suggestion that the ideas held by anthropologists, like the ideas held by the peoples they study, might be determined by social environment. With regard to substantive issues, however, Saliba's (1975) excellent review of the debate makes it clear that most of Leach's critics were concerned only with establishing two points: first, the Christian belief in the Virgin Birth is not really comparable to beliefs about parthenogenesis found in some nonliterate societies, and second, there really are some societies that are ignorant of the causal link between sexual intercourse and reproduction. Leach's very specific hypothesis about the Mary cult—that it is most likely to flourish in societies where the gap between ruler and ruled is large—was ignored, and it has continued to be ignored. Even Leach himself, after having mentioned the idea, never seems to have picked it up again. This neglect is unfortunate, if only because the hypothesis seems so compatible with the results of a number of anthropological investigations concerned with the study of patronage and patron-client relationships.

The term "patronage" has been used to encompass a wide variety of social relationships, and sorting out the different types of patronage has been a major goal of people working in this area (cf., for example, Kahane, 1984). Most reviews of the literature, however, suggest that the type of patronage to flourish in the Latin countries bordering on the Mediterranean is centered upon the "patron/client" relationships (Bennet, 1968: 475; Eisenstadt and Roniger, 1980: 61-71). This is a relationship between two individuals that is nonascriptive (for example, not based on kinship), diffuse, highly particularistic, and that involves an exchange of services. In the typical case, the client offers loyalty, labor, or votes, and receives from the patron protection and the patron's willingness to intervene on the client's behalf with the centers of political and economic power that transcend the local community. Implicit in the patron/client relationship is the belief (which may or may not be justified) that the client does not have direct access to the centers of power, and thus needs the patron to act as a mediator on his behalf. It is this last belief that makes the material on patronage in Mediterranean countries relevant to Leach's argument about the Mary cult.

A society in which clients feel that they have no direct access to the centers of political and economic power sounds very much like Leach's "society where the gap between the rulers and the ruled is large." We would therefore expect to find the Mary cult flourishing where patronage—at least, patronage defined in terms of the patron/client relationship—flourishes and, of course, we do. The Mary cult is particularly strong in Italy and Spain, where patron/client relationships are extensive. Leach does not mention patronage, but it is relatively easy to develop a version of his argument that incorporates this element: a religious world view that encourages prayers to Mary asking her to intervene with God is easily seen as a structural reflection of society in which clients ask their patrons to intervene on their behalf with higher powers.

Appealing as the structuralist argument is, there are nevertheless problems with it. For instance, if the structure of a religious ideology does reflect the structure of the important social relationships in a society, what can we expect of a religion in the case of a society characterized by extensive patron/client relationships? At best, only that the religious world view will emphasize supernatural beings who mediate between humankind and God. There is nothing in the structuralist argument that allows us to predict the nature of these supernatural mediators, or that the most important such mediator will be a virgin mother or even a female.

We should remember, as well, that although Mary may be the most important supernatural mediator in the Roman Catholic tradition, she is by no means the only one. At least since the third century A.D. it has been a part of Catholic tradition that the saints in heaven can intercede with God on behalf of those who pray to them (O'Neil, 1967). In fact, demonstrating that a deceased person is capable of interceding with God in order to produce some miraculous benefit has become one of the formal prerequisites for canonization.

But though the saints are supernatural mediators, they are not associated with either virginity or femaleness. Weinstein and Bell (1982), for instance, have examined the biographies of 864 saints who lived during the period 1000-1700 and coded these biographies according to a number of variables, including sex. Their sample included not only all the saints of this period who have been canonized by the Church, but also a number of individuals who were considered saints on the basis of local tradition alone. What these investigators found was that only 151 of these saints (18 percent of the total) were female. In the case of the saints, then, it appears that supernatural mediation is overwhelmingly associated with maleness, not femaleness.

Weinstein and Bell also addressed the issue of chastity, by which they meant abstention from sexual intercourse. They found that this issue was raised in saintly biographies in two ways. In the case of 97 saints (11 percent of the total), their biographies mention a struggle to remain chaste despite strong pressures to the contrary. The biographies of 104 saints (12 percent of the total) mention conversion to a life of sexual continence after an initial period of noncontinence. But the most important finding from our perspective is that "chastity" is not an issue in the vast majority of biographies in the Weinstein/Bell sample.

In the end, then, what can we conclude? On the one hand, the fact that both the Mary cult and the cult of the saints are popular in those areas of Europe (such as southern Italy and Spain) where patron-client relationships are extensive does lend some support to the structuralist argument that the prevalence of patron-client relationships leads to a religious emphasis upon supernatural mediators. On the other hand, the Weinstein and Bell findings on the cult of the saints make it clear that there is no association in the Catholic world view between being a supernatural mediator and being either female or chaste. In other words, even if the prevalence of patron-client relationships might lead to an emphasis upon supernatural mediators, this would not explain why the most important of these is a virgin mother. Thus, although the structuralist argument must be considered a useful complement to any theory about the Mary cult, it does not in itself provide us with an adequate explantation of that cult.

ONE GODDESS UNDER MANY NAMES

A number of scholars have suggested that "the Virgin Mary" is simply a new name for a single goddess who has in the past been worshiped under a variety of different names. In his comprehensive survey of Mediterranean goddesses, for instance, James (1959) makes a point of referring to "the goddess cult" rather than to "goddess cults." The idea is by no means a new one. In the second century A.D., the Roman author Lucius Apuleius advanced a similar idea in *The Golden Ass*. This novel, written in the first person, tells of how Lucius Apuleius was transformed into an ass and how he attempted to regain his human form. Toward the end of the story, Lucius (still an ass) confronts a goddess who tells him that although she is called Mother of the Gods by the Phrygians, Minerva by the Athenians, Venus by the Cyprians, Diana by the Cretans, Proserpine by the Sicilians, Ceres by the Eleusians, and so on, it is the Egyptians who know her by her true name, Isis. Adding the "Virgin Mary" to the list does not change the basic hypothesis that underlies this passage, namely, that all these goddesses are in some sense the same goddess. But my own reading of those scholars who express similar sentiments suggests that there are, in fact, several different and distinct versions of the hypothesis that one goddess exists under many names. In particular, there are three versions that seem to be especially popular, and each must be considered separately.

Mary and the Mother Archetype

Perhaps the most well known hypothesis is that developed by C. G. Jung and his students, who see the Virgin Mary and most other mother goddesses as deriving ultimately from one or more of the archetypes buried in the unconscious of all human beings. This argument is simply an application of Jung's more general theory, which sees the content of all religious and mythological thought as having been shaped by such archetypes. We must know, of course, what an "archetype" is before we can evaluate his arguments relating to the Virgin Mary—and therein lies a problem. Despite the centrality of the concept to Jungian psychology, and even though it has long since passed into common usage, it is, as Anthony Storr (1973: 39) has noted, extraordinarily difficult to give the term "archetype" an adequate definition.

Although Jung often complained that others were misusing the concept, his own work provides few guidelines as to what would constitute proper usage. To be sure, Jung often tells us what an archetype is not (it is not an unconscious idea, it is not something that fully determines the content of our thought, and so on,) but he devotes surprisingly little attention to telling us, in detail, just what an archetype is. We must define this concept before we can evaluate Jung's arguments about the Virgin Mary, however, and so I will offer my own definition (though there will almost certainly be Jungians who will challenge it): an archetype is a predisposition for certain qualities and attributes to cluster together in the unconscious. In Jungian theory this clustering in the unconscious has the effect of influencing, in the sense of shaping, our conscious thought. Thus Jung would explain the Virgin Mary, say, by arguing that our conscious image of Mary has been shaped, at least in part, by an unconscious archetype. Actually, Jung developed two quite separate arguments that derive Mary from two different archetypes.

In the better known of these two, Jung (1970a: 9-44) derives our image of Mary from the mother archetype. Jung's attempt to specify the general properties of the mother archetype is long and rambling, and very difficult to summarize. The basic idea seems to be that positive qualities and attributes such as femininity, magical power, solicitude, wisdom, helpfulness, fertility, and sympathy, as well as negative qualities and attributes such as secretiveness, darkness, a tendency to devour, seductiveness, and terribleness all tend to cluster together in our unconscious, and the tendency of these particular qualities and attributes to cluster together is what for Jung constitutes the mother archetype. What he is suggesting, I think, is that when we associate one of these attributes and qualities with a conscious image, we will tend to associate some of the other of these qualities and attributes to the same image. Thus, if we see our real mother as being, say, helpful and sympathetic, then there should be some tendency to see her as being, say, seductive as well. In fact, an important part of Jung's theory of socialization is that many of the qualities that we associate with our image of our mother are qualities that we have projected onto our real mothers under the influence of the mother archetype.

None of this is to say, however, that all the qualities and attributes that define a given archetype will be present in every conscious image that has been shaped by that archetype. On the contrary, archetypes are only predispositions, nothing more. In any given image that has been shaped by a particular archetype, some of the qualities and attributes that define the archetype will be more prominent than others. Thus, Jung argues, the mother archetype has given rise to conscious images as diverse as the Virgin Mary, the Greek goddess Demeter, the Hindu goddess Kali, and the Wicked Witch and Wicked Stepmother characters that so often appear in fairy tales.

Jung's second and less well known argument relating to the Virgin Mary has to do with what he calls the "quaternity." In its most general sense, the quaternity is an unconscious predisposition to associate two pairs of opposites in a balanced composition. In discussing the Godhead (by which Jung seems to mean "the sacred"), Jung argues that the particular quaternity that will shape our conscious thoughts is one that predisposes us to think in terms of a balanced union of two specific contrasts, namely, male vs. female and good vs. evil. Carried to its logical extreme, of course, this particular quaternity would produce four conscious images associated with the Godhead: the good male, the bad male, the good female, and the bad female. But because archetypes (and the quaternity clearly functions as an archetype for Jung, even if he rarely calls it that) only shape our thoughts, all four images will not usually be found in all religions. On the contrary, Protestants, Jung argues, typically recognize only the good male (God, Jesus Christ) and the bad male (Satan). Catholic theology, on the other hand, has gone further by including a good female into the Godhead—the Virgin Mary. Jung, as far as I know, does not give an example of a system in which all four images of the quaternity are associated with particular persons, but a good example might be the Hebrew traditions discussed by Patai (1967), which have recognized a good male (Yahweh), a bad male (Satan), a good female (Wisdom, the Matronit), and a bad female (Lilith).

Since Jung relates devotion to the Virgin Mary to archetypes buried in the unconscious of all human beings, it might seem that Jung's analysis cannot explain variation in Marian devotion over time and across different social settings. Such a criticism, however, would be misleading. As Jung's discussion of the quaternity makes clear, his theory does have the potential for dealing with variation of this sort, since he explicitly says that not all elements of the quaternity (or any archetype) will be present in all religious systems.

The real problem with Jung's theory is that neither he nor his students have been much concerned with explaining such variation in any systematic way. Thus, Jung tells us that the "good female" aspect of the quaternity is not present in Protestant thought, but fails to tell us why this should be so. Why, in other words, should the "good female" be less evident in the Protestant societies of northern Europe than in the Catholic societies of southern Europe? Similarly, why should the "good female" have been submerged during the first four centuries of the Christian era, only to emerge in the fifth? These are the questions that we must be able to answer if we are to understand the Mary cult.

The problem of variation also emerges in connection with Jung's first argument, which derives our image of Mary from the mother archetype. One of the things we want to explain is why Mary, unlike most of the mother goddesses in the world, is disassociated from sexuality. Nothing in Jung's arguments would allow us to do this.

In the end, then, I cannot say that Jung's theory is falsified by the evidence; I can only say that this theory, at least as it is presently formulated, does not seem capable of explaining those observations about the Mary cult that we have defined to be important.

Mary and the Paleolithic Mother Goddess

During the nineteenth century, most anthropologists were social evolutionists, and most social evolutionists believed that the earliest human societies had been matriarchal (that is, societies in which women held the balance of political power), matrilineal (societies in which descent was traced through the female line), and had worshiped mainly female deities. After a while, the existence of such a "matri-centered" stage of social evolution came to be challenged; the ensuing debate lasted a long time and was extremely acrimonious before being settled. Today, the issue is not particularly controversial. Although a few popular authors like Davis (1972) try occasionally to resuscitate a belief in the existence of such an evolutionary stage, most anthropologists now consider matrilineal descent an adaptation to a particular set of ecological conditions, and believe that true matriarchies have never existed. There are, however, several modern scholars who still adhere to at least part of the original nineteenth-century position, in that they believe that the earliest human religions were organized around female deities.

James (1959), for instance, argues that the earliest forms of religion developed in two stages, and in each stage female deities predominated. Early humans, James suggests, would have been concerned with the regeneration and fertility of the natural world. On the analogy with human birth, he argues, and assuming that such people would be ignorant of the male role in procreation, they would naturally associate the regeneration and fertility of nature with an all-powerful mother goddess. Later, as awareness of the male role in procreation increased, this goddess would come to be associated with a male counterpart. In the usual case, James suggests, the mother goddess would become associated with the earth, while her male counterpart would become associated with the sky, since the sky is the source of the rain that fertilizes the earth. Gimbutas (1982) makes a similar argument, but locates the process more precisely in time and space. In Gimbutas' account, the most important goddess of Old Europe (which for her includes Greece, the Balkans, southern Italy, and Western Anatolia) between 6000 B.C. and 3500 B.C. was an all-powerful goddess that Gimbutas calls the "Great Mother." It was only under the impact of the great Indo-European invasions, says Gimbutas, that the cult of the Great Mother came to be supplanted by cults organized around an Earth Mother who was paired with a Sky God. Others who argue in favor of an Old World goddess cult that had its origins in the Paleolithic include Branston (1957), Hultkranz (1961), and Neumann (1963).

The relevance of these arguments to the Mary cult lies in the fact that the people making these arguments often see the Mary cult as a simple continuation of the primordial mother goddess tradition. For instance, after mentioning that devotion to the Great Goddess of Old

Europe was never extinguished entirely, even by the Indo-European invasions, Gimbutas (1982: 200) concludes by noting that "village communities worship her to this day in the guise of the Virgin Mary." James (1959: 192–227) devotes an entire chapter in his book to establishing the same point.

In linking the Mary cult to a goddess cult that originated in the Upper Paleolithic (c. 35,000–10,000 B.P.), both Gimbutas and James seem to be using a form of explanation that was popular among nineteenth-century social anthropologists, and that supplied the basis of Frazer's *The Golden Bough*: something is explained by showing it to be a "survival" of a practice that originated at an earlier stage of social evolution. A number of scholars, including myself, would now reject such an explanation in principle on the grounds that a proper explanation of a continuing social practice must be in terms of some ongoing social or psychological processes. Yet even if we take the "survival" argument on its own terms, it is suspect, since there are no solid grounds for believing that a goddess cult *did* exist in the Paleolithic.

Without exception, all the scholars who argue for a goddess cult in the Upper Paleolithic rest their case almost entirely upon the evidence provided by the so-called "prehistoric Venuses." These are statuettes (and a few engravings) that have been found at Gravettian sites (c. 27,000–20,000 B.P.) scattered from Siberia to Western Europe. The particular Venuses reproduced in most textbooks tend to portray females with sagging breasts, protruding stomachs, and large buttocks and thighs—all of which have suggested to a great many commentators that these Venuses are somehow associated with fertility. It is fairly easy, then, to see such statuettes as representing a fertility goddess of some sort (a conclusion facilitated by the very fact that they are called Venuses). But however reasonable such a conclusion may seem, it quickly runs into several difficulties.

First, most of the art that dates from the Upper Paleolithic is not "portable" art, like the Venus figurines, but rather "parietal" art, which is the term given to the paintings and engravings found in various caves such as Altamira in Spain and Lascaux in France. The inaccessibility of these caves, plus the fact that they were clearly not used for day-to-day living, has suggested to any number of prehistorians that they were religious sanctuaries. If there was indeed a widespread goddess cult in the Paleolithic, then surely we should find some evidence of that cult in Paleolithic parietal art. But we don't. The vast bulk of this art consists of depictions of recognizable animals (such as horses, bison, and mammoths) and abstract geometric designs. Human representations, by contrast, are quite rare. For instance, in surveying the parietal art found in seventy-two different Paleolithic caves in Western Europe, Leroi-Gourhan (1967) found recognizable animals in 2,058 different depictions, whereas humans were portrayed in only 106. Furthermore, among those relatively few depictions of humans, males outnumbered females by a ratio of nearly five to one. Since Leroi-Gourhan's pioneering work, Ucko and Rosenfeld (1972) have conducted a more extensive survey of human representations in Paleolithic parietal art, and have found that 21 percent of these representations are clearly male, 24 percent are clearly female, 39 percent are apparently sexless, and the remaining 15 percent are so damaged that determination of sex is impossible. Parietal art, then, provides no evidence that Paleolithic religion had a feminine emphasis, and certainly no evidence to support the existence of a cult devoted to a particular goddess.

Even if we ignore the parietal art and focus entirely upon the Venus figurines themselves, there is still no basis for adducing a goddess cult in the Paleolithic. Rice (1981), for instance, has examined 188 prehistoric Venuses in what is the most comprehensive study of such figurines to date. She looked at five physical characteristics (size and shape of breasts, shape of stomach, shape of hips, size and shape of buttocks, degree to which face is lined) in order to sort the Venuses into four categories. These four categories were: young (prereproductive) female, female of reproductive age, but not pregnant, female of reproductive age and pregnant, and old (postreproductive) female. One finding from Rice's study is that only about 23 percent of the Venuses in her sample could reasonably be called pregnant. Thus, although pregnant Venuses seem to be reproduced in textbooks more often than any other type, they are atypical. The major finding of Rice's study, however, is that the variation among these figurines with respect to age and reproductive status is exactly what you would expct to find if these figurines represented a cross-section of women drawn from a typical population of hunter-gathers. The fact that the figurines represent not just pregnant females, but females of all ages and all reproductive stages, leads Rice (1981: 409) to conclude that these figurines were not associated with fertility, let alone with a fertility goddess. Just as importantly, Rice notes, so much variation among the physical appearance of these figurines makes it highly unlikely that they represent the idealized representation of a single goddess of any sort.

In summary, then, whether we look at parietal art or the Venus figurines, there is no evidence suggesting that a goddess cult existed during the Paleolithic. In fact, the evidence seems to suggest that such a cult did *not* exist. If the Mary cult does derive from a longstanding tradition (and that has by no means been established), that tradition did not originate—as James and Gimbutas claim—in the Paleolithic.

Mary as Earth Mother

When we come to the agricultural societies of the Neolithic, however, we find a veritable explosion of goddesses. At Catal Hayuk, for instance, a Neolithic settlement in western Turkey that dates from the sixth to seventh millennium B.C., archeologists have uncovered evidence of "shrines" or "cult rooms" in which representations of a goddess (or goddesses) figure prominently (Singh, 1974: 88-89; Mellaart, 1975: 108-110). The first great goddesses to whom we can attach names are those like Inanna and Ishtar, who appear in the religions of those agricultural societies that developed in the Fertile Crescent during the third millennium B.C.

The suggestion that agriculture promotes the development of a goddess cult is not new. In a well known article originally published in German in 1905, Albrecht Dieterich argued that the development of agriculture fosters the development of an Earth Mother religion, and Dieterich's argument has been repeated by a number of scholars over the intervening eighty years. Even those scholars who trace a goddess cult back to the Paleolithic concede that the development of agriculture changes the nature of this cult by transforming the goddess into an Earth Mother. As we might expect, some scholars have established, fairly casually, an identification between these agricultural Earth Mothers and the Virgin Mary (Bord and Bord, 1982: 4).

Yet despite the popularity of this hypothesis linking agriculture to goddesses, I know of no attempt to test it with anything other than anecdotal data. Such a test is possible, however, using data from the sccs. Most of those societies coded for "sex of supernatural beings" in Whyte (1978b) have also been coded for "degree of dependence upon agriculture for subsistence" by Murdock and Provost (1973: column 3). For this analysis an "agricultural society" was defined as a society in which agriculture contributed more than any other subsistence activity to the food supply (codes 3 and 4 in column 3; Murdock and Provost, 1973). Whyte's (1978b) variable, "sex of supernatural beings," was again conceptualized as reflecting an emphasis upon the feminine among supernatural beings, and was dichotomized as before (codes 1 and 2 = low and codes 3 and 4 = high). The data showing the relationship between agriculture and an emphasis upon the feminine among supernatural beings is given in Table 2-3.

The data in this table do provide some support for the hypothesis being tested, since there is a moderately strong correlation between agriculture and a relatively high emphasis upon female supernatural beings (phi = .24), and the overall distribution is statistically significant, though just barely (p = .05, using Fisher's Exact Test, one-tailed).

But although the hypothesis linking agriculture to the feminine in religion receives some support, the explantation of this linkage is not obvious. For instance, those authors who have written on "Earth Mother religions" seem to imply that agricultural peoples would naturally be concerned with the fertility and the regeneration of the earth, and would (on the analogy with human birth) naturally tend to think of the earth in feminine terms. Taken together, these "natural" predispositions would result in the earth being personified in the form of an Earth Mother goddess. In a penetrating critique of the "Earth

TABLE 2-3

Relationship between a Reliance on Agriculture for Subsistence and a Relative Emphasis upon Female Supernatural Beings, for sccs Societies

| | *Relative Emphasis upon Female Supernatural Beings* | |
	low	*high*
Agricultural societies	19	26
All other societies	15	7

NOTE: phi = .24, p = .05, using Fisher's Exact Test, one-tailed.

Mother" tradition, however, Pettersson (1967) has brought out several problems with this argument. First, there is no evidence to suggest that the most important goddesses of the Classical world were directly associated with the earth. Second, those goddesses who were directly associated with the earth, such as the Greek goddess Gaia, were not the focus of popular cults. Finally, the argument assumes that the earth would "just naturally" be conceptualized in female terms. Although this was true in Greece and Rome, it was not true in ancient Egypt (Pettersson, 1967: 82-84), and so the universality of this assumption must be questioned.

Even if we do not understand *why* agriculture promotes an emphasis upon the feminine in religion, an association between these two variables does seem to exist. Nevertheless, we must remember (again) that Mary's complete disassociation from sexual intercourse makes her quite unlike the mother goddesses that were popular in the great agricultural societies of the ancient world. In other words, although there might be something about agriculture that promotes the development of mother goddess cults in general, there is nothing in the present discussion that would allow us to explain why certain agricultural societies (like Italy and Spain) are attracted to the Virgin Mary, whereas other agricultural societies (like, say, ancient Sumer and Akkad) were attracted to such sexually promiscuous mother goddesses as Inanna and Ishtar.

GEOFFREY ASHE:
THE MARY CULT AND THE COLLYRIDIANS

Although most of the hypotheses about the origins of the Mary cult have been put forward by investigators who have not been much concerned with documenting their hypothesis in any precise manner, there is an exception to this pattern, to be found in the work of Geoffrey Ashe. Ashe is a British scholar known primarily for a number of semipopular books and articles that he has written on the historical origins of the Arthurian legends.[2] One of his books, however, is about

[2] For a sampling of Ashe's work on the Arthurian legends see Ashe (1957) as well as the articles by Ashe in Ashe (1968). Ashe has also published a novel that might be of interest to some readers (1973), because he uses it as a vehicle for explaining the Arthurian legends (among other things) using Jungian concepts.

the Virgin Mary. Entitled simply *The Virgin*, it is the only work I know of that tries to account for the historical origins of the Mary cult using a reasonably systematic methodology. Just as importantly, perhaps, *The Virgin* was written for a popular, rather than a scholarly, audience, and so is very likely the most widely read of all modern works on the Mary cult. Yet despite the high visibility of Ashe's book and the fact that it has been reviewed in a few scholarly journals (Wilson, 1976; E. Carroll, 1978), Ashe's theory has not as yet been subjected to any substantial degree of critical scrutiny.

Ashe organizes his book in much the same way that I have organized the first half of this one: he sets out some facts about the Mary cult that seem puzzling, and then develops an explanation that accounts for these facts. For Ashe, one of the most important observations to be made about the Mary cult is that there is so little justification for it in the New Testament. To establish this, Ashe spends most of the first half of his book developing exegeses of New Testament passages that refer to Mary. In this endeavor, Ashe shows no great awareness of modern Biblical scholarship, and tends instead to take the accounts in the New Testament at face value. But it would be wrong to criticize him too strongly on this point. Since most early Christians also took the New Testament at face value, Ashe is justified in trying to demonstrate that such an approach to the New Testament would not in itself have given rise to the Mary cult. The other observation that Ashe discusses was also dealt with in the first chapter of this book: there is little evidence of the Mary cult during the first four centuries of the Christian era.

Having established that the Mary cult could not have derived from the official traditions preserved in the New Testament, and that it did not make its appearance in the Church until at least the fifth century A.D., Ashe concludes that there must have existed an independent Marian Church, that is, a widespread and organized group that venerated Mary, that existed side by side with the official Church during the first four centuries of the Christian era and that was assimilated by the official Church sometime during the fifth to sixth centuries. Ashe then claims to find evidence of just such a Marian Church in the writings of Epiphanius, who was bishop of Salamis (in Cyprus) during the latter part of the fourth century.

Epiphanius' best known work, and the one that Ashe is concerned with, was his *Panarion*, also called "A Medicine Chest of Remedies against Heresies." Epiphanius' goal in this work was to list and describe all the heresies that had existed since the earliest days of Christianity, and he discusses eighty of them, in chronological order. The heresy of importance to Ashe is Epiphanius' seventy-ninth, which was associated with a group called the Collyridians. According to Ephiphanius, the Collyridians were a sect composed mainly of women, and which admitted women to the priesthood. They were originally from Thrace, though they had spread north into Scythia and south into Arabia, and their central ritual involved the offering up of "small cakes." (In Greek, "small cake" or "small loaf" = *collyris*; hence the name Collyridians.) But most importantly for Ashe, Epiphanius describes the Collyridians as worshiping the Virgin Mary. Ashe regards the Collyridians as being the tip of a Marian iceberg, and the existence of this group constitutes the entirety of his evidence in support of the assertion that there was an organized and widespread Marian religion during the first four centuries of the Christian era.

Having established the existence of the Collyridians in the late fourth century, Ashe sets out to provide them with a past and a future—and, in each case, he admits that his historical reconstructions are pure speculation that cannot be verified in any detail. As to the past, Ashe traces the Collyridians back to the Virgin Mary herself. In Ashe's account, the historical Mary, rebuffed by the early leaders of the Church, left Jerusalem and founded a community of holy women in some wilderness area. This community continued to flourish after Mary's death, especially in those areas (like Scythia, Thrace, and Arabia) where the influence of the early official Church was little felt.

In discussing the post-fourth century history of the Collyridians, Ashe assumes that sometime during the fifth century or so, the Church assimilated the Marian Church of which the Collyridians were a part. As part of the mutual accomodation involved in this assimilation, the Church accepted a greater emphasis upon the veneration of Mary, while the Collyridians accepted the view that the priesthood should be limited to males. According to Ashe, it was this organizational amalgamation that produced the sudden appearance of the Mary cult within the Church during the fifth and sixth centuries.

What Ashe needs to explain, of course, is why the Church would want to assimilate such an independent Marian Church in the fifth and sixth centuries—and he does. Ashe instructs us to consider the tremendous social upheavals that were taking place during this period,

(43)

and points to a number of barbarian invasions as evidence of such up-heavals. During such trying times, Ashe argues, people would natu-rally yearn for the sense of security provided by a mother goddess like Mary. The Church's choice then (according to Ashe) was either to ca-ter to this yearning by assimilating the Marian Church or to lose out to the Marian Church in the competition for followers.

In evaluating Ashe's argument, it cannot be emphasized too strongly that Epiphanius is the only commentator prior to the sixth century who mentions the Collyridians. They are mentioned in a few later accounts, but in every case that I have examined, these accounts cite Epiphanius as their source. Moreover, this general neglect of the Collyridians is not due to the fact that the *Panarion* is the only survey of early heretical sects available to us. On the contrary, heresy was an important issue in the early Church, and several such surveys were put together during the Patristic period. Prior to the *Panarion* (which was published c. A.D. 377), for instance, Iranaeus had completed (c. 225) his well known *Against Heresies*, and Eusebius had completed (c. 312-325) his *Church History from A.D. 1-324*. Both of these works de-scribed and discussed dozens of heresies. Subsequent to the *Panarion*, continuations of Eusebius' *Church History* were published both by Socrates Scholasticus (c. 439) and Sozomen (c. 445), and Theodoret published (c. 453) his *History of Heresies*. None of these works men-tions the Collyridians, nor do they mention any heretical group that worshiped Mary. It strains credulity to believe that the "Marian Church" described by Ashe could have been as widespread as his ar-gument requires, and yet be ignored by all those who commented upon early heresies other than Epiphanius.

It almost goes without saying that we also have no documentary record of a key event in Ashe's theory, namely, the assimilation of the Marian Church into the official Church. Though we have a fairly good record of how the various councils and synods of the Church treated most other heresies of the period, we have no record of any council or synod that dealt with the Collyridians, and certainly no record of the Collyridians being assimilated into the Church.

In summary, then, there is no evidence at all to support Ashe's con-tention that the Collyridians were the tip of a widespread Marian Church that existed side by side with the official Church during the first four centuries of the Christian era, and no evidence that the two Churches were merged in the fifth century. If anything, the lack of references to the Collyridians in the early literature on heresy suggests that they were an obscure sect of no great importance.

Having said all this, we are still confronted with the fact that Epiphanius does mention those Mary-worshiping Collyridians. It would be far easier to reject Ashe's argument if we could provide the Collyridians with a past and a future (relative to Epiphanius) congruent with the history of some known heresy. In fact, this is easily done.

There were two characteristics that most distinguished the Collyridians, according to Epiphanius: they worshiped the Virgin Mary and they admitted women to the priesthood. Epiphanius himself uses the Collyridians as much to argue against the idea of female priests as to argue against the worship of Mary. But the fact that the Collyridians admitted females to the priesthood establishes a clear similarity between this group and an early heretical sect called the Montanists. Unlike the Collyridians, the Montanists have a well documented history.[3] They were discussed by all the Church historians mentioned earlier, including Epiphanius, as well as by Patristic commentators such as Tertullian (who was himself a Montanist for a while) and Jerome.

Montanus was a Christian who lived in Phrygia (now west-central Turkey) toward the end of the second century A.D. Some accounts make him an ex-priest of the Magna Mater cult who had recently been converted to Christianity; other accounts suggest that he was in fact a Christian bishop. In any event, Montanus claimed the gift of prophecy, and he attracted two women, Maximilla and Priscilla, who claimed the same gift. The claim to prophecy did not in itself make the early Montanists heretics; only much later, and mainly in reaction to Montanism, did the Church decide that the age of prophecy was over.

In fact, all commentators agree in suggesting that the early Montanists did not differ from the Church over any point of doctrine. They were noted only for their emphasis upon prophecy, for their belief in the imminence of the Parousia (the Second Coming), and for their excessive asceticism. (It was this last point that made Montanism especially popular with Tertullian, who was their most famous convert.) The Montanists believed that during the Parousia, Christ would appear at Pepuza, a town in western Phrygia that they called the New Jerusalem. For this reason, the Montanists were often called Pepuzi-

[3] The Patristic literature dealing with the Montanists is extensive. For a review of that literature, see Chapman (1911), Kidd (1922: 278-296), and Schaff (1910: 415-427).

ans. I might mention that Epiphanius lists both the Montanists and the Pepuzians (they are his forty-eighth and forty-ninth heresies, respectively), and considers them to be related distinct sects. Most other commentators, however—both in the Patristic period and in the present—use the terms "Montanist" and "Pepuzian" interchangeably.

Over time, however, the Montanists/Pepuzians did come to espouse a doctrine that was clearly heretical: they allowed women to become priests, and even bishops. This, of course, is one of the things that establishes a similarity between the Pepuzians of the second and third centuries and the Collyridians of the late fourth century.

I can find no reference to the Pepuzians worshiping the Virgin Mary. There are, however, a number of observations that—when put together—suggest that their beliefs had some affinity with Maryworship. First, "Virgin" seems to have been a formal rank among the Pepuzians, and it was a title claimed by both Priscilla and Maximilla. (Since both women had been married, the label obviously did not refer to physical virginity, but rather to abstinence from sexual intercourse past a certain point in their lives.) Women holding the title Virgin also played a part in some Pepuzian rituals (Chapman, 1911: 523). Second, Pepuza was identified as the New Jerusalem because it was at Pepuza that Christ appeared to Priscilla in a dream. What is most interesting about this dream in the present context is Priscilla's report that Christ had appeared to her in the form of a woman. Finally, we know that during their ceremonies the Pepuzians prayed to Eve (Chapman, 1911: 523), and Eve was widely regarded in the Eastern Church as the precursor of Mary.

At this point, then, two possibilities suggest themselves. On the one hand, it seems plausible to suggest that an emphasis upon a virgin foundress, upon virginity, upon Christ in the form of a woman, and upon Eve might cause at least a few Pepuzian groups to develop—over the course of two centuries—into groups who worshiped the Virgin Mary. Another possibility is that Epiphanius' account of the Collyridians is simply a garbled account of a run-of-the-mill Pepuzian sect. In other words, it seems plausible to suggest that an account of some fourth-century group of Pepuzian ancestry, which claimed a virgin foundress, emphasized virginity, talked of Christ in the form of a woman, and so on, might be transformed—if repeated often enough—into a description of a sect that worshiped the Virgin Mary. This description might then have been picked up by Epiphanius, who did not recognize the Pepuzian connection.

Finally, I might note that there is some basis for associating the Pepuzians with Thrace, which according to Epiphanius was the original home of the Collyridians. "Thrace" was the name given to that part of modern Bulgaria which lies directly north of modern Turkey, and this in itself means that Thrace was relatively close to Phrygia (where the Pepuzians originated), located in what is now west-central Turkey. There is, however, at least one reference in the Patristic literature that establishes an even closer connection between the Pepuzians and Thrace, in Eusebius' *Church History*. In his section on Montanism, Eusebius makes several references to the prophetesses Maximilla and Priscilla, but only twice associates either one with a specific geographical location. In one passage (Chapter 18: v. 13), however, Eusebius tells us that Maximilla was opposed by a local bishop while she "was pretending to prophesy in Pepuza," and in a later passage (Chapter 19: v. 3), Eusebius records the report of another bishop who mentions Priscilla. The full text of this second passage is:

[from] Aelius Publius Julius, bishop of Debeltum, a colony of Thrace. As God liveth in the heavens, the blessed Sotas in Anchialus desired to cast the demon out of Priscilla, but the hypocrites did not permit him.

Aelius Publius Julius and Sotas are unknown outside of this passage, but Debeltum and Anchialus are identified as cities in Thrace. This passage therefore very clearly suggests that the Montanist prophetess Priscilla was sufficiently active in some areas of Thrace to have attracted the opposition of "the blessed Sotas" (whoever he might have been) and a local bishop.

One advantage of identifying the Collyridians as deriving from the Montanist tradition is that it allows us to explain the absence of earlier references to them: the group that became the "Collyridians" had been described, but under the "Montanist/Pepuzian" heading. Such an identification also allows us to provide the Collyridians with a future, since we know that Montanism achieved a widespread popularity (at least in Asia Minor and North Africa) that seems to have peaked around the fifth to sixth centuries.

It might be argued, of course, that the history of Montanism actually lends some degree of support to Ashe's argument. The Montanist movement did constitute something like a parallel Church, and it did admit women to the priesthood—as did the "independent Marian Church" whose existence is posited by Ashe. Had the Montanist movement been assimilated into the Church around the fifth century, it would be relatively easy to develop a variant of Ashe's theory that does account for the emergence of the Mary cult during that century. But such an assimilation never occurred. Starting as early as the end of the second century, the Montanists were regularly condemned by several synods and councils of the Church, and a reconciliation between the Montanist Church and the official Church never took place. In A.D. 601, for instance, Pope Gregory the Great still felt it necessary to warn the Spanish clergy about the invalidity of baptisms performed by Montanist priests. Even as late as the ninth century, the patriarch of Constantinople complained to the Emperor about the need to do something about the Montanists.

I have devoted so much attention to the possible link between the Collyridians and the Pepuzians because Epiphanius' reference to the Collyridians is the only piece of concrete evidence that Ashe can adduce in support of his theory. If the Collyridians can be accounted for plausibly under the hypothesis that they were Pepuzians, then there is nothing left to recommend Ashe's theory.

CONCLUSION

In reviewing theories about the Mary cult offered by previous investigators, my goal has been to see if any of them can explain important observations about the Mary cult. In fact, we have found that two of these theories do appear to be of some use in this regard. Thus, it does appear, first, that patronage (at least of the Latin Mediterranean variety) does promote an emphasis upon supernatural mediators, and second, that a heavy reliance on agriculture does promote devotion to female deities. We would therefore expect that a goddess-mediator like Mary, once introduced into a society characterized by patron/client relationships or by a heavy reliance on agriculture, would tend to become popular; and this appears to be so.

Having said this, I must emphasize once again that neither the "patronage" hypothesis nor the "agriculure" hypothesis seems capable of explaining Mary's complete disassociation from sexual intercourse or the relative absence of the Mary cult during the first four centuries of the Christian era. To explain these things, then, we must look elsewhere.

SOME PSYCHOANALYTIC
HYPOTHESES

We have so far noted several times that the Mary cult is especially strong in southern Italy and in Spain.[1] On the basis of the evidence reviewed in the last chapter, this can be attributed in part to the facts that patron-client relationships are extensive in these regions and that both regions had traditonally relied heavily upon agriculture. Yet anyone who is familiar with the vast literature on the anthropology of the Mediterranean that has accumulated over the past twenty-five years[2] cannot help but wonder if the extraordinary devotion to Mary in these regions is not also connected with other cultural traits that characterize these same societies.

It is now fairly well established, for instance, that the *machismo* complex, though found in several Mediterranean countries, is especially strong in southern Italy and Spain.[3] The *machismo* complex is a male-centered ideology that encourages men to be sexually aggressive, to brag about their sexual prowess and their genital attributes, and to dominate women sexually. It leads to a view of the ideal man as being a man totally under the control of his testicles. One of the informants questioned by Gilmore (1983: 244) in his study of an Andalusian agricultural town expressed the basic idea by saying that a *macho* is "a man who would instantly make love to a shovel if you dressed it like a woman." Gilmore also points out that the *Machismo* world view contrasts sharply with the sexual ideology that prevails in, say, the Muslim countries that border the Mediterranean, where it is

---

[1] The argument developed in this chapter is a somewhat modified version of the argument that was presented in Carroll (1983). Permission to reprint some of the passages from Carroll (1984) has been granted by the Society for the Scientific Study of Religion, which holds the copyright to that article.

[2] For some critical reviews of this "anthropology of the Mediterranean" tradition see Gilmore (1982) and Herzfeld (1984).

[3] For a review of the literature dealing specifically with the *machismo* complex in Mediterranean societies, see Gilmore and Gilmore, 1979: 281-283 and Saunders (1981).

usually the female who is seen as being subject to barely controllable concupiscence.

Saunders' (1981) review of the literature relating to the *machismo* complex in the Mediterranean area makes it clear that most scholars see this complex as a compensatory response on the part of males to a conflict produced by an early feminine identification followed by a later masculine identification. There also seems to be some consensus that this psychic conflict is somehow linked to the dynamics of the father-ineffective family. By definition, a father-ineffective family is a family-type characterized by the concentration of de facto authority within the home in the hands of the mother, and is usually considered to be a result of the widespread economic marginality of males.

The basic argument is that sons raised in a father-ineffective family will tend to identify initially with their mothers, thus acquiring a feminine identification. As these sons mature, however, they will discover that the larger society expects them to act like males. Their early feminine identification will therefore produce in these sons an insecurity about their masculinity, and they react to this insecurity by engaging in exaggerated masculine behavior. This exaggerated masculinity is the *machismo* complex.

Under this argument, the fact that the *machismo* complex is especially strong in such areas as southern Italy and Spain is traceable to the fact that the father-ineffective family is especially common in these regions (Saunders, 1981: 456). The father-ineffective family is, of course, by no means unique to southern Europe. It is precisely the same family type that Oscar Lewis (1959; 1965) long ago documented as characteristic of the lower classes in such New World Hispanic societies as Mexico and Puerto Rico. Lewis too, I might add, traced the *machismo* complex to the intrapsychic conflicts that develop in males raised in such a family.

Scholarly consensus breaks down, however, over the issue of how the father-ineffective family produces an early feminine identification. For instance, the father-ineffective family is usually associated with frequent absence of the father, either because he is away pursuing the few jobs that are available or because his ineffectual status within the household causes him to seek the company of other adult males outside the household as much as possible. There is a longstanding tradition in a psychological anthropology, associated with John Whiting and his associates, which argues that this absence of the father produces the early feminine identification in sons. Several scholars working in the Whiting tradition, therefore, have suggested that the *machismo* complex derives ultimately from absence of the father (see Burton and Whiting, 1961). But unfortunately for the Whiting argument, there is much evidence to suggest that absence of the father (whatever its other effects might be) does not lead to an early feminine identification (see the review in Parker, Smith, and Ginat, 1975).

My own view is that the father-ineffective family probably produces an early identification with the mother because of her status as authority figure. I assume that sons in the father-ineffective family, like all sons, come to develop a sexual desire for their mother and, driven by castration anxiety, feel that this desire must be repressed. (How the nature of the father-ineffective family affects the strength of the son's desire for the mother, and the strength of his castration anxiety, will be considered in the next section.) But sons raised in a father-ineffective family, like all sons, will face the problem of how to carry out this repression.

In discussing the normal (in the sense of usual) Oedipal process for males, Freud argued that sons will repress their desire for the mother by identifying with the father.[4] He argued that since the father is an authority figure within the home, identification with him means that the son can introject the father's authoritativeness (that is, bring it into his own mind and surround his image of himself with this same sense of authoritativeness), and then use this introjected authority to order himself to repress his desire for the mother.

But in the father-ineffective family, it is the mother who is the authoritative figure, and so (assuming Freud's general argument to be correct) the only way that a son can obtain the introjected authority to repress his desire for the mother is to identify with the mother. It is this, I argue, not the absence of the father, that produces an early feminine identification in sons raised in a father-ineffective family.

I should point out that neither the interpretation just offered nor that offered by Whiting and his associates exhausts the range of possible hypotheses linking the father-ineffective family to an early feminine identification in sons. Gilmore and Gilmore (1979), for instance, in their discussion of the *machismo* complex, trace the son's early feminine identification to a variety of pre-Oedipal processes.

---

[4] Though Freud presented his views on the Oedipal process for the male in several of his works, I have relied mainly upon Freud (1964 [1932]).

THE FATHER-INEFFECTIVE FAMILY AND OTHER
ASPECTS OF THE OEDIPAL PROCESS

Although Mediterranean scholars have devoted a great deal of attention to the issue of how the father-ineffective family affects the son's early identification (and how this, in turn, leads to the *machismo* complex), they have not been much concerned with how this family structure might affect other psychological variables. The major exception is the late Anne Parsons (1969), a pioneer in the application of the psychoanalytic perspective to the study of Mediterranean family structures. Before summarizing her argument, however, we must make explicit the distinction between "identification" and "sexual attachment." Though the distinction is clear in psychoanalytic literature, it is too often blurred in other discussions.

"Identification" is easy to define: it refers to the process of adopting the characteristics of someone else, and includes adopting them only in one's own mind. When a son imitates his father's behavior, or surrounds himself with the sense of authoritativeness that he associates with his father, we say that the son is identifying with his father. To understand "sexual attachment," however, we must first understand Freud's use of the term "sexual," since the discrepancy between his use of this term and common usage has always been one of the major barriers to a wider understanding of Freud's theories.

Freud argued that we all experience a continuous buildup of sexual (or "libidinous") energy, and that unless this energy is periodically released in some way, we experience tension. Any activity that allows us to release this built-up sexual energy is, by definition, a sexual activity. The release of tension that accompanies sexual activity (so defined) inevitably produces a diffuse sense of physical pleasure. As a result, Freud tended to see any activity that produced a diffuse sense of physical pleasure as a sexual activity. Sexual intercourse is a sexual activity in this sense, but so are a variety of other activities. Kissing, holding, touching, caressing, and so on, are usually associated with a diffuse sense of physical pleasure and so are usually considered by Freud to be sexual activities. Even being in the presence of someone you love can often produce a diffuse sense of physical pleasure, and so it too is a sexual activity in Freud's view.

Given this view of sexuality, it seems obvious that the young child will experience a variety of different sexual activities and will associate those activities with certain individuals more than with others. The more the young child associates a particular individual (say, the mother) with sexual activities, the more the child will invest that individual with sexual energy, a process that Freud calls "cathexis." The more the young child cathects a given individual, the more he or she will seek out additional sexual activities with that individual. When this occurs we say that the child has become sexually attached to that individual. The division of labor that prevails in most societies insures that mothers are generally the ones who have primary responsibility for raising their children. This means that mothers are the ones most likely to hold, touch, and caress those children, which in turn means (for Freud) that the first sexual attachment of both the son and the daughter will usually be to the mother.

It is this psychoanalytic perspective on sexuality that informs Parsons' (1969) study of the father-ineffective family among the working class in Naples. Parsons is well aware that this family type diverges considerably from that implicit in Freud's own studies. But instead of rejecting Freud out of hand, she asks how the structure of the father-ineffective family would affect the variables that define the Oedipal process that Freud describes. One of her conclusions is that the father-ineffective family should intensify the son's sexual attachment to his mother, as a result of the greater amount of interaction between the son and his mother. The hypothesis that the absence of the father increases the son's sexual attachment of the mother (unlike the hypothesis that the father's absence promotes identification with the mother) has received a substantial amount of empirical support (Stephens, 1962: M.P. Carroll, 1978).

But apart from identification and sexual attachment, there is a third variable that would be dramatically affected by the structure of the father-ineffective family. This is castration anxiety, and the discusson linking the father-ineffective family to castration anxiety will be especially important when we return to explaining the Mary cult.

Consider how and why castration anxiety develops. In the family situation considered by Freud, both the father and the mother are present in the home on a fairly regular basis. Given this, the son will eventually perceive that the father is a rival for the sexual favors of the mother, that is, the father—like himself—wants to hold, touch, caress, and be in the physical presence of the mother. But in the eyes of his son, a father is no ordinary rival, but a giant associated with enormous power. Facing such an omnipotent rival, the son will come to fear that the father will retaliate against him for daring to want what the father also wants. When the son becomes aware of the anatomical difference between the sexes, he will suddenly know the likely form of this retaliation: someone will detach his penis just as someone had detached the penis of his mother and his sisters. Freud, somewhat misleadingly, used the term "castration anxiety" to describe the young son's fear of "penis-detachment."

Driven by this fear, the son will act to eliminate the perceived threat from his father by repressing his desire for his mother, that is, he will drive the sexual desire for his mother into his unconscious mind. This repressed desire for the mother will remain latent in the unconscious until puberty. At that time hormonal changes will energize all the son's sexual desires, including those in the unconscious. The strength of the mother-son incest taboo (that is, the strong sense that intercourse with a mother is morally wrong) will insure that his sexual desire for the mother cannot enter his conscious mind directly, so it comes to consciousness in the form of a generalized desire for women.

How would the nature of the father-ineffective family affect this basic process? We must remember that the absence of the father associated with the father-ineffective family does not mean that the father is absent for years at a time. On the contrary, although he might be absent during the day, or even for a period of several days or weeks, he does return to the household on a regular basis throughout the year. In other words, the son is still confronted with the father on a regular basis. On these occasions, then, the son will still see the father as a rival, and, more importantly, will still believe that the father sees *him* as a rival. The special nature of the father-ineffective family, however, will affect the nature of this rivalry.

The fact that the son's desire for the mother in this situation is especially strong should in itself intensify the son's sense of rivalry with the father, and thus should intensify the son's fear of retaliation from the father. Remember too that the father facing the son in this situation is a man under the influence of the *machismo* ideology, which means that he defines himself (and is likely to be defined by his son) as sexually aggressive. Such a father would almost certainly be regarded by the son as a more dangerous rival than the sort of father who would be found in the middle-class Viennese families studied by Freud. Consistent with all this is the finding, which emerges clearly from the various projective tests that Parsons (1969: 73-77) gave to her Neapolitan subjects, that the father-son relationship in the father-ineffective family is characterized by a great deal of overt hostility.

In the end, then, I am suggesting that the association of males (and thus fathers) with sexual aggressiveness in areas like southern Italy and Spain should have the effect of intensifying a son's fear of castration. This intensified castration anxiety should in turn insure a stronger repression of the son's sexual desire for the mother than is usually the case. Thus I agree with those Mediterranean scholars who have argued that the father-ineffective family results in the *machismo* complex, and I accept Parson's suggestion that this same family structure intensifies the son's sexual attachment to the mother. I add only the suggestion that the son's sexual desire for the mother in this situation will not only be strong but also strongly repressed.

It is now time to demonstrate how all of this helps us to understand the Mary cult.

THE PSYCHOANALYTIC ORIGINS OF THE MARY CULT

At the most general level, devotion to the Virgin Mary is an example of a religious devotional practice, and Freud (1959 [1907]) long ago provided the standard psychoanalytic perspective on such practices. He argued that the desires in our unconscious are constantly struggling to enter the conscious mind; the repression of these desires requires a nearly continual supply of psychic energy. If a desire in our unconscious is exceptionally strong, then the psychic energy required to keep it fully repressed is correspondingly great, and constantly to divert this amount of psychic energy to the process of repression would be wasteful. A compromise solution is to allow the energy that builds up to be discharged through some activity that represents the disguised fulfillment of that unconscious desire. According to Freud (1959 [1907]), this is the process that gives rise both to the obsessive rituals associated with neurosis and to the devotional practices associated with religion. This argument is more or less identical to the argument that he developed to explain dreams (Freud, 1953 [1900]) and hallucinations (1961a [1923]), since he saw these phenomena, too, as reflecting the disguised fulfillment of unconscious wishes.

The unconscious desires that give rise to religious devotions, obsessions, dreams, and hallucinations must be disguised because to allow them to enter the conscious mind in an obvious way would be to defeat the whole point of repression. Freud used the term "dreamwork" to describe the various processes that disguise our unconscious desires, and dreamwork includes such well-known psychoanalytic processes as displacement, condensation, negation, symbolization, and projection. But though the unconscious desires that give rise, say, to religious devotional practices are disguised by dreamwork, there usually remains some degree of similarity between the practice and the desire that gave rise to it.

Given Freud's views on religious devotional practices in general, given what we know about the Mary cult, and given the discussion about the effects of the father-ineffective family on the Oedipal process, three hypotheses about the Mary cult suggest themselves. My argument will be clearer, I think, if I first present and discuss each of these hypotheses, and only then proceed to demonstrate how they can be used to explain a range of observations about the Mary cult.

The first hypothesis is fairly straightforward.

> *Hypothesis 1.* Fervent devotion to the Mary cult on the part of males is a practice that allows males characterized by a strong but strongly repressed sexual desire for the mother to dissipate in an acceptable manner the excess sexual energy that is built up as a result of this desire.

I claim no great originality for this hypothesis, and suspect that it has been offered, at least in passing, by any number of investigators; certainly it seems implicit in Parsons (1969), though she never states it as baldly as I have. I also suspect that any psychoanalytically inclined investigator who gave the Mary cult any thought would probably regard this hypothesis as self-evident.

But there is a corollary to this hypothesis that will probably seem more problematic to most readers:

> *Hypothesis 2.* The distinctive features of the Mary cult over the centuries have been shaped primarily by the son's strong but strongly repressed desire for his mother.

The problem with this second hypothesis, of course, is that it sees the content of the Mary cult as having been shaped only by the desires found in the male unconscious, even though we know that the cult receives the support of both males and females.

The fact is that virtually every psychoanalytically inclined investigator who has studied religion has argued that the content of religion is shaped by impulses and desires found in the male unconscious. Freud himself, for instance, traced the content of myth, and the content of religion generally, to impulses and desires created in the male during the Oedipal period. Malinowski (1955) found that Trobriand mythology reflected the son's hostility toward his mother's brother. Dundes (1962) found that the Earth-Diver myth reflected a male's envy over the ability of females to give birth. Spiro (1979) found that the Bororo myth he was analysing reflected the son's Oedipal desires. Carroll (1982) saw the Rolling Head myth found among North American Indians as reflecting a son's fear of castration—and so on. This tendency to trace the content of religious belief back to the male unconscious is taken for granted by these investigators; it is never justified. Some would see in all this nothing more than a reflection of the fact that these investigators are themselves male. Possibly. But the tendency is evident even when the psychoanalytic investigator is female, as with Nadelson's (1981) study of Mundurucu mythology.

In the end, the issue can only be resolved by empirical research. Ideally, this means developing two different interpretations of the same set of religious beliefs, one tracing those beliefs back to the masculine unconscious and the other back to the feminine unconscious, and then determining which interpretation is better supported. For instance, elsewhere (Carroll, 1985a) I have considered a myth found among a large number of the Indian societies of North America. The central incident in this myth is a Trickster father who lusts after his own daughter, feigns death, and then reappears as a stranger in order to marry her. There would seem to be two obvious psychoanalytic interpretations of such a myth. First, the myth could be seen as a projection of the daughter's incestuous desires for her father, and second, it could be seen as a straightforward reflection of a father's incestuous desires for his own daughter. Using data from the *Ethnographic Atlas* relating to those societies in which this myth was found, each hypothesis was developed and tested. Only the hypothesis that traced the content of the myth to the father's incestuous desire for his daughter received any support. Here, then, is a case in which it seems difficult to argue that a male-oriented interpretation of the data was imposed on that data.

A single test, of course, never proves very much. But this test, together with the fact that most previous investigators have found the assumption that religious beliefs are most shaped by the male unconscious to be useful, leads me to adopt that assumption here in the form of Hypothesis 2.

Yet this hypothesis says only that the *content* of the Mary cult will be shaped by the son's strong but strongly repressed desire for the mother. We must still develop female analogue to Hypothesis 1, that is, we must still explain why the Mary cult, once established, attracts female devotees. The key here, I think, lies with a well-established observation: in those areas where the Mary cult is strong, females are encouraged to emulate the Virgin Mary in both her roles, as virgin and as mother (cf. Warner, 1976). But this means that the attitude of female devotees toward Mary is quite different from that of males. The latter, after all, are not encouraged to be either virgins or mothers—and, in fact the *machismo* ideology works directly against remaining a "virgin."

The question we must ask ourselves, then, is why identification with the Virgin Mary would be of any value to females. The answer lies in Freud's discussion of the Oedipal process for females.[5] He argued that a daughter's first sexual attachment, like that of the son, will be to the mother. But the daughter will very quickly become aware of the anatomical difference between the sexes. Because the genital region is so intimately associated with sexual stimulation and because the daughter (like all children) operates under a "bigger is better" principle, the daughter will feel generally inferior. The daughter then turns to the father in the hope that he can provide her with the wished-for penis. She quickly realizes that this is impossible, and so her "wish for a penis" from the father becomes a "wish for a baby" from the father. The daughter may not be fully cognizant of the nature of the reproductive act, but she will know that "making a baby" involves close physical contact between a man and a woman. Her desire for a baby

---

[5] Freud's view of the Oedipal process for females changed several times over the course of his career (although his views on the Oedipal process for males remained relatively constant). The summary I have presented here reflects his final position, which was outlined at various places in Freud (1964 [1932]).

from the father, then, inevitably brings along with it a desire for close contact with the father, which Freud calls a desire for sexual contact with the father.

We can now understand the value to females of identifying with the Virgin Mary. Remember Leach's comment about Mary: she was a mere mortal with whom God the Father had a mystical relationship, and from whom she received a baby, Jesus Christ. That is, the Virgin Mary experienced what must be regarded as the ultimate fulfillment of every daughter's Oedipal desires, to have intercourse with the father and receive from him a baby. This leads to the third and final hypothesis.

> *Hypothesis 3.* Identifying strongly with the Virgin Mary allows women to experience vicariously the fulfillment of their desire for sexual contact with, and a baby from, their fathers.

As mentioned at the beginning of this book, the value of any hypothesis can only be demonstrated by showing how it can be used to make sense out of the data. It is now time to do just that.

EXPLAINING THE CENTRAL OBSERVATIONS

Hypotheses 1 and 2, taken together, provide the basis for explaining the thing that makes Mary so distinctive in comparison to earlier mother goddesses, namely, her complete disassociation from sexuality. We have already noted that if an obsessive practice is to be effective in discharging the sexual energy built up from strongly repressed sexual desires, it must be disguised. Disassociating Mary from explicit sexual intercourse is a way of effecting such a disguise. In other words, excessive devotion to a mother figure associated with sexual intercourse would be too obvious a reflection of the son's unconscious desire for his mother; excessive devotion to a mother figure who is disassociated from sexual intercourse, however, is not.

Explaining the strong historical association between the Mary cult and Latin Catholic areas like Spain and southern Italy must be done in two steps dealing, respectively, with males and with females.

Freud's general theory leads us to expect that all males in all societies will develop some degree of sexual desire for their mothers, and that in almost all cases, this desire will undergo some degree of repression. If Marian devotion is a way of discharging the sexual energy that builds up from such a repressed desire, then the Mary cult should have some appeal to males in all societies. But Hypothesis 1 leads us to expect that Marian devotion among males should be especially strong in those societies where the prevailing family structure produces in sons a desire for the mother that is especially strong and especially strongly repressed. As we have already seen, the father-ineffective family characteristic of proletarian settings in Spain and southern Italy is just that sort of family structure. Hypothesis 1 therefore leads us to expect that Marian devotion among males would be especially strong in these areas.

Similarly, Freud's general theory leads us to expect that daughters everywhere will come to desire their fathers to some degree. If identification with Mary by a female is indeed a vicarious fulfillment of the daughter's Oedipal wishes (as Hypothesis 3 suggests), then again we would expect the Mary cult to have a universal appeal, this time among females. But Hypothesis 3 also suggests that when the prevailing family structure in a society intensifies the daughter's desire for her father, then devotion to Mary among the females in that society should be correspondingly strong. In the case of females, then, we could explain the intensity of the Mary cult in areas like southern Italy and Spain if we could argue that the father-ineffective family intensifies the daughter's Oedipal desires for the father just as it intensifies the son's Oedipal desires for the mother. Can a reasonable case to this effect be made?

For Parsons (1969: 83-86), there is little doubt: she argues that the incestuous attraction between the daughter and the father in the typical Neapolitan working-class family is both strong and overt. That such a desire is overt comes as no surprise, since the daughter's desire for the father, unlike the son's desire for the mother, never comes to be strongly repressed. Parsons supports her conclusion here by pointing to various kinds of evidence: the overtly sexual references that were included by all her respondents in the descriptions of the TAT card illustrating a father and a daughter; the fact that her respondents seemed relatively tolerant of actual instances of father/daughter incest; the general perception among her respondents that daughters often seduced their fathers; and the extremely strong interest that fathers showed in the courtship of their daughters, which Parsons interprets as a projection of the father's own incestuous desires.

Parsons never explains why the father-ineffective family should intensify the daughter's Oedipal desires for the father; such an explanation, however, is not difficult. Remember that one consequence of the father-ineffective family is the *machismo* ideology, part of which emphasizes male sexuality and male genitalia. Parsons (1969: 30) notes that it is not uncommon among the families in her sample to allow very young boys to go about naked from the waist down and to have their penises singled out for teasing admiration by adults. Brandes (1980) has likewise documented the prevalence of the "big penis" motif in Andalusian folklore. But it is a sense of genital inferiority that leads the daughter to drop the mother as a sexual object and to turn to the father, first for a penis, and then for sexual intercourse and a baby. An ideology that emphasizes the male genitalia would presumably heighten a daughter's sense of genital inferiority and thereby intensify her attraction to the father.

In summary, then, though the process works differently for males and for females, in the end the father-ineffective family intensifies Oedipal desires in both sons and daughters, and so promotes Marian devotion. The association of the Mary cult with southern Italy and Spain can therefore be traced to the prevalence of the father-ineffective family in these regions.

Thus far the argument developed here explains two of the central observations about the Mary cult outlined in Chapter One, the association of the cult with southern Italy and Spain and the disassociation of Mary from sexual intercourse. It will be best to explain the third observation, the sudden appearance of the Mary cult in the fifth and sixth centuries A.D., in a separate chapter. For the moment I want to demonstrate that the argument developed so far can explain some aspects of the Mary cult not yet discussed.

MARIAN MASOCHISM

One of the most common criticisms directed against psychoanalytic explanations of the sort being presented here is that a committed psychoanalyst will be able to construct such an explanation no matter what the data. This criticism is often valid, and any psychoanalytically inclined investigator who ignores it will end up talking only to the already converted. But two possible responses have already been indicated in Chapter One: one may derive precise predictions from psychoanalytic arguments and test them using quantitative data; and one may develop psychoanalytic arguments that are capable of explaining a wide range of observations using a small number of theoretical principles. There is also a third response: having committed themselves to a particular psychoanalytic formulation, investigators must commit themselves to *all* the logical consequences of that formulation, and then check to see if those logical consequences obtain in data not yet gathered. An example should clarify this point.

Freud, on several occasions (1955a [1919]; 1961b [1924]; 1961d [1930]; 1964 [1932]), considered the psychic effects of an unconscious desire that was both strong and strongly repressed, and he quite consistently argued that such a desire produces a strong sense of guilt and a strong need for punishment. For Freud, guilt is produced because the super-ego knows that there is a strong but forbidden desire in the unconscious. Such guilt in turn produces a desire, usually unconscious, for expiation, and it is this desire to expiate guilt that gives rise to a need for punishment. This need in turn gives rise to accident-proneness and masochistic behavior. Freud (1961b [1924]) specifically considered the case of concern here—that of a son with a strong but strongly repressed desire for the mother. He argued that the resultant need for punishment would usually become a need for castration, since sons inevitably realize that castration is the most fitting form of punishment for their incestuous desires. Freud recognized, of course, that few males ever castrate themselves. He did argue, however, that a strong but strongly repressed desire for the mother will usually give rise to a need for symbolic castration, which for Freud meant bodily mutilation of some sort.

If, then, excessive Marian devotion on the part of males derives from a strong but strongly repressed sexual desire for the mother, then these same males should exhibit a masochistic need for punishment. In other words, we would expect to find an association between excessive Marian devotion and masochism. Though the evidence is sketchy, I think that evidence of such an association does exist.

Let us start with the responses given by Parson's Neapolitan subjects to the mother/son card in the TAT that was administered to them. According to Parsons (1969: 78) the following responses were typical:

> The son is asking forgiveness of the mother, repenting of the evil he has done.

Maybe he did something very serious, probably he went away and so now he has come back to ask her forgiveness and the mother no longer wants to receive him.

The mother has a son she has not seen for many years. . . . He returns after having done many bad things, stealing and other things. He returns to the family to ask forgiveness. Who knows whether or not the mother will give it to him but I think she will.

The son is asking forgiveness for something. . . . A mother would always forgive her son, even if he were an assassin, even if he were Chessman.

The penitent son who returns to the mother and the mother cannot or does not know how to forgive him.[6]

These responses do not show any evidence of overt sexuality, but we would not expect them to. What they do show is evidence of guilt, that is, of wrongdoing being attributed to the son in the presence of his mother. Parsons tells us that these responses were more likely to be elicited from male respondents than from female respondents, and that only the mother/son card elicited such attributions of guilt.

This attribution of such guilt to the son is exactly what Freud's theory leads us to expect if indeed the father-ineffective family does create in the son a strong but strongly repressed desire for his mother. On the other hand, I can find nothing in Parson's summary of her data to provide direct support for the predictions that the son's excessive guilt should produce a need for punishment, and in particular, a need for symbolic castration. But if we examine descriptions of how the Mary cult actually functions in southern Italy and Spain, not only do we find some support for this prediction, but we can make sense out of some otherwise puzzling observations.

Consider, for instance, Tentori's (1982) account of the rites associated with the sanctuary of the Madonna of the Arch near Naples—one of the few detailed accounts of a major Marian festival in southern Italy written by a social scientist. The central rites associated with the Madonna of the Arch take place on the Monday following Easter, and the central participants in those rites are called *fujenti* (those who flee). The *fujenti* are organized into groups that function as social clubs throughout the rest of the year. There are 310 of these groups in the

---

[6] These passages from Anne Parsons' (1969) *Belief, Magic and Anomie* are reprinted here with the permission of Macmillan Publishing Company, which holds the copyright.

Naples area alone, and the total number of *fujenti* is around 30,000.
On the day of the rites, each group of *fujenti* forms a "squadron" of its
members near the sanctuary. These squadrons are composed mainly
of males, and they proceed, one at a time, to the sanctuary. The resulting procession is observed by a large number of pilgrims who do
not take a direct part in the ceremonies. (In 1972, the year that Tentori
observed the rite, there were about 25,000 *fujenti* and 100,000 pilgrims.)

Tentori's account of the interaction between the *fujenti* and the surrounding crowd suggests that, at least until recently, the *fujenti* engaged in self-flagellation.

> The members of each company proceed in double file. Some of
> them wield rods with which they are allowed to keep the crowd
> of onlookers from blocking the passage of the column: this is
> why the devotees of the Madonna of the Arch who take part in
> the ritual are known as *vattienti* (*battenti*, "beaters") as well as *fu-*
> *jenti* (*fuggenti*, "those who flee"). *It is said that the vattienti once dealt*
> *blows to themselves rather than to the crowd, as a sign of pentience, but*
> *this is no longer the case.* (p. 101, emphasis added)

Masochistic behavior then, is evident in the "Madonna of the Arch"
rites not only by virtue of the fact that the members of the crowd willingly submit to beatings by the *vattienti*, but also in the fact that, until
recently at least, the *vattienti* were expected to beat themselves. Additional displays of masochistic behavior have occurred when the *fu-*
jenti reach the church itself. Here they fall upon their knees in order to
cross the threshold, and some remain upon their knees and crawl to
the central altar. In previous years, we are told, the *fujenti* would "lick
the floor with their tongues as they crawled to the main altar."
Though Tentori's account does suggest that the masochistic elements
in the behavior of the *fujenti* have been diluted in recent times, it is
worth noting that of the 25,000 who took part in the 1972 rites, 1,000
needed to be treated at the first-aid station.

Evidence of a masochistic need for punishment is also found in the
origin legends associated with the Madonna of the Arch. One of these
earliest legends, for instance, relates that in the fifteenth century, a
ballplayer engaged in the game of pall mall became angry and hurled
his ball against an image of the Virgin. As a result, the image started
to bleed, and the local populace was outraged. The player was given a

summary trial and hanged from the tree that held the Virgin's image. A somewhat later legend tells of how a middle-aged woman cut her foot and promised to make a votive offering to the image of the Virgin if the foot was healed. The wound did heal and the women did start to make the promised offering. The offering, however, fell from her hands, and the woman—in anger—trampled on it. That woman subsequently contracted gangrene, and both of her feet simply detached from her legs. The detached feet were placed in a basket, and it proved impossible to remove them from that basket, which was taken as a miracle. This basket, with the feet that were miraculously stuck to it, was displayed in the sanctuary of the Madonna.

Tentori (1982: 106) notes that the image of Mary conveyed in these legends is in sharp contrast to the image of Mary promoted by the official Church. The "official" Mary is usually portrayed as a beneficent mother figure, whereas these legends clearly associate the Madonna of the Arch with violence and brutal punishment. Under the interpretation being presented here, of course, the association of the Virgin Mary with violence and brutal punishment can be seen as reflecting the masochistic desires that result from the son's strong but strongly repressed desire for the mother. Notice, by the way, that in the case of each legend, the particular punishment meted out involves bodily mutilation (a neck being broken, feet being detached), which seems consistent with the prediction that the son's strong but strongly repressed sexual desire for the mother should produce a need for symbolic castration.

The fact that the character who experiences symbolic castration in one of these origin legends is a female is obviously not consistent with my argument. But though my argument cannot account for all the data, it seems capable of accounting for most of it. In particular, the interpretation offered here allows us to account for those observations about the Madonna of the Arch that appear most problematic, that is, the association of Mary with bodily mutilation in both origin legends and the masochistic behavior associated with the *fujenti* rites themselves. Finally, my argument requires that the *fujenti* rites should be most popular with Catholics, especially male Catholics, who have been raised in father-ineffective families; this seems consistent with Tentori's (1982: 96) report that most of those attending the rites are of working-class origin, which is the stratum in which the father-ineffective family is most prevalent.

One case study does not warrant a generalization, and my argument would be stronger if I could demonstrate that the masochistic behavior evident in the *fujenti* rites is evident in most of the Marian festivals celebrated in southern Italy. Unfortunately, I have been unable to locate reports on local religion in southern Italy that provide the sort of detail that characterizes Tentori's account. In the case of Spain, however, where we also expect an association between Marian devotion and masochistic behavior, detailed information on local religion is more readily available. This is mainly due to a series of excellent studies by William Christian (1972; 1981a, 1981b).

Using a variety of documentary records, such as chapel dedications, the dedications associated with major shrines and curing sites, and formalized religious requests ("vows"), Christian's work makes it clear that local religion in Spain has been characterized by a relatively strong emphasis upon devotion to Mary and to the saints since at least the sixteenth century. Over the period 1580-1780, however, Christian (1981a: 181-210) argues that we can also detect an increasing emphasis upon devotion to Christ himself. What is of particular interest to us is the form that this took: it consisted almost entirely in an emphasis upon Christ's Passion, that is, upon the scourging, the crowning with thorns, and the crucifixion. One of the most common of the devotional practices during this period was self-flagellation in imitation of the scourging of Christ. Flagellation was by no means unique to Spain, and organized groups of flagellants were quite common in many areas of Europe at least from the thirteenth century onward. In the case of these early flagellants, however, information on the relative size of the movement is sketchy, and it is not clear that their emphasis upon flagellation was connected with a devotion to the Passion of Christ. Furthermore, most of the medieval flagellant groups were quickly defined to be heretical and so expelled from the Church.

In the case of the flagellant movement in Spain from the sixteenth century onward, however, information on the relative size of the movement is available, and the movement was an integral part of the Spanish Church. Christian's review makes it clear, in fact, that the flagellant brotherhoods (and most of flagellant groups in Spain were composed of men) became enormously popular with both clergy and laity almost as soon as they were introduced. "By 1575, in the larger cities thousands of flagellant brothers participated in the Holy Thursday and Good Friday processions, were a regular component of peti-

tionary processions, and operated hospitals, orphanages and other social services" (1981a: 185).

Even by itself, the prevalence and popularity of self-flagellation in
Spain would probably provide some evidence in support of the prediction that a strong Marian emphasis among males will be associated
with a strong need for punishment. But self-flagellation was only the
most extreme of the practices associated with a general emphasis
upon Christ's Passion which (if Christian's account is correct) per-
meated Spanish religion for centuries. It is this general emphasis upon
Christ's Passion that, in my view, provides the best evidence in support of the prediction that Spanish religion should be associated with
a need for punishment.

The key here is to remember who Jesus Christ is in the Christian
tradition and why his Passion is so important: Jesus is the Son sent to
earth by God the Father to suffer and be crucified in order that humankind might be redeemed. Another way of saying this is that
Christ was a son who experienced bodily mutilation and death at the
instigation of his father. If the structure of the Spanish family produces sons with a strong but strongly repressed desire for the mother,
which in turn gives rise to a strongly masochistic need for punishment
then identifying with a son (like Jesus Christ) who has been mutilated
and killed at the instigation of his father can be regarded as an obvious
symbolic fulfillment of that wish. If this identification involves the actual mutilation of your own body (as occurs during self-flagellation),
then so much the better for wish fulfillment.

In summary, then, I am suggesting that both a general emphasis
upon Christ's Passion (that is upon the scourging, crowning with
thorns, and crucifixion of Christ) and the practice of self-flagellation
derive from the masochistic need for punishment that arises in response to a son's strong but strongly repressed desire for the mother.
Since it is this same desire that gives rise to intense Marian devotion,
a masochistic emphasis upon Christ's Passion will be most evident in
those regions where support for the Mary cult is strongest.

MORE MASOCHISM

Most adherents of the Mary cult, in most countries, do not flagellate
themselves, but we would not expect them to. Under the argument
offered here, extremely masochistic behavior should appear only

in those societies where the repressed desire for the mother is particularly intense. On the other hand, since I am arguing that a son's repressed desire for the mother (however strong) is everywhere the mainstay of the Mary cult, we would expect to find some traces of masochism, however muted, wherever the Mary cult is established. This expectation, I think, can help us to understand some features of the cult that might otherwise be puzzling.

Consider, for example, the association of the Mary cult with cloth scapulars. A scapular consists of two rectangular pieces of cloth held together by strings. The strings must be of sufficient length that when placed around the neck, one piece of cloth rests upon the chest and one upon the back. Usually, a picture or a message of some sort will be stitched to one or both of these pieces of cloth. There are eighteen different scapulars that have been approved by the Church, the titles of which are listed in Table 3-1. As is clear, more scapulars are associated with Mary than with either Christ or any of the saints. More importantly, the one that has over the centuries proven to be the most popular of all is a Marian scapular, the Brown Scapular of Our Lady of Mt. Carmel.

The association of the Mary cult with scapulars in general and the Brown Scapular in particular cannot be overemphasized. The Blue Army of Our Lady, which is probably the largest and most active of the modern organizations trying to promote Marian devotion, promotes two devotional practices above all others. The first of these is saying the rosary and the second is wearing the Brown Scapular.

According to tradition, it was the Virgin Mary herself who gave the first Brown Scapular to St. Simon Stock in the year 1251, during the course of an apparition. She is supposed to have said that "Anyone who dies clothed in this shall not suffer eternal fire, and if they die wearing it, they shall be saved." Pope John XXII, in a Bull issued in 1322, supposedly amplified the Virgin's promise by promulgating the "Sabbatine Privilege," which says that those who wear the scapular consistently and die with chastity and prayers to Mary, will be freed from Purgatory on the first Saturday after their death.

The use of the Brown Scapular and the associated Sabbatine Privilege have been a source of great controversy in the Church. Most Catholic scholars, for instance, now regard the Bull supposedly issued by Pope John XXII as apocryphal, and agree that the use of the Brown Scapular seems to come into widespread use only in the six-

TABLE 3-1

List of the Cloth Scapulars Approved by the Church

1.	The Scapular of the Most Blessed Trinity
2.	The Scapular of Our Lady of Ransom
3.	The Brown Scapular of Our Lady of Mt. Carmel
4.	The Black Scapular of the Seven Dolors of Our Lady
5.	The Blue Scapular of the Immaculate Conception
6.	The Scapular of the Most Precious Blood
7.	The Black Scapular of the Passion
8.	The Red Scapular of the Passion
9.	Scapular of the Blessed Virgin Mary under the title of "Help of the Sick"
10.	The Scapular of the Immaculate Heart of Mary
11.	The Scapular of St. Michael the Archangel
12.	The Scapular of St. Benedict
13.	The Scapular of the Mother of Good Counsel
14.	The Scapular of St. Joseph
15.	The Scapular of the Most Sacred Heart of Jesus
16.	The Scapular of the Sacred Hearts of Jesus and Mary
17.	The Scapular of St. Dominic

SOURCE: Hilgers (1912)

teenth century, several centuries after the alleged apparition to Simon Stock. At the moment, the official position of the Church is that it is permissible only to preach that those who fulfill the conditions of the Sabbatine Privilege will secure the protection of Mary after their death, and that this protection might make itself especially felt on Saturdays, since that is the day of the week most consecrated to her.

But this official position notwithstanding, the literature of organizations like the Blue Army go to great lengths to promulgate the original text of Mary's message to Simon Stock. (". . . who dies clothed in this shall not suffer eternal fire"). Likewise, though the Blue Army does in its longer publications give both the traditional interpretation of the Sabbatine Privilege and the official position of the Church, a number of its smaller pamphlets present the traditional interpretation alone. The following excerpt from one of these shorter pamphlets is typical:

Members of the Blue Army can obtain THE SABBATINE PRIVILEGE: Mary's promise of release from Purgatory soon after death for all those who: 1) wear the scapular; 2) observe chastity

(69)

according to their state in life; and 3) pray the daily rosary. (Emphasis in original)

Taken together, Mary's original promise and summaries of the Sabbatine Privilege like the one just given imply strongly that use of the Brown Scapular will enable one to avoid Hell and spend only a minimal amount of time in Purgatory. This alone would explain why the Brown Scapular has been so popular over the centuries. Still, what has not as yet been explained is why Mary's promise and the Sabbatine Privilege have come to be associated with a cloth scapular, rather than, say, a medal or an icon, or why such cloth scapulars are more associated with Marian devotion than with, say, devotion to Christ and the saints.

An explanation that flows quite naturally from the argument presented here is that cloth scapulars have become such an important part of the Mary cult because they are uncomfortable to wear. Their use therefore entails a certain masochistic discomfort of the sort that we have come to expect to find associated with the Mary cult. Such an interpretation seems consistent with the fact that at least until the first decades of this century, the Church has always insisted that the two rectangular pieces of cloth forming each scapular had to be made of wool, rather than cotton or any other material. Whatever the theological justification for this traditional insistence, it seems evident that a wool scapular would, on the average, be more uncomfortable than, say, a cotton one.

Lest readers think that I am making too much of the discomfort caused by the scapular, consider the case of the scapular medal. Since 1910, Catholics who have been invested with a cloth scapular (which can only be done by a priest) may later substitute a scapular medal for the cloth scapular. The scapular medal has a portrayal of Mary on one side and of Christ on the other. The use of the scapular medal, however, is discouraged by the Blue Army. In justifying its position, the Blue Army Manual (1982: 9) says in part:

> One of the great disadvantages of the medal, which is one of the major reasons why the Blue Army does not advocate its use in place of the cloth, is that we can so easily forget it. The cloth "insists" that we remember the fact that we have, of our own choice, become officially set aside as a special child of the Queen of Heaven.

It seems that the Blue Army is saying what I am saying: the cloth scapular should be worn because it is more uncomfortable than the scapular medal. It argues only, of course, that the discomfort associated with the cloth scapular serves to remind us that it is there. I am suggesting that wearing something uncomfortable is an obvious instance of masochism, and that this has always made the wearing of cloth scapulars particularly appealing to members of the Mary cult. Viewing the use of a cloth scapular as minor exercise in masochism also seems to explain the Church's insistence that the scapular be worn continuously, and that taking it off and putting it aside for any length of time invalidates all the benefits that might otherwise be gained.

THE MARY CULT AND BILATERAL DESCENT

One great conceptual danger for anyone who uses psychoanalytic principles to explain cultural practices is teleology, which in this context means explaining a cultural practice only by reference to the psychological functions served by that practice. For instance, I have argued that excessive Marian devotion on the part of males serves to discharge the excess sexual energy built up by a strong but strongly repressed sexual desire for the mother. Yet it seems clear that there must be a wide range of practices that might serve to discharge such excess sexual energy just as well. We must explain, therefore, why excessive devotion to Mary in particular is chosen as the means of discharging this energy in societies like Spain and Italy.

Furthermore, if we take seriously the methodological injunction that in using Freud's theory to explain the Mary cult we must embrace all the consequences of that theory, then we must confront the fact that there is one alternative way to discharge the excess sexual energy built up by repression that is especially important in Freud's theory. That is the participation in, and the maintenance of, strongly cohesive social groups that extend beyond the nuclear family.

What I am referring to is the view of social evolution that Freud developed at length in his *Civilization and Its Discontents* (1961d [1930]). Freud's argument in that book is that the advance of civilization depends upon the formation of highly cohesive social groups that transcend the nuclear family. But maintaining the sense of attachment or, alternatively, the sense of social solidarity needed to insure the existence of such groups requires an enormous amount of psychic energy—so much, in fact, that it is beyond the innate capabilities of most human beings. It was Freud's view that the psychic energy needed to maintain social solidarity must be created, and this is done by repression. The final argument, then, is that the repression of sexual or aggressive desires creates excess psychic energy, which can then be diverted to the task of maintaining the solidarity of groups that transcend the nuclear family. It was this line of reasoning that led Freud to emphasize the importance of the incest taboo in human social evolution in *Totem and Taboo* (1955b [1913]). In Freud's view the incest taboo created the first instance of sexual repression, and thus the introduction of that taboo, by creating excess sexual energy that could then be diverted to the task of maintaining social solidarity, was the decisive first step in creating civilization.

Freud's argument forces us to make a clear prediction about the Mary cult. If the maintenance of highly cohesive social groups (which in a traditional society are usually based upon kinship) is indeed an alternative procedure for discharging excess sexual energy, then Marian devotion should be negatively correlated with the presence of such groups. That is, all else being equal, societies characterized by highly cohesive corporate kin groups that transcend the nuclear family should be less characterized by Marian devotion than societies in which such kin groups are absent. "All else being equal" implies that we are dealing only with societies that have had some historical exposure to the Mary cult and in which a son's repressed desire for the mother is both strong and strongly repressed. The value of this prediction is that it allows us to explain an observation about Mediterranean societies reported—without explanation—quite some time ago by Wolf (1969).

Wolf's goal in that article was to contrast the Latin Catholic societies of the northern Mediterranean (by which he meant mainly Italy and Spain) with the Islamic societies of the southern Mediterranean with regard to social organization and religious symbolism. According to Wolf, two striking contrasts emerge from such an analysis. The first has to do with kinship. In Latin Catholic countries, descent is usually reckoned bilaterally, the conjugal relationship tends to be the most important kinship bond, and kin relationships outside the nuclear family tend to be dyadic, producing a loosely defined network of extended kin ties. What is generally not found in Latin Catholic countries are highly cohesive corporate kin groups that function beyond the level of the nuclear family. Islamic societies, on the other hand, tend to be associated with patrilineal descent and with the presence of highly cohesive corporate kin groups formed along patrilineal lines.

Correlated with this difference in kinship organization, says Wolf, there is a difference with respect to what he calls "the female element" in religion. His point is that the emphasis upon the female element in religion found in Latin Catholic countries, and most evident in the Latin Catholic emphasis upon Mary, has no real counterpart in Islam. Wolf is well aware that some Sufi groups occasionally use a female terminology when talking of the sacred, and that there is in Islam, especially in what he calls "folk Islam," some emphasis upon devotion to Fatima, the daughter of the Prophet. His argument is not that Islam completely lacks feminine emphasis, only that this does not approach the emphasis upon the feminine found in Latin Catholicism. Wolf himself simply reports this correlation between the absence of cohesive kin groups and the Mary cult; he makes no attempt to explain it. It is, however, exactly the sort of correlation that we might have expected from Freud's argument.

The present discussion forces an important modification of the theory being presented in this book. So far I have linked Marian devotion to a son's strong but strongly repressed desire for the mother, and linked such a desire in turn to the father-ineffective family common in proletarian settings in southern Italy and Spain. But the father-ineffective family is almost certainly not the only type of family to produce in sons a strong but strongly repressed desire for the mother. For instance, in many Islamic societies women are excluded from the public domain (Eickelman, 1981: 105-174), and there are solid psychoanalytic arguments (Slater, 1968) and ethnographic case studies (Kiray, 1976) which suggest that this exclusion leads mothers to develop an especially close and indulgent relationship with their sons, since it is only through their sons that they can achieve success—albeit vicariously—in the outside world. It seems reasonable to conclude that one effect of an especially close and indulgent mother/son relationship would be an intensification of the son's sexual desire for the mother. I further assume that in Islamic societies, as in European societies, this desire will be repressed.

If the presence of a strong and repressed desire for the mother in

sons were sufficient to give rise to the Mary cult, then we would expect to find such a cult or its analogue in Islamic societies. But we do
not. Under the interpretation offered here, this is because the emergence of a strong Mary cult requires two preconditions: not simply a
strong but strongly repressed desire for the mother in sons, but also
the absence of cohesive kin groups that transcend the nuclear family
and that can serve as vehicles for the discharge of excess sexual energy.

HISTORICAL ORIGINS

The hypotheses presented in the previous chapter have enabled us to account for two of the three central observations about the Mary cult discussed in Chapter One: Mary's status as a mother goddess completely disassociated from sexuality and the fact that Marian devotion seems especially intense in southern Italy and Spain. But can the theory presented so far explain the fact that the Mary cult seems to have been generally absent in the Church during the first four centuries of the Christianity era? To answer this question, let us reconsider the Ashe hypothesis that the relatively sudden appearance of the Mary cult suggests that the cult derived from the sudden absorption into the Church of a group of Mary worshipers, whom he identified as the Collyridians. Although Ashe's views linking the Mary cult to the Collyridians are probably incorrect, he might well be right in believing that support for the cult was connected with absorption into the Church of some new group or groups. What makes this line of reasoning so appealing is that even conventional histories of the Church make it clear that the fourth century A.D. (the period just prior to the emergence of the Mary cult) was a period in which a variety of new groups were absorbed into the Church.

THE GREAT TRANSFORMATION

All historians agree in asserting that until the early part of the fourth century, Christianity was a minority religion within the Roman Empire, concentrated mainly in urban areas, and at a tremendous legal disadvantage with respect to pagan cults.[1] In the latter part of the third century and during the first decade of the fourth, emperors such as Decius (who reigned 249-251), Gallus (251-253), Valerian (253-260),

[1] The account of the changes that took place in the Church during the fourth and fifth centuries presented in this section is necessarily brief. For more detailed accounts of these changes, see Baus (1980), Kidd (1922), Latourette (1937), and Schaff (1910).

and Diocletian (284-305) had subjected Christians to the most brutal and extensive persecutions that they had to that point experienced. Yet within the course of a single century, all this changed. Christianity, from being an often-persecuted minority religion, became the professed religion of a majority in both the East and the West, and the legally dominant religion of the empire.

This great transformation began during the reign of the Emperor Constantine (306-337). In 313, for instance, Constantine issued his famous Edict of Milan. Exactly what was done at Milan is a matter of some dispute among historians, but all agree that the decisions made there had the effect of easing the legal sanctions against the practice of Christianity. Apart from the Edict of Milan, we know of a number of laws passed between 313 and Constantine's death in 337 that explicitly benefited Christianity. Christian clergy, for example, were exempted from taxation; childless and celibate clergy were allowed to inherit; private citizens could make out wills naming the Church as beneficiary; bishops were given the right to adjudicate certain legal matters, and their decisions were binding on the civil authorities; Sundays and other Christian festivals were given the same legal status as pagan festivals; and so on. The emperor himself financed the building of many new Christian churches and the repair of several others.

Although Constantine did not give the Christian Church any legal advantage over the pagan cults, he did give it a legal advantage over heretical or schismatic Christian groups. For instance, he explicitly excluded the clergy associated with such groups from the privileges conveyed upon the "orthodox" Christian clergy. Furthermore, when heretics or schismatics broke with the Church, they were denied legal title to any Church property that they might be using. Constantine was prepared to back up this last order with military force, as he did in North Africa when the Donatists left the Church but refused to give up their church buildings.

Gradually, in the seventy years following Constantine's death, his policy of ensuring legal equality between the Christian Church and the pagan cults gave way to a policy of ensuring the legal supremacy of Christianity. Sacrifices, an integral part of almost all pagan rituals to that point, were outlawed, whether they were performed in public or in private. Large numbers of pagan temples were either dismantled or converted to secular use, and pagan priests (unlike Christian ones) were no longer entitled to receive support from the state. Private citizens were prohibited from making wills naming a pagan cult as beneficiary. All pagans were barred from holding office in either the state administration or the army. Army officers who themselves professed Christianity to retain their rank but who made no attempt to dissuade their families from paganism were to have their property confiscated. Finally, the death penalty was specified for baptized Christians who lapsed into paganism, and the wills of such people were considered null and void.

It is true that there were brief intervals during this period during which the anti-pagan legislation was relaxed or even reversed. The resurgence of interest in the pagan cults during these intervals—especially during the brief reign of Emperor Julian (called the Apostate)—is evidence that popular support for paganism was still strong in the general population. Nevertheless, the fact remains that by the first decade of the fifth century, Christianity had become at least the professed religion of the majority, and was the only religion that could be practiced openly with impunity. The fact that the Mary cult emerged immediately following this great transformation in the social status of the Church can hardly be coincidental, though as far as I know no previous commentator has suggested a direct causal link between the two events.

I think that such a link does exist, and that the key to understanding it lies in the observation that the transformation of the Church during the fourth century was qualitative as well as quantitative. There was, in other words, not just an increase in the number and proportion of people within the empire who were Christian, but a change in the type of person who was now a member of the Church. I suggest that it was the incorporation of people from new social strata (and not the incorporation of preexisting religious groups like the Collyridians) that led to the emergence of the Mary cult. But to understand the nature of these new groups, and how their incorporation led to the emergence of the Mary cult, we must first understand the social composition of the Christian Church during the first three centuries of the Christian era.

CHRISTIANITY AND CLASS IN THE PRE-CONSTANTINE ERA

The question of the class origins of the early Christians is a very old one. Until recently, the dominant view—held both by Christians themselves and by historians—seems to have been that the early Christians were drawn disproportionately from the unpropertied lower classes, that is, from the "poor" in the usual sense of that term. In large part this view was probably shaped by the many passages disparaging wealth in the New Testament. It also seems consistent with the well known description of the Corinthian Church in 1 Corinthians 1: 26-29: "not many of you were wise according to worldly standards, not many were powerful, not many were of noble birth; but God chose what is foolish in the world to shame the wise. . . . God chose what is low and despised . . . so that no human being might boast in the presence of God" (May and Metzger, 1973).

Malherbe (1977: 29-59), however, points out that a new consensus is emerging among historians that the early Christian Church may well have been more of a middle-class movement than was previously thought. Although no one has suggested that the early Christians were *all* of middle-class origin, many now think that this class was the dominant group in the Church, and that most of the "poor" were likely to have been dependent in some way upon the middle class. Thus, for instance, it is now generally assumed that most of the "poor" discussed in 1 Corinthians 1: 26-29 were either domestics in a middle-class household or clients under the protection of a middle-class patron.

Meeks (1983: 73) expresses this new consensus by suggesting that both the extreme top and the extreme bottom of the Roman social scale were missing from the early Christian Church. He points out that what he calls the "poorest of the poor" were the tenant farmers, agricultural slaves, and agricultural day laborers. Living in rural areas, these groups would have had little to do with a church that was almost entirely urban.

If the urban middle class dominated early Christianity, then the absence of the Mary cult in the early Christian Church would most easily be explained (given the logic of this book) by arguing that the middle-class family in the early empire did not produce in sons the strong but strongly repressed desire for the mother from which support for the Mary cult derives. Was this the case?

We encounter some difficulties in trying to answer this question. First, our knowledge of family life in ancient Rome is fragmentary, and derives largely from various anecdotes recorded by literary authors. But more importantly, it seems obvious that most such descriptions are of the senatorial and equestrian classes, that is, the Roman aristocracy.[2] The merchants, artisans, and other professionals who composed the Roman bourgeoisie, on the other hand, were drawn primarily from the nonaristocratic freedman or plebian classes.

To proceed any further, then, we must assume that the type of family typical of the middle class in ancient Rome was similar to that of the aristocratic classes; many might not be willing to make that assumption. But in the Roman Empire, class membership in the legal sense (that is, whether you belonged to the senatorial class, the equestrian class, the plebian class, and so on) was not always correlated with wealth. For instance, a variety of conditions made it more likely that freedmen (that is, manumitted slaves) than free-born citizens would become merchants and artisans. Thus a very large number of freedmen became as rich, if not richer, than most members of the aristocratic (senatorial or equestrian) classes.[3] If we grant that economic position is a major determinant of family organization (and here again, some might not), then the suggestion that the Roman middle-class family would be similar to the type of family associated with the aristocratic classes seems plausible.

With all this in mind, was there anything about the Roman family that would have produced in sons a strong but strongly repressed desire for the mother? The answer would seem to be "no." The Roman family was, in fact, the very opposite of the father-ineffective family that produces such a desire. Both by law and by custom, a Roman father exerted tremendous authority over his wife and children (although that authority has often been exaggerated). Roman fathers also tended to work in or around their homes, and there seems to have been some expectation that they would spend a substantial amount of time in the company of their sons. The Roman son, then, had considerable contact with an authoritative father. Roman mothers, on their part, were not secluded in the household (in the manner of women in Classical Greece), and polygyny was not widely practiced in the Roman world. Thus two factors, seclusion of wives and polygyny, that have been mentioned by some modern commentators as promoting an especially strong sexual attachment to the mother in the son were

[2] See, for instance, the accounts of Roman family life presented in Balsdon (1969; 1983 [1962]) and Johnston (1973 [1932]).

[3] For some of the reasons why low legal status might actually have worked to insure relatively high economic status, see Duff's (1958) discussion of freedmen in the early Roman Empire.

absent in Rome. Rather than resembling the "father-ineffective" family, then, the Roman family resembles far more the northern European middle-class family studied by Freud at the turn of this century.

But if there was nothing about the Roman family that would produce in sons an especially strong but strongly repressed desire for the mother, and if indeed the early Church was dominated by the middle class, then we have no theoretical reason for believing that a virgin mother goddess like Mary would have had any particular appeal to most early Christians. From this perspective, then, the absence of the Mary cult during the first four centuries of the Christian era is not problematic.

THE ROMAN POOR

But if the great transformation of the fourth century changed Christianity from a middle-class movement to one that incorporated people from all levels of Roman society, then one of the "new" groups brought into the Church at this time would have been the Roman proletariat, notably the rural proletariat, and it is likely that this group *was* characterized by the father-ineffective family. I cannot base such an assertion upon actual descriptions of family life among the Roman proletariat; such descriptions do not exist. But the economic processes that give rise to the father-ineffective family in the modern world were operative in the Roman world, as well.

In the case of modern southern Italy and Spain, for instance, investigators (like Gilmore and Gilmore, 1979; Saunders, 1981) almost inevitably attribute the emergence of the father-ineffective family to widespread and chronic unemployment among males in a wage economy. Oscar Lewis made a similar argument in explaining the presence of the father-ineffective family among the poor in Mexico (Lewis, 1959) and among poor Puerto Ricans in both Puerto Rico and New York City (Lewis, 1965). The widespread economic marginality of males in a wage economy has also been identified as a factor leading to the emergence of the father-ineffective family in the case of a variety of Caribbean societies (Smith, 1956; Clarke, 1957), the poor in the United States (Yorburg, 1983), and blacks in Lesotho, South Africa (Murray, 1981).

Although the work by Oscar Lewis and others on the "culture of poverty" has generated a great deal of controversy over the last twenty-five years, few if any critics have challenged the only hypothesis from the "culture of poverty" argument that concerns us here, namely, that the economic marginality of males in a wage economy is a sufficient condition for producing the father-ineffective family. If we grant that this hypothesis is likely to have been as valid for ancient Rome as it is for modern Mexico, the modern Caribbean, modern South Africa, and so on, then we can make some educated guesses as to the likely prevalence of the father-ineffective family among the Roman poor by considering the degree of economic marginality among the Roman poor. On this issue there is some information.[4]

The economy of the early empire (that is, the pre-Constantine empire) was for the most part agricultural. Starting in the first century B.C., and continuing for the next three to four hundred years, virtually all commentators agree that several trends in Roman agriculture resulted in a continually increasing impoverishment of the rural poor. First, Roman agriculture tended to move away from purely subsistence farming, toward commercial farming. This movement was accompanied by a trend toward successive amalgamation of individual farms into larger and larger units, resulting in the proliferation of the large commercial farms called *latifundia* throughout the empire. Initially, these *latifundia* (which had first made their appearance in the second century B.C., just after the Second Punic War) had been worked by slaves, aided occasionally by contract labor. But with the drying up of the slave supply under Augustus (mainly due to the cessation of Roman territorial acquisition and the high rate of manumission), the labor on these commercial farms was supplied by tenant farmers and migrant workers. Finally, there was a substantial increase in absentee ownership, which siphoned off to urban areas the wealth that had previously been spent in the local farming communities. Over the course of the first few centuries of the empire, all these trends produced an increasing impoverishment of the countryside, and were a major factor in provoking the rural-urban migration that produced the mobs so characteristic of the great cities of the empire: Rome itself, Alexandria, Antioch, and so on.

---

[4] The overview of Roman economic history that follows is based mainly upon Rostovtzeff (1926) and the various essays in Frank (1938); I have also taken into account remarks on the Roman economy found scattered throughout more general works like Haywood (1967), Heichelheim and Yeo (1962) and Sinniger and Boak (1977).

Some idea as to the extent of poverty in ancient Rome can be had by looking at the steps taken by the state to alleviate it. Perhaps the most well-known of these was the grain dole, whereby free grain was distributed to Roman citizens. The number of those eligible to receive free grain was set at 200,000 in the latter part of the first century B.C., and was maintained at that level thereafter. In evaluating that figure we must remember that the grain dole was only available to those citizens who could prove that the city of Rome was their ancestral home, and so the dole would not have been available to many (possibly most) of the migrants who came to the city from other parts of Italy and the empire.

The problem of poverty was also addressed by the "alimentary institution" established for the Italian peninsula during the first century A.D. This was a state-run bureaucracy set up to loan money to farmers at a low rate of interest—5 percent. The profits from these loans were to be used for the maintenance and education of impoverished children in the region where the loan was made. The goal was to provide a direct subsidy to the poor while simultaneously providing funds that could be used to revitalize the agricultural economy in a region. The success of the alimentary institution is a matter of some debate among historians; the institution itself, however, operated in Italy until at least the end of the third century A.D., when exceedingly high rates of inflation led to the program's abandonment.

The grain dole and the alimentary institution, to be sure, operated only within the Italian peninsula. But since all commentators agree that the impoverishment of the rural poor was an empire wide phenomena, this means only that those outside Italy were probably worse off than those in the peninsula.

It should be noted that what we have just described suggests only that there was probably an increase in the economic marginality of the poor, especially the rural poor, over the course of the first few centuries of the empire. Nothing can be inferred from these facts about the relative size of the poor in contrast to other segments of Roman society, and yet the issue of relative size is directly relevant to the argument here: the larger the proportion of the general population that was poor, the more dramatically would the middle-class nature of the early Christian Church have been changed when Christianity was extended to all segments of Roman society. Unfortunately, historians have written little on the economic classes of the Roman Empire. One of the few to discuss the economic class structure of ancient Rome is MacMullen (1974), who presents data from a variety of sources which indicate that the distribution of wealth in ancient Rome was "sharply vertical"—which means the rich were very rich and very few, whereas the poor were very poor and very numerous. Defining a poor person as someone in "habitual want, that is, he devoted the vast bulk of each day's earnings to his immediate needs and accumulated no property to speak of," MacMullen estimates that the poor constituted—at minimum—one third of the general population. His analysis of the distribution of farming plots of different sizes in different parts of the empire suggests that in some areas the poor might have constituted as much as 60 to 80 percent of the local population. Even granting that MacMullen's estimates are only gross approximations, it seems obvious that the poor did constitute a large segment of the Roman population.

THE BIRTH OF THE MARY CULT

At this point, then, we are in a position to survey some of the effects that would have accompanied the great transformation of the Church in the fourth century. First, it seems clear that the relatively sudden extension of Christianity to all levels of Roman society would have flooded the middle-class Church with significant numbers of the Roman proletariat. In fact, given the relative size of the proletariat, these new Christians may well have constituted a sizable proportion of the Church's membership. If we grant that the economic conditions characteristic of the early empire make it likely that many (possibly most) of these new proletarian Christians would have been raised in father-ineffective families, then the arguments presented in the last chapter suggest that at the beginning of the fifth century the Church incorporated within its ranks, for the first time, a large number of males who were characterized by a strong but strongly repressed desire for the mother. Since it is precisely this desire that gives rise to Marian devotion, the relatively sudden emergence of the Mary cult in the early part of the fifth century comes as no surprise.

I am suggesting, then, that from the end of the fifth century forward, the development of the Mary cult can be seen as the result of an interaction between the Church hierarchy and one fairly large segment of the Church's new constituency, Christians drawn from the urban or rural proletariat. So long as the Mary cult did not directly challenge any of the central Christological doctrines of Christianity, Church leaders would have seen in the Mary cult a way of maintaining the allegiance of these new Christians by, in effect, giving them a type of Christianity that they wanted.

This view of things leads us to reconsider some key events in the history of the fifth-century Church. Take, for example, the Council of Ephesus in 431 A.D. All Catholic commentators agree in asserting that Marian devotion increased dramatically after Ephesus. But why? The central theological issue debated at Ephesus had to do with the two natures of Christ. One faction, led by Nestorius, the Patriarch of Constantinople, argued that the human and divine natures of Christ were "conjoined" within the framework of a single personality. The other faction, led by Cyril, patriarch of Alexandria (and supported by the Pope, Celestine), argued that the two natures of Christ were in fact merged in a "hypostatic union." Cyril's faction won out, and the Nestorians were defined as heretics. But it was a dispute over Mary that ignited the entire controversy. Increasingly, at least in the East, Mary had been called by the title *Theotokos*, which many people of the time interpreted as "Mother of God." Nestorius objected to the use of this term on the grounds that it made little sense to suggest that a creation (like Mary) could be mother to her Creator. For Nestorius, *Anthropotokos* (Mother of the Man) or *Christotokos* (Mother of Christ) made more sense. It was the debate over the precise meaning of *Theotokos*, and over the appropriateness of this term as a Marian title, that gave rise to the debate over the relationship between Christ's two natures.

For most ordinary Christians in the empire, it seems doubtful that the Council's decision to endorse Cyril's notion of a "hypostatic union" would have had any impact at all. One modern commentator (Hardon, 1975: 136), trying to explain the concept to a lay audience, puts it thus: "It means that the two natures of Christ are united personally, in such a way that while the source from which the union was effected was two distinct natures, which remained essentially unchanged, the being in which the union was completed was one individual (in Greek, *hypostasis*), which individual was divine." The difference between this view and the Nestorian view (which talked of "conjunction") would almost certainly not have been understood by the mass of Christians throughout the empire. What would have been understood by most Christians, however, is that a bishop had tried to deny Mary a title (*Theotokos*) that implied a close association between Mary and God, and that views of this bishop had been denounced by the official Church. In the eyes of most Christians, then, the only important result of the Council of Ephesus would have been that Mary's relatively high status in the Christian pantheon was affirmed. Thus I suggest that at Ephesus the Church showed itself willing to make Mary a far more important goddess than she had previously been, and that this was a response to the fact that Mary was a figure who appealed to a large segment of the Church's new constituency.

The events surrounding the Council of Chalcedon in 451 A.D. can be interpreted in a similar manner. Here again, the important theological issues debated were impeccably Christological. In reacting against Nestorianism, some Church leaders, led by the monk Eutyches, had argued that the Incarnate Christ had really only had a divine nature and had not possessed a human nature at all. At Chalcedon, this position was defined as heretical, and the conclusions at Ephesus concerning the two natures of Christ were reiterated. The reason that Chalcedon was important for the Mary cult lies in what is traditionally called the *Tome of Leo*. This is a collection of essays written by Pope Leo the Great, in which he set out the orthodox position regarding the two natures of Christ. It was by accepting this document that the Council of Chalcedon rejected the "divine nature only" arguments of Eutyches. Leo's tome, however, was accepted in its entirety, and since Leo had touched upon Mary, however incidentally, his statements on Mary also became the official position of the Church. Leo had referred both to Mary's *in partu* virginity and to her perpetual virginity. Although these two beliefs had been common in the early Church, they had never before been given official endorsement by the Church hierarchy meeting in council.

In other words, when the Roman proletariat flooded into the Church at the end of the fourth century, they found a mother goddess who was almost completely disassociated from sexuality. The Virgin Birth had always been a part of Christian dogma, and most Church authorities endorsed a belief in Mary's *in partu* virginity and her perpetual virginity. But a doctrine advocated by most Church leaders is not quite as compelling as an official doctrine of the Church approved by a Church council. By making a belief in Mary's *in partu* virginity and in her perpetual virginity official, then, Chalcedon made Mary's disassociation from sexuality complete—and she became that much more appealing to males characterized by a strong but strongly repressed desire for the mother. The fact that the major theological issues discussed at both Ephesus and Chalcedon were Christological would have provided Church leaders with a ready-made reassurance against any fears they might have had about encouraging the development of a goddess cult that would, in time, come to overshadow the Christ cult itself.

MASOCHISM AGAIN

I have argued that Marian devotion and masochism should be associated because each derives from the same source, namely, a son's strong but strongly repressed desire for the mother. I have also argued that in those areas where the Mary cult was especially entrenched, this masochistic emphasis often took the form of an intense emphasis upon the Passion of Christ, and in particular upon the scourging and crucifixion of Christ. Given all this, we might expect that if the influx of the Roman rural proletariat into the Church in the fourth century did give rise to the Mary cult in the fifth, then we should also find in the fifth century an increased emphasis upon Christ's Passion. We do.

Because the image of Christ crucified seems now to be so much a part of Catholic tradition, it is easy to overlook the fact that representations of the crucifixion are completely absent from Christian art during the first four centuries of the Christian era. Christ is portrayed quite often in, say, the art of the catacombs, but not in connection with his crucifixion or any other aspect of the Passion. Surveys of catacomb art (van der Meer, 1967: 81-90; Gough, 1973: 10-48; Stevenson, 1978) show that the depiction of Christ in this period is symbolic (as in the symbol of a fish), allegorical (under the guise, for example, of the "good shepherd," a very common motif in early Christian art), or in a New Testament scene unconnected with the Passion (the raising of Lazarus, the Sermon on the Mount, and so on). In fact, in all of catacomb art, there is only one depiction of any aspect of the Passion, and that occurs in a single fresco in the catacomb of Praetextatus, which seems to depict the crowning with thorns. Even then, the crown of thorns has clearly been transformed into a less painful laurel wreath (Stevenson, 1978: 106).

It is only in the latter part of the fourth century that we begin to see any interest in the Passion in Christian art, and even then the emphasis is muted. Scenes from the Passion do appear on a number of sarcophagi (the so-called "Passion sarcophagi") carved during this period. The earliest of these has been dated to c. 340; most are dated closer to A.D. 400 (Lowrie, 1947: 86-104, as well as Plates 1-5 in Schiller, 1972). Even these sarcophagi, however, tend to emphasize those aspects of the Passion that do not involve great physical suffering. Lowrie (1947: 98), for instance, reports that the most common scenes are those involving the kiss of Judas, the arrest of Jesus, and the judgment of Pilate (which is especially frequent). The only scene with a clearly masochistic emphasis that appears with any frequency is the crowning with thorns, and here again the crown of thorns is usually depicted as a laurel wreath. The crucifixion itself does not appear on any of these sarcophagi, nor on any other example of Christian art from the fourth century.

This apparent reluctance to portray the crucifixion is especially surprising in that the cross itself came into widespread use as a Christian symbol during the first part of the fourth century. The traditional explanation of this greater iconographic emphasis upon the cross is that the Emperor Constantine had placed the cross on his personal banner, and that Constantine's mother, St. Helena, had discovered fragments of the True Cross in Jerusalem. Some scholars, however, have argued that neither of these stories has any historical basis, and so it seems equally plausible to suggest that the stories may have been a response to, rather than the cause of, an increased use of the cross as a Christian emblem.

But it is not until we come to the early part of the fifth century that we find the earliest known examples of the crucifixion in Christian art. One of the wooden panels on the doors of the Church of S. Sabina in Rome shows a crucified Christ between two crucified thieves, and these doors are usually dated to c. 420-440. Even here, there is a muting of the grislier aspects of the crucifixion. For instance, although the nailheads in Christ's hands are clearly visible, his hands are nailed only to wooden blocks (not a true cross) and his feet are shown resting on the ground. The only other representation of the crucifixion that dates from this period is found among the scenes carved onto a small ivory box now in the British Museum. The scene shows Christ nailed to a true cross, with his feet suspended above the ground. A picture of Judas hanging from a nearby tree is in the same scene. Gough (1973: 130) dates this box to c. A.D. 400, but most scholars (Hutter, 1971: 56; Schiller, 1972: 9) prefer a somewhat later date, c. 420-430, which would make the box more or less contemporaneous with the crucifixion panel from the doors of S. Sabina—and with the Council of Ephesus. I must emphasize that these two examples are the *only* depictions of the crucifixion that date from the early part of the fifth century. It is only toward the end of the fifth century, and continuing into the sixth, seventh, and eighth centuries, that representations of the crucifixion become more common in Christian art. The relatively sudden appearance of this iconographic emphasis upon the Passion in general and the crucifixion is particular "just happens" to coincide with the sudden influx of the Church of the Roman proletariation and the subsequent emergence of the Mary cult.

There is one other important feature of the post-Constantine Church that can be related to the masochism of sons raised in father-ineffective families: clerical celibacy. Celibacy, of course, had been voluntarily embraced by many Christian clerics since the earliest days of the Church. Nevertheless, although there is some debate about the matter, the available evidence (reviewed in Thurston, 1908; Rehage, 1967; Delhay, 1967) seems to suggest that during the Church's first three centuries a majority of priests and deacons (though probably a minority of bishops) were married and so not celibate.

What is certain is that there were no formal regulations whatsoever requiring clerical celibacy in any region of the Western Church until c. A.D. 300. At that time the Spanish Council of Elvira imposed celibacy upon bishops, priests, and deacons. This rule, however, applied only to Spanish clerics, and it was an isolated case. When a Spanish bishop tried to have the Council of Nicea (A.D. 325) adopt a general rule requiring clerical celibacy, the council instead adopted the position of the Egyptian bishop Paphnutius, who argued that such a rule would be both difficult to administer and imprudent (Delhay, 1967: 370).

The movement to impose celibacy upon the clergy began in earnest only toward the end of the fourth century. In the period between 384 and 458 there were thirteen different decrees (listed in Delhay, 1967: 371-372) issued by a variety of popes and local councils on the issue of clerical celibacy. As a result of these decrees, celibacy came to be required of all clerical orders—bishops, priests, deacons, and subdeacons—in all areas of the Western Church by the middle of the fifth century.

What I am suggesting, of course, is that voluntary celibacy, that is, the decision to abstain from enjoying sexual pleasure for the remainder of one's life, is a form of masochism. This suggestion is in itself by no means novel. Ernest Jones (1951d [1930]: 206), for instance, long ago suggested that the celibacy of the Christian clergy be viewed as a form of "symbolic castration." The practice of this symbolic castration became widespread in the Church during precisely the same historical period that has been important to us in our argument.

CONCLUSION

The influx of the Roman proletariat into the Church during the fourth century, the relatively sudden emergence of the Mary cult in the fifth century, the increased emphasis upon the Passion of Christ in the late fourth and early fifth centuries, the sudden insistence upon clerical celibacy during this same period—all these trends have been noted before by historians of religion, art historians, social historians, and so on. But no one, to my knowledge, has suggested that all these phenomena are interrelated in a very precise way.

If we grant that the father-ineffective family was common among the Roman proletariat, and that such a family structure does produce in sons a strong but strongly repressed desire for the mother, then we would expect that the sudden absorption of the Roman proletariat into the Church during the great transformation of the fourth century should produce in the Church an increased emphasis upon masochism (in Church art, in clerical practice, and so on) and the appearance within the Church of a cult centered around a mother goddess disassociated from sexuality.

MATER DEUM MAGNA

On the face of it, the task set out in Chapter One would seem to be complete. All three of the central observations associated with the Mary cult—Mary's unique status as a Virgin Mother, the association of the cult with southern Italy and Spain, and the relatively sudden emergence of the cult in the fifth century—have been accounted for using a consistent and parsimonious set of psychoanalytic principles. Along the way, this same set of principles has been used to shed some light on other features of the Mary cult—the relationship between Marian devotion and masochism, for instance, and the previously un-noticed association between the rise of the Mary cult and an increased emphasis upon graphic portrayals of the crucifixion. But if we agree that psychoanalytic investigators should commit themselves to all the consequences of their argument, then there is one such consequence that must now be confronted.

If the father-ineffective family was as widespread among the Ro-man proletariat as I have suggested, if this type of family produces a strong but strongly repressed desire for the mother in sons, and—fi-nally—if this desire gives rise to a religious devotion focused upon a mother figure disassociated from sexuality, then we should very clearly expect to find that just such a mother goddess played an im-portant role in Roman religion in the pre-Constantine period. This prediction would seem to contradict a point established in Chapter One, that Mary is unique among the mother goddesses of the ancient world. But remember that Farnell (1907: 305-306) did suggest that there might have been one (but only one) Classical goddess who was a virgin mother just like Mary. That goddess was Cybele.

THE CULT OF CYBELE

There is no doubt in the mind of modern scholars, just as there was no doubt in the minds of Roman scholars, that the cult of Cybele originated in Asia Minor, and in particular, in Phrygia (which is the area where Montanism later developed). Most of the information about the early historical origins of the Cybele cult in Asia Minor is derived from the archeological record. For instance, during the Greco-Roman period, it was conventional to represent Cybele as a goddess sitting on a throne, holding a tympanum, and associated with lions—either two lions flanking the throne or a single lion across the goddess's lap. Excavations at Catal Hayuk, a Neolithic settlement in Asia Minor that dates from the sixth millennium B.C. has yielded a terracotta statue of a woman seated on a throne and flanked by two lions. On the analogy with the known iconography of Cybele in the Classical period, this statue is therefore taken to be the earliest known representation of the goddess. Sometime around the beginning of the first millennium B.C. (which corresponds more or less to the period of the Trojan wars described by Homer), the archeological record also indicates that the Cybele cult spread from Asia Minor to Greece.

Conventional histories have assigned a very precise date to Cybele's arrival in Rome: a stone representing the goddess arrived in the city of Rome on the sixth of April in the year 204 B.C. The conditions that led up to her arrival in Rome, and the arrival itself, have been described by any number of Roman historians. The most frequently cited account seems to be that in the twenty-fifth book of Livy's massive *History of Rome*, which was composed sometime toward the end of the first century B.C. According to Livy, the story of Cybele's introduction at Rome started just at the end of the third century B.C., when Hannibal's army was still ravaging parts of southern Italy. The social disruptions caused by Hannibal eventually led Roman leaders to consult the Sibylline books. The books declared that the foreigner (Hannibal) would be driven from Italy only when Italy received the Mother of Mt. Ida (a mountain in Asia Minor, and long known as a center of the Cybele cult). A Roman delegation was sent to Asia Minor to obtain the stone that was worshiped as the Mother. Having done this, the delegation made its way back across the Mediterranean and landed at Ostia. From there, the boat carrying the goddess made its way up the Tiber to Rome, arriving there on April 6, 204 B.C. Although the earliest histories (including Livy) suggest very clearly that the original image of the goddess was an irregularly shaped stone, most graphic representations of the goddess's arrival in Italy (see, for instance, Showerman, 1901: 228) show the ship approaching the dock at Ostia with a statue of an enthroned Cybele on its deck. Some authorities have questioned the literal accuracy of the story presented in Livy, but the archeological record (reviewed in Vermaseren, 1977: 38-69) does indicate that the cult first achieved popularity in the second century B.C., in the period immediately following the Second Punic War.

Because of the unsavory nature of the rites associated with the Cybele cult (which will be considered later), Roman citizens were initially forbidden to become priests of the cult, and activities of the cult were more or less restricted to the Palatine Hill. This meant that most of Cybele's priests, called *galli*, and certainly all of her high priests, called *archigalli*, were initially of Phrygian origin, and the cult itself was probably not very prominent in comparison to other Roman cults. By the middle of the first century A.D., however, the Cybele cult had become so popular that the restrictions against Roman citizens becoming *galli* had been lifted, and sanctuaries dedicated to Cybele had spread throughout Italy and other parts of the empire. Moreover, the primary festival devoted to Cybele, the *Megalensia*, held on April 4th to commemorate the goddess's arrival at Ostia had by the first century A.D. become the most important religious festival in the Roman religious calendar.

But now the key question: was Cybele, like Mary, a goddess who was both mother and virgin? The first part of this question is easy to answer: Cybele was definitely a mother goddess—the most important of the mother goddesses in the Roman pantheon. This is evident in the titles by which she was addressed. According to Showerman (1901: 296), for instance, the three most common of her titles were *Magna Mater* (Great Mother), *Mater Deum* (Mother of the Gods), and *Mater Deum Magna Idaea* (Great Mother of the Gods of Mt. Ida). Other common titles were usually some combination of *Mater* with a geographic place name such as *Mater Idaea, Mater Illiaca*, and so on. The sense in which Cybele was a mother is more difficult to determine. Some classical authors clearly tried to assimilate Cybele to Roman state religion by making her literally mother of the gods, and the mother of Jupiter in particular. In other cases, she was assimilated to preexisting agricultural goddesses, like Ceres, and was thus "mother" because she was associated with agricultural fertility. In still other cases, Cybele seems to have been considered a mother simply because of some vague sense that she had called forth life in all its forms.

But for whatever reason, Cybele *was* a mother. Was she also a virgin? This is the question that Farnell found so difficult to answer in his own study of the Cybele cult in the Greek states, and it is just as difficult to answer it in connection with the cult of Cybele in the Roman world. As a start, we might examine the characteristics attributed to Cybele in Greco-Roman mythology.

There are two Cybele myths that seem to have been especially widespread in the Classical world, and that must therefore be examined here. The first of these goes like this:

The Great Mother is sleeping on Mt. Agdus (or Mt. Ida or Mt. Dindymus) in the form of a rock, or (in some versions) in the form of the earth itself. Her son, Jupiter/Zeus, overcome by lust, approaches and tries to rape her. The mother resists, but Jupiter/ Zeus ejaculates and his semen falls upon the rock/earth. As a result, the Mother becomes pregnant. The offspring that results is an androgynous creature called Agdistus, who grows up to become a raging monster. The gods, intent upon taming Agdistus, get him drunk, and when he falls asleep, they tie his testicles to a tree. When Agdistus awakes, he leaps up and castrates himself. On the spot where his testicles fall, there arises a pomegranate/ almond tree. One day, Nana, daughter of the river-god Sangarius, picks some fruit from the tree and holds it to her bosom, where it promptly disappears. As a result Nana becomes pregnant and gives birth to a boy, called Attis. Attis grows to manhood and falls in love with a nymph. He prepares to marry her, but Agdistus (now female, remember) is so incensed at the impending marriage that she intervenes and drives Attis mad. In a frenzy, Attis castrates himself. Agdistus then repents of her actions, and prevails upon Zeus to preserve Attis's body from decay, which is done.

The second myth is similar to this first, and obviously related to it, but there are two important differences. First, it starts simply with Jupiter/Zeus ejaculating on the ground. There is no personification of the ground as the Mother, and no suggestion that Jupiter/Zeus was intent upon raping anyone (let alone his mother). Second, after Agdistus is castrated, he/she/it *becomes Cybele*. In this second myth, then, Agdistus and Cybele are the same person, which means that it is Cybele who is incensed at Attis's impending marriage, and Cybele who drives Attis to self-castration. Notice that in the first story Cybele does not willingly submit to her son's sexual advances, and in the second, Cybele's love for the younger Attis, though intense, is never consummated. Together, then, these myths might justify the assertion that Cybele was not associated with any strong desires for sexual intercourse.

But there is another story about Cybele that does associate her with willing sexual intercourse. It was related by the Roman historian Diodorus, who wrote in the first century B.C. According to Diodorus, all the legends about Cybele are derived from an actual historical incident. Long ago, he tells us, a daughter was born to the wife of a king, and the king caused his daughter to be abandoned on a mountain. The daughter, however, was suckled by wild animals and survived. Since the mountain was called Cybelon, the girl was called Cybele. She grew up and fell in love with a shepherd named Attis, by whom she became pregnant. Cybele was then reunited with her father. Incensed that his daughter would have fallen in love with a lowly shepherd, the king had Attis killed.

If the story related by Diodorus were widely held in the Roman world, of course, it would be difficult to sustain the argument that Cybele was disassociated from sexuality. Classical scholars, however, generally agree that Diodorus often invented stories in order to provide a "rationalistic" explanation of popular myths (Hammond and Scullard, 1970: 347). Rose (1928: 17) has suggested that the Cybele story presented by Diodorus is just that, a rationalistic invention, and that the story should therefore be ignored in studying the myths concerning Cybele.

If we do as Rose suggests, and set the Diodorus story aside, then the two myths—which were the two most prevalent of all the myths involving Cybele—would seem to justify portraying Cybele as a "chaste" goddess, where chaste means only that she was not associated with any strong or indiscriminate sexual desires. This conclusion is by no means novel. Showerman (1901: 300-301), in particular among Cybele scholars, has gone to great lengths to argue for Cybele's chastity on the basis of the mythological evidence.

But being chaste is not the same as being virginal. It would obviously strengthen my case if Cybele, like Mary, was more directly associated with virginity. In this connection, it will be useful to look at a story associated with the introduction of the Cybele cult at Rome in 204 B.C., and repeated in one form or another by any number of Classical authors, including Livy, Cicero, Ovid, Suetonius, and Pliny.

In its most complete form (as in Ovid's *Fasti*, IV: lines 291:326), the story begins by relating how the boat carrying Cybele to Italy, after arriving at Ostia, is stuck in the mud and cannot be moved despite the greatest efforts of those present. At this point, a woman named Claudia Quinta steps forward and tells the goddess that she (Claudia) has been falsely accused of being unchaste. She then asks for a sign from the goddess that will prove that she is as chaste as the goddess herself. Frazer (1929: 213) translates the relevant line as: "But if I am free of crime, give by your act a proof of my innocency, and chaste as you are, do you yield to my chaste hands." Claudia then takes the rope attached to the ship's prow and with but a gentle tug, pulls the ship free. By this miraculous act Claudia's chastity is vindicated. In relating the story, Ovid (*Fasti*, IV: line 236) tells us that though the story may seem strange, it has been "attested by the stage"—presumably a reference to the fact that a reenactment of the incident involving Claudia Quinta was a part of one or more of Cybele's festivals (Frazer, 1929: 241-242).

What was the precise nature of Claudia's chastity, and thus by implication, of Cybele's? As Frazer (1929: 239) points out, most accounts of the miracle of Claudia Quinta, including the accounts of Livy and Ovid, clearly identify her as a Roman matron, that is, as being married. This would create the impression that she had been accused of adultery. On the other hand, Frazer also notes that there are three Classical authors—Aurelius Victor, Herodian, Julian—who explicitly call Claudia a Vestal Virgin. Since these three authors are "not corroborated by Livy and other ancient authorities," Frazer concludes that their versions of the miracle of Claudia Quinta are in some sense wrong. But precisely because the three authors mentioned by Frazer *are* relatively late authorities (Herodian wrote in the third century, A.D., Aurelius Victor and Julian in the fourth), an obvious hypothesis suggests itself: that the story of the miracle of Claudia Quinta started out portraying her as a matron, but that over the centuries the content of the stories changed and Claudia "became" a virgin, in order to reflect an increased emphasis upon Cybele's virginity.

I realize, of course, that the available evidence is far too meager to substantiate this hypothesis: I am only arguing that the changes in the

Claudia story suggest that something like this might have occurred. Even then, the case is by no means clear-cut, since there are several late authors who repeat the Claudia story and keep Claudia a matron. Still, this line of thinking does suggest that if we are ever to find Cybele associated directly with the "virgin" label, then we would do best to focus primarily upon sources written relatively late, that is, in the third and fourth centuries A.D.

In fact, if we do focus our attention upon third- and fourth-century material, then we do find a direct association between Cybele and virginity, and it occurs in a familiar source: Epiphanius's *Panarion*, written in the fourth century A.D. In speculating upon the name of the goddess Cybele, Epiphanius argued that the name meant simply "virgin" (Vermaseren, 1977: 22). At the very least, this suggests that by the fourth century A.D. there was some basis in the minds of at least some people, like Epiphanius, for associating Cybele with virginity.

THE GREAT MOTHER AND CASTRATION

If the case for Cybele's disassociation from sexuality rested entirely upon the evidence presented so far, then the case would be very weak. On the other hand, perhaps we have been looking for the Great Mother's disassociation from sexuality in the wrong places. Given the modern Western bias toward defining religion in terms of belief (or theology or philosophy), to focus upon the ideational components of the Cybele cult—the myths and legends associated with it—might seem eminently reasonable. But as W. Robertson Smith (1894) reminded us long ago, the key elements in traditional religion are the rites and rituals associated with religious practice. This view leads us to expect that if Cybele were indeed disassociated from sexuality in the minds of most Romans, then most likely this disassociation would have been effected by the rites associated with her cult.

In the case of the Great Mother's cult, there seems no question but that the associated rites did far more to shape Roman attitudes toward Cybele than the myths and legends in which this goddess appeared. Consider, for example, the case of St. Augustine (A.D 354-430). Augustine devoted a large part of his *City of God* to commenting upon a now-lost work on Roman cults by the Roman author Varro, and in the course of this commentary, he often spoke of the cult of the Great

Mother. The following passage is typical of his attitude toward this goddess and her cult:

> The Great Mother has surpassed all her sons, not in greatness of deity, but of crime. To this monster not even the monstrosity of Janus is to be compared. His deformity was only in his image; hers was the deformity of cruelty in her sacred rites. . . . This abomination [the Great Mother] is not surpassed by the licentious deeds of Jupiter, so many and so great. He with all his seductions of women, only disgraced heaven with one Ganymede; she [the Great Mother] . . . has both defiled the earth and outraged heaven. (*City of God*, Book VII, Chapter 26)

It seems clear from this and other passages that Augustine considers the cult of the Great Mother to be the very worst of all the pagan cults. But why? What was the "deformity of cruelty in her sacred rites" to which Augustine refers?

Augustine tells us, in fact, the basis of his revulsion on several occasions: the *galli*, that is, the priests of the Great Mother, were supposed to work themselves up into a frenzy and castrate themselves. Augustine's attitude toward the *galli* is clear, when he talks (in the same chapter) of the "effeminates [who] not later than yesterday, were going through the streets of Carthage, with annointed hair, whitened faces, relaxed bodies, and feminine gait, exacting from the people the means of maintaining their ignominious lives." Likewise, later in the same passage he talks sarcastically of "the Great Mother of the gods [who] has brought mutilated men into Roman temples . . . to promote the strength of the Romans by emasculating their men." But Augustine is by no means the only source to mention the self-castration of the *galli*. On the contrary, this is the one thing that is mentioned by virtually all the Classical authorities who discuss the cult of the Great Mother. For instance, sources as diverse as Pliny's *Natural History* (XXXV, 46: 165), Juvenal's *Satires* (VI, 514), and Martial's *Epigrams* (III, 81:3) mention, if only in passing, that the *galli* castrate themselves, using a piece of broken pottery. The self-castration of the *galli* is also dwelt upon in those Classical accounts which treat the cult of the Great Mother at length, notably the accounts in Apuleius's *The Golden Ass* (Book VII: 24-31, Book IX: 1-10) and Ovid's *Fasti* (Book IV: 179-372). It seems obvious from these accounts that the self-castration of the *galli* was the thing about the cult of the Great Mother that most impressed itself upon the Roman mind; it certainly was what, more than anything else, led to early attempts to restrict the cult in Italy.

I must emphasize that here I am concerned with psychological associations, that is, with the elements (like "self-castration") that the average Roman would have associated with the cult of the Great Mother. In fact, not all *galli* were actually castrated. When Roman citizens were finally allowed to become *galli* (in the first century A.D.) they were still forbidden to castrate themselves. Though the law was apparently violated in a few cases, a substantial number of *galli* probably retained their testicles. Nevertheless, whatever the reality, it seems clear from any number of commentaries that the *galli* were associated with self-castration, and it is this association, I now want to argue, that served to disassociate the Great Mother from sexuality. If we think of the *galli* as being surrogate sons in relation to the Great Mother, then who was the Great Mother? She was, in effect, a mother who had surrounded herself with sons who were intensely devoted to her but who by their self-castration had gone out of their way to disassociate this devotion from any taint of overt and obvious sexuality. To the extent that the average male member of the Great Mother's cult identified with *galli*, then to that extent could they devote themselves to the service of a mother goddess without allowing into their conscious mind the suggestion that this devotion was inspired by sexual impulse.

In the end, then, I am arguing that devotion to a mother goddess surrounded by castrated "sons" is an effective way to discharge the excess sexual energy produced in sons by a strongly repressed desire for the mother. Very likely, in fact, devotion to the Great Mother of the gods is a more effective way of discharging such energy than devotion to Mary, the Mother of God. Mary, after all, is only disassociated from sexuality in general, but the self-castration of the *galli* insures that the Great Mother is disassociated very specifically from a son's sexual desire for his mother.

Since I am deriving the cult of the Great Mother from the *son's* unconscious desires, we would expect the cult to have been primarily associated with males, and it was. There were a few priestesses, but the overwhelming majority of the Great Mother's ministers were priests (the *galli*). Likewise, most of the lay sodalities charged with organizing and staging the festivals associated with the Great Mother are explicitly described in the Classical literature as being brotherhoods

(Showerman, 1901: 275-276). The male-centeredness of the Great Mother's cult is worth emphasizing, if only because it was not true of goddess cults in general. We know, for instance, that the Isis cult—which is the only other goddess cult to approach the cult of the Great Mother in popularity—appealed mainly to women (MacMullen, 1981: 116).

MASOCHISM

In connection with our discussion of the Mary cult, I argued that the guilt produced by a strong but strongly repressed desire for the mother should produce a need for castration, and more generally, a need for punishment. This led us to expect an association between the Mary cult and masochistic behavior, and the same reasoning leads us to expect a similar association in connection with the cult of the Great Mother. The tremendous emphasis placed upon the castration of the *galli*, of course, is by itself sufficient grounds for adducing elements of masochism in the Great Mother's cult.

But castration is a one-time-only event, and since the son's strong but strongly repressed desire for the mother is continually operative, we might expect to find that other—more repeatable—masochistic activities characterize this cult. It comes as no surprise, then, to learn that the *galli* regularly practiced self-flagellation using a leather scourge studded with knuckle-bones (Vermaseren, 1977: 115; for a picture of this scourge, see Showerman, 1901: 272). The best known self-flagellations took place on March 24, called the *dies sanguinis*, or day of blood. On this day the *galli* were supposed to flagellate themselves about the arms and chest until sufficient blood oozed from their wounds that it could be used to annoint various altars and images in the temple. (The *dies sanguinis*, as one might expect, was also the day on which a would-be *galli* was supposed to castrate himself.)

But cult festivals aside, the *galli* could lapse into a range of masochistic behavior in response to any number of daily events, a tendency that was often mocked. Thus, the Roman orator Octavius (cited in Showerman, 1902: 306) ridiculed an *archigallus* who began flagellating himself in order to salute the emperor, not realizing that the emperor had died seven days before. But perhaps the most graphic description of the masochistic behavior associated with the *galli* comes from Apuleius. At one point in *The Golden Ass*, Lucius the Ass is sold to a group of *galli*, and he describes their behavior as they enter a house:

> They would bend down their necks and spin round so that their hair flew out in a circle; they would bite their own flesh; finally, each of them took his two-edged weapon and wounded his arms in several places. . . . [One] took a whip . . . and . . . scourged his own body . . . so that you could see the ground to be wet with the womanish blood that issued out abundantly with the cutting of the swords and the blows of the scourge. (*The Golden Ass*, Book VIII: 27-28)

Since the argument that I am making suggests that the masochism of the *galli* was ultimately addressed to a continuing "need for castration," I might note that at least one Latin author (cited in Showerman, 1901: 306) described the practice of the *galli* lacerating themselves as "castrating also their arms."

ON FREUDIAN INTERPRETATIONS IN ANCIENT ROME

When the dream of a patient undergoing psychoanalysis has been analyzed, it is standard practice for the analyst to present his or her interpretation of that dream to the patient to see if the interpretation makes sense. Similarly, it becomes reasonable to ask if the interpretation of the Great Mother's cult just given would make sense to a Roman, or at least to some Romans. For instance, how would an adherent of the cult have responded to my suggestion that the emphasis upon the castration of the *galli* derives from a strong but strongly repressed desire for the mother? Probably not very well.

As Ovid tells us (*Fasti*, Book IV: lines 215-246), members of the Great Mother's cult gave a very straightforward explanation of the castration: it was done to commemorate the self-castration of Attis after he had been driven insane by Agdistus/Cybele. A modern commentator, of course, might suggest that the myth developed in order to rationalize the practice. But there is nothing in this that supports the suggestion that the castration of the *galli* derives from the sense of guilt produced by a strong but strongly repressed desire for the mother. Nevertheless, it is not difficult to develop an interpretation of the myth that shows it to be a disguised fulfillment of just such a desire.

In the myth, for instance, what is the proximate cause of Attis's self-castration? He is driven insane by Cybele on account of the strong love that she has toward him. And what is Cybele's relationship to Attis? Though she is not, strictly speaking, his mother (his mother is Nana, daughter of King Sangarius), Cybele is nevertheless a "female parent" (since it was the testicles of Agdistus, later Cybele, that gave rise to the fruit that impregnated Nana). To derive the basics of the Attis myth, then, we need only assume that a son's strong but strongly repressed desire for the mother becomes—through projection—a mother's strong desire for her son, and that the nature of the mother-son relationship be somewhat disguised by making a "mother" into a "female parent." Thus, the need for castration that derives from a son's desire for the mother becomes a need brought about by a female parent's strong desire for her son, and that, of course, is what the Attis myth is all about.

The transformations just discussed have the effect of disguising the son's strong but strongly repressed desire for the mother, and this makes sense in psychoanalytic terms, since this desire must be disguised before being allowed into the conscious mind, or the whole point of repression would be evaded. On the other hand, the very fact that the myth is a *disguised* reflection of the son's strong but strongly repressed desire for the mother means that the myth itself cannot be taken as evidence that that desire exists—a simple methodological point usually ignored by psychoanalytic investigators.

There is, however, one classical myth which, though not common, does seem to establish a link between the self-castration of the *galli* and a son's desire for his mother in a fairly direct manner, and which would thus seem to suggest that at least a few Romans saw this link to be as obvious as I have suggested here. This myth is related by Arnobius in his *Adversus Nationes*, usually translated as "Against the Pagans." Arnobius had been born a pagan, but was converted to Christianity in the late third century A.D. He wrote *Adversus Nationes* as a way of validating his conversion in the eyes of the local bishop. As a result, his work is a polemic designed to demonstrate the inferiority of the pagan cults. Modern commentators seem to feel that Arnobius had few theological skills, and that much of his work is characterized by logical inconsistency. But I am interested here only in Arnobius's description of the cult of the Great Mother, not in his commentary on it.

In Book v, Arnobius considers how adherents of the Great Mother's cult justify the self-castration of the *galli*. He first presents the standard explanation: they do it in commemoration of Attis's self-castration. In discussing this justification, Arnobius relates the myth that begins with Jupiter assaulting his mother while she sleeps, and ends with Attis's castrating himself as a result of having been driven insane.

A bit further on, however (Book v: 20–21) Arnobius relates a second version of this same myth that I have been unable to locate in any other source. Here, Jupiter is overcome with guilt for having violated his mother, and finding that nothing will mollify her, he finally cuts off his own testicles. Then,

> approaching his mother with downcast looks, and as if by his own decision he had condemned himself, he casts and throws these [testicles] into her bosom. When she saw what his pledge was, she is now somewhat softened. (Arnobius, 1886: 497)

Subsequently, and as a result of the initial rape by Jupiter, the Mother of the gods bears a daughter called Proserpine. Jupiter, eventually returning to his old ways, tries to seduce Proserpine (his daughter) in the form of a giant snakelike dragon.

Since Arnobius presents this myth in the context he did, the suggestion is very strong that at least some of these individuals saw the castration of the *galli* as a commemoration of Jupiter's self-castration, which had been prompted by his guilt over having raped his mother. Such a justification, I suggest, is not very different from the account offered here, namely, that it derives from the guilt produced by a strong but strongly repressed desire in sons for their mothers.

Lucretius, a Roman poet who wrote in the first century B.C. (and thus nearly three and a half centuries before Arnobius) is a second Classical author who may have linked the self-castration of the *galli* to a son's sexual desire for his mother. The relevant passage occurs in *De Rerum Natura* ("On the Nature of Things"), a long poem that for the most part presents an atomic theory of matter. In the middle of Book II of that work, Lucretius devotes about seventy-five lines to a description of the Great Mother of the gods and her cult. When he comes to the *galli*, he says:

> gallos attribuunt, quia, numen qui violarint
> matris et ingrati genitoribus inventi sint,
> significare volunt indignos esse putandos,
> vivam progeniem qui in oras luminis edant.

The following is typical of how this passage has been translated by Classical scholars in the nineteenth and early twentieth centuries:

> They assign to her also the *galli*; because they wish to intimate that those who have violated the sacred-respect due their mother, and have been found ungrateful to their fathers, are to be thought unworthy to bring living offspring into the realm of light. (Translation by Mason, 1851: 129)

What Lucretius is telling us in this passage is, of course, why the *galli* are castrated: because they have "violated the sacred-respect due their mother," and have thus been "found ungrateful to their fathers." Notice that he is very definitely not attributing this self-castration to the Attis myth.

The key phrase is obviously "numen qui violarint matrix." Although this can with much justification be translated "who violate the sacred-respect [or sacred majesty] of the mother," a quick check with the *Oxford Latin Dictionary* (1968) indicates that "violo" is a transitive verb that was used by a number of Classical authors in the sense of "to violate sexually," that is, "to rape." In other words, this passage could just as easily be translated as saying that the *galli* are castrated because there are sons who rape their mothers. In fact, Humphries' (1968: 69) translation of this passage comes very close to this:

> They give her eunuch priests to demonstrate that men are sometimes found unworthy of their fathers, ravishers of the maternal godhead, and such men must not send offspring to the shores of light.

It is impossible to know for certain just what Lucretius meant in this passage. But if his meaning was in any way similar to what is expressed in the Humphries translation, this is as close an approximation to the hypothesis being offered here as we are likely to find two thousand years before the age of Freud.

PROLETARIAN SUPPORT FOR THE GREAT MOTHER'S CULT?

The larger argument here suggests that the Great Mother's cult should have been especially popular with the Roman proletariat, notably the rural proletariat, since this is the stratum most likely to have been characterized by the father-ineffective family. In trying to establish this, we again run afoul of the fact that most Classical scholars, and certainly most Classical authors, have ignored the issue of class in the economic sense of the word. Although there are any number of conventional accounts of Roman religion which suggest that the Mother's cult was especially popular with the "lower" classes (Pascal, 1964: 56-57; Rose, 1959: 274-276), the references are clearly to legal classes, slaves and freedmen, which were not necessarily correlated with economic status. Some authorities (Altheim, 1938: 309-326) have emphasized the high degree to which the aristocracy was involved in the Mother's cult; it was, after all, one of the very few "Oriental" cults ever to achieve the status of a state cult.

The fact is that I cannot establish with any degree of certainty that the cult of the Mother drew its support disproportionately from the ranks of the impoverished Roman proletariat. All I can say is that this possibility is not ruled out by the available evidence. We know, for instance, that the Mother was regarded as the "foundress of cities," and that her greatest temples were located in urban areas. On the other hand, she was clearly an agricultural goddess, as well (usually as a result of having been merged with a goddess like Ceres or Demeter), and that her festivals were regularly celebrated in the countryside (Vermaseren, 1977: 38-125; Ferguson, 1980: 17). The Roman countryside was also dotted with a number of natural grottos that had been modified to serve as sanctuaries of the Mother (Vermaseren, 1966: 9). There are, as well, bits of evidence which suggest that the Mother's cult was organized in such a way as to achieve as much contact as possible with all levels of Roman society, including the poor. For instance, we know from sources as diverse as Ovid (*Fasti*, Book IV, 349-352) and Augustine (*City of God*, Book VII, Chapter 26) that the *galli* supported themselves by begging "small coins" from the public at large. We also know that the *galli* made use of "traveling sanctuaries," that is, groups of *galli* carried aloft a statue of the Great Mother, and were sent into the countryside for the express purpose of visiting the small villages. It is precisely to such a group of traveling *galli* that Lucius the Ass is sold, and Lucius complains mightily of having to bear the image of the Mother as the group moved from village to village in the countryside.

Finally, there is some epigraphic evidence which suggests that in Italy itself the Mother's cult was especially strong in the southern and western sections of the peninsula (MacMullen, 1981: 220), and these were the areas most affected by the development of the large agricultural estates.

Nevertheless, all this is highly circumstantial. Only one bit of evidence links the Mother cult to the rural proletariat in any direct way, and that is provided by Livy. In describing the events that led Roman leaders to consult the Sibylline books, and eventually to import the cult of the Great Mother into Italy, Livy (Book XXV, Chapter 1: 6-8) says:

> As the war [with Hannibal] dragged on and on . . . superstitious ideas, for the greater part from abroad, spread widely among the citizens. . . . Not only were Roman rites abolished in secret . . . but even in public. . . . Sacrificial priests and augurs had got a hold on the citizens, and their number was increased by the arrival of the country people who, driven from their fields, . . . had come to the city. (Translation in Vermaseren, 1977: 38)

In the context of Livy's overall account, this passage suggests that the cult of the Great Mother was imported in response to the influx into Roman cities of "country people, who, driven from their fields, uncultivated and unsafe as a result of the long war, had come to the city" (Vermaseren, 1977: 38). These people are, in effect, the rural proletariat. Livy is implying, then, that the image of the Great Mother was especially appealing to members of the rural proletariat.

If my argument is correct, then it provides a new perspective on why the cult of the Great Mother first appeared in Italy in the second century B.C. It is during this period that we first encounter the growth and development of large commercial estates, the *latifundia*, on the Italian peninsula (Heichelheim and Yeo, 1962: 159-162; Scullard, 1982: 18-21). What began to emerge then in rural areas in the second century B.C. are precisely those economic conditions that give rise to the father-ineffective family. If this type of family does produce in sons a strong but strongly repressed desire for the mother, and if support for the Great Mother's cult derives from this desire, then the fact that archeological evidence of this cult's popularity in Italy first appears in the latter half of the second century B.C. makes sense. This interpretation, by the way, suggests that the story concerning the Great Mother's arrival at Rome (the consultation of the Sibylline books, the delegation sent to Asia Minor, and so on) is likely to have been a later invention designed to explain the sudden appearance of a fairly bizarre cult among the Roman proletariat.

Here again we have provided an explanation of a previously unnoticed, but easily demonstrable, correlation. We have seen that the emergence of the Mary cult seems to have coincided with an increased emphasis on a graphic representation of the crucifixion, and have explained this by suggesting that the two events were produced by the same underlying psychological processes. In the present case, although any number of historians of Rome had mentioned the rise of the *latifundia* in the second century B.C., and although others have pointed to the rise of the Great Mother's cult in Italy during the same period, no one has suggested a direct link between the two events. By relating the rise of the *latifundia* to the father-ineffective family, and the father-ineffective family to the Great Mother's cult, we have been able to do just that. In general, uncovering causal links between elements previously thought to be unrelated is one of *the* most important results of the psychoanalytic method.

SOME PSYCHOANALYTIC ALTERNATIVES

It seems obvious that a popular cult organized around a mother goddess who requires self-castration of her priestly sons would attract the attention of psychoanalytically inclined investigators. In fact, this cult has probably been mentioned, if only in passing, by any number of psychoanalytic investigators, and three investigators have developed a fairly detailed psychoanalytic interpretation. The first of these was Ernest Jones, who played a major role in the early history of the psychoanalytic movement.

Jones wrote several essays on religion (most of which can be found in Jones, 1951a), and he usually interpreted religious belief as a form of denial. More importantly, perhaps, Jones argued that this denial was in almost all instances directed at the same thing: the son's desire to castrate or kill his father, in order that he (the son) might gain exclusive possession of the mother. Religious belief, in other words, was for Jones usually a form of denial that arose in response to hostility toward the father and sexual attraction toward the mother, which were universally engendered in sons by the Oedipal process.

For instance, Jones (1951d [1930]: 204-206) saw the goddess cults of the ancient world, with their overwhelming emphasis upon all-powerful female deities like Isis, Cybele, and Astarte, as denying the son's hostility toward the father by minimizing the father's presence. Simultaneously, of course, these cults allowed the son to gratify his desire to possess the mother exclusively. But an emphasis upon an all-powerful mother goddess was not—for Jones— the only way to deny the son's hostility toward the father. A quite different way is to emphasize the son's complete submission to the father's will. This was, for Jones (1951b [1914]: 356; 1951d [1930]: 207-209), the solution adopted by Christianity, which stresses that Christ was so willing to submit to his Father's will that he allowed himself to be crucified. This Christian emphasis upon submission to the father's will also explains why Christianity expunged the feminine element in the Godhead. Thus, although pagan pantheons always included deities corresponding to the Oedipal triad—Father, Mother, and Son—Christianity replaced the "Mother" with the more masculine "Holy Ghost" (Jones, 1951c [1922]).

Given our concerns here, I see at least two problems with the sort of argument that Jones advances. First, because Jones tends to lump all mother goddess cults into a single category, he cannot show why the Virgin Mary, unlike all previous mother goddesses save Cybele, is disassociated from sexuality. Yet this is one of the central observations that we are trying to explain. But there is a second problem that is far more general and more serious. Since Jones insists upon seeing all religious practices as attempts to cope with the same thing, the son's desire to eliminate the father in order to possess the mother, his argument provides no clear basis for explaining variation among religions. For instance, how does Jones explain why some societies respond to the son's Oedipal wishes by emphasizing all-powerful mother goddesses and deemphasizing the masculine in religion, whereas other societies respond to these same wishes by emphasizing the son's absolute submission to the father? It "probably depends upon the type of civilization present, whether light or serious minded, and on whether its predominant note is matriarchal or patriarchal" (Jones, 1951d [1930]: 205). Jones does not define what he means here by the terms "matriarchal" and "patriarchal." Why did Christianity replace the mother with the Holy Ghost? Because this was consistent with the patriarchal emphasis that Christianity inherited from the Hebraic tradition (Jones, 1951c [1922]: 371-372). Why has there been an increasing emphasis upon the Virgin Mary within the Catholic tradition, whereas the Protestant tradition has chosen to denigrate Mary? Because (Jones 1951c [1922]: 372-373) the Protestant tradition is reinforcing the original patriarchal tendencies inherent in Christianity, whereas the Catholic tradition has "adulterated" these tendencies. At best, arguments such as these are too vague to be of any use; at worst they are tautological.

While I have immense respect for the insights of Ernest Jones in other regards, in the area of religion his tendency to see opposites (such as the Catholic emphasis upon Mary and the Protestant deemphasis of her) as different responses to the same problem is precisely the sort of analysis which has acted as a barrier to the wider use of psychoanalytic theory in the study of religion.

Norman Reider (1959) offers an interpretation of the Cybele cult in the middle of an article concerned with the universal appeal of the game of chess, and in many ways his interpretation falls midway between that presented here and the one developed by Jones. For Reider, the various myths about Cybele are concerned with the standard Oedipal drama described by Freud, even though the father is not explicitly mentioned. According to Reider, representing the Oedipal drama by focusing only upon the mother-son relationship is to be expected in "matriarchal" societies, a term that he—like Jones—does not define. Like me, Reider sees the masochism evident in the Cybele cult as arising from guilt, but for Reider this guilt derives from the son's repressed desire to eliminate the father rather than his repressed sexual desire for the mother.

Although Reider does draw some comparisons between Cybele and Mary, he does not explicitly address the issue of Mary's (or Cybele's) disassociation from sexuality. Similarly, Reider's argument, like Jones', cannot in any obvious way explain variation across historical periods and across geographical areas with regard to support for the cults of Cybele and of Mary.

By contrast, the interpretations offered by Edith Weigert-Vowinkel (1938) *do* provide a basis for explaining variation. In the first part of her article, Weigert-Vowinkel relies mainly upon Classical sources to provide a historical overview of the Cybele cult as it functioned throughout the ancient Mediterranean world. In the second half, however, she does what I have done here: she relates support for the Cybele cult to a particular type of family structure.

Like Jones and Reider, Weigert-Vowinkel argues that the Cybele cult arose in the "matriarchal" societies of the ancient Near East. Unlike them, however, she speculates in detail on the form of family structure likely to have characterized these "matriarchal" societies. In her reconstruction, the mother in the matriarchal family was not simply a source of nurturance and love, but also the forbidding figure. By "forbidding," Weigert-Vowinkel seems to mean that the mother, not the father, was associated with both authority and punishment. Sons raised in such a family, she argues, would develop a strong desire for union with this forbidding mother, by which she seems to mean sexual union (certainly that is how her argument has been interpreted; see Reider, 1959: 328). Cybele was a projection of the forbidding mother, and so devotion to her cult allowed sons to gratify this desire for union. Once established in these matriarchal cultures, the Cybele cult later spread to more patriarchal cultures, like Rome, where it appealed primarily to disadvantaged groups.

In retrospect, it seems clear that some parts of this argument have to be modified. Few if any anthropologists today believe that matriarchy was a stage that preceded the development of patriarchy (a premise clearly implicit in Weigert-Vowinkel's discussion). Many commentators would also take issue with her contention that familial authority in the cultures of the ancient Near East was concentrated overwhelmingly in the hands of the mother. Still, what Weigert-Vowinkel calls the matriarchal family bears a striking resemblance to what has in this book been called the "father-ineffective" family. So even if we put aside the social evolutionary elements in Weigert-Vowinkel's argument, and the issue of whether or not the matriarchal family was widespread in the ancient Near East, we still find that she reached a conclusion similar to the one reached here: the Cybele cult should have been especially appealing to sons raised in families where the father's influence was negligible and in which all effective authority was concentrated in the hands of the mother.

There is, however, one important theoretical difference between my interpretation of the Cybele cult and the one offered by Weigert-Vowinkel, and it lies in the way we each explain the masochistic elements associated with that cult. I have suggested that this masochistic emphasis derives from the guilt produced in sons by their strong but strongly repressed desire for the mother. Weigert-Vowinkel, by contrast, sees such masochism primarily as a mechanism used by sons to win the approval of the forbidding mother. The son, she argues, will see masochism as a way of winning approval for several different reasons. First, it is seen by the son as a way of indicating his willing acceptance of the punishment that he associates with her and this, he feels, will please her. Second, he will also attempt to win the mother's approval by identifying with her. This desire to identify with the mother leads the son to imitate her, and so to inflict upon himself the punishment that he expects her to inflict upon him. For Weigert-Vowinkel, the self-castration associated with the *galli* also derives from the son's desire to identify with his mother, since castration makes the son more like the mother, in an obvious way. Finally, castration is also the son's way of denigrating the male role, and this too, he believes, will please his forbidding mother.

I know of no way to decide which of these two explanations of the masochism associated with the Cybele cult is the more correct. In support of my own argument I can only point to the fact that Freudian theory leads us to expect that a strong but strongly repressed desire for the mother will lead to guilt and, subsequently, to masochism; and to the fact that the Rohrschach data gathered by Parsons in her study of the father-ineffective family seem to show evidence of this guilt in sons. It is also true that the same argument which allowed us to explain the masochism evident in the Cybele/Mary cults also allowed us to explain the disassociation of Mary and Cybele from sexuality. Thus, the strong repression which is instrumental in producing guilt also makes it imperative that no overt sexuality be associated with the goddess in the conscious mind. Weigert-Vowinkel does not explicitly address the issue of repression, and nothing in her argument would lead us to expect that Cybele (and by extention, Mary) would be disassociated from sexuality. On the other hand, nothing in Weigert-Vowinkel's explanation of the masochism associated with the Cybele cult directly contradicts my own explanation of that masochism, and I see no reason not to believe that both the processes described by Weigert-Vowinkel and those described here may work to produce masochism in sons raised in father-ineffective families.

GETTING BEYOND THE OBVIOUS

The point that there were certain obvious similarities between the cult of Cybele and the cult of Mary has been made before. It is commonplace, for instance, to point out that many churches dedicated to Mary were erected on the ruins of temples devoted to Cybele, and that there is an obvious similarity between the title "Great Mother of the gods" and the title "Mother of God" (Vermaseren, 1977: 182; Ferguson, 1970: 239). Nevertheless, the interpretation being offered in this chapter differs in several ways from earlier attempts to link these two cults.

Most importantly, perhaps, I have chosen not to focus upon these or other obvious similarities. It seems clear that to do so easily leads to conclusions that are not defensible. For example, if we put aside the fact that the goddess Isis was associated with sexual promiscuity, then there are far more obvious similarities between the Mary cult and that of the Isis cult than between the Mary cult and that of the Great Mother. Several commentators (Ferguson, 1970: 239; Hyde, 1946: 54) have noted that Marian iconography was influenced by portrayals of Isis far more than of any other pagan goddess. In particular, the early portrayals of the Madonna with child seem to have been heavily influenced by portrayals of Isis with her young son Horus. Isis and Mary share any number of titles (see Witt, 1971: 272-273, for a complete list), many more than Mary shares with the Great Mother.

If we paid attention only (or even primarily) to obvious similarities, then we would be likely to conclude that the Mary cult was somehow derived from the Isis cult rather than from that of the Great Mother. In fact, when a pagan precursor to Mary is proposed, it is more often Isis than anyone else. In Warner's (1976) popular work, for instance, the relationships between Mary and Isis are often discussed; Warner's references to Cybele are fewer and more likely to be made only in passing. Witt (1971: 269-281), in particular, has argued Isis, alone of all the pagan goddesses, was the "great forerunner" of the Virgin Mary.

Yet if we put superficial similarities aside, and if by "Mary's precursor" we mean a goddess who drew her support from the same psychological wellsprings as Mary herself, then it is difficult to derive the Mary cult from the Isis cult. First, Isis was associated with sexual promiscuity (cf. Chapter One), whereas one of Mary's most distinctive features is her complete disassociation from overt sexuality. This alone suggests that Isis and Mary drew their support from different psychological sources. Second, we know that the Isis cult appealed mainly to women; no such sex-bias is evident in the Mary cult. On the contrary, if anything the Mary cult over the centuries has probably appealed more to males than to females. Finally, there is nothing in the

Isis cult that corresponds to the masochistic emphasis that has been associated with the Mary cult since its inception. If there was a precursor to Mary in the classical pantheon, then, it would have to be a mother goddess disassociated from sexuality, who appealed as much to males as to females, and whose worship entailed masochism. The only such goddess is Cybele, not Isis.

In summary, I have argued that the father-ineffective family produced in Roman proletarian sons a strong but strongly repressed desire for the mother that found its expression in the Cybele cult. When males of this sort began moving into the Church in large numbers during the Great Transformation of the fourth and fifth centuries, they created a demand for a goddess who was like Cybele. Although the middle-class sensibilities of the Church hierarchy forced a muting of the masochism associated with Cybele, these newcomers did get the goddess they wanted. She is Mary.

PART II
MARIAN APPARITIONS

MARIAN APPARITIONS

To the believer, nothing so testifies to Mary's importance as the fact that she intervenes directly in the affairs of this earth by appearing face to face with ordinary Catholics.[1] Mary, of course, is not the only supernatural being in the Christian pantheon who makes such appearances. Over the centuries, any number of Catholics have come face to face with Jesus Christ himself, several angels (St. Michael the Archangel seems to have been seen quite frequently), a variety of saints, and the Devil. Still, apparitions of the Blessed Virgin Mary seem to have occurred especially often, and this seems even more true in the modern age than previously. For instance, in his discussion of the theology of apparitions, Rahner (1963: 72-73) points out that during the Middle Ages appearances of saints, prelates, and the infant Jesus were much more common than they are now. Rahner's implication, probably correct, is that Marian apparitions now account for a larger share of all apparitions.

Certainly, Marian apparitions have been important to Marian devotion. Several of the most important Marian shrines, for instance, are associated with these apparitions. A million and a half people a year visit 140 Rue du Bac in Paris, where the Virgin appeared to Catherine Labouré in 1830; four and a half million visit Lourdes, where the Virgin appeared to Bernadette Soubirous in 1858; nearly two million visit Fatima, where the Virgin appeared to three children in 1917; and an incredible twelve million people a year visit the Basilica of Our Lady of Guadalupe in Mexico, where the Virgin appeared to Juan Diego in 1531. Even the shrines associated with less well-known apparitions remain popular: the shrine associated with the apparitions at Beauraing, Belgium, in 1932-1933 continues to attract about 500,000

[1] Some of the material in this chapter is taken from Carroll (1984), and is reprinted here with permission of the Society for the Scientific Study of Religon; most is presented here for the first time.

visitors a year, while the shrine associated with the Marian apparitions at Banneux, Belgium, in 1933 still attracts 600,000 visitors a year.[2]

In addition to the Catholics who actually visit these shrines, there are millions more who have worked to promote the devotions associated with some particular "Mary." During the last century, for instance, the Children of Mary, a sodality founded to spread devotion to the Miraculous Medal that the Virgin gave to Catharine Labouré in 1830, was one of the largest lay religious organizations in the world, and tens of millions of Miraculous Medals were distributed through their efforts. Today, the largest lay organization associated with Marian devotion is probably the Blue Army, which as recently as the 1970s claimed a membership of twenty-five million in 110 different countries (Geisendorfer, 1977: 46). The Blue Army is specifically devoted to spreading the message given by the Virgin Mary during her apparitions at Fatima in 1917.

Another measure of the close tie between Marian devotion and apparitions is the fact that the three cult objects most associated with this devotion—the rosary, the Brown Scapular of Our Lady of Mt. Carmel, and the Miraculous Medal—are all, according to pious tradition, supposed to have been introduced by the Virgin Mary herself during the course of an earthly apparition.

This great concern on the part of Mary's devotees with apparitions is all the more surprising in that the Church is very conservative about such matters, and only a very few of the thousands of Marian apparitions that must have occurred over the centuries have ever been given ecclesiastical approval. Such approval, when it is given, indicates only that there is nothing associated with the apparition that is clearly contrary to Catholic faith or morals, and that there is sufficient evidence to justify a purely human faith in the reality of the apparition (Graef, 1963a: 83-84). Even apparitions that have been investigated by the Church and denied such approval, however, can attract a large following among Catholics. In the early 1950s, for instance, thousands of Catholics flocked to Necedah, Wisconsin, to hear the message of

---

[2] All figures relating to the number of pilgrims attracted annually to the various European shrines listed in this paragraph are taken from the 1984 edition of *Quid*, the French-language almanac (Fremy and Fremy, 1984). The figures relating to the shrine of Our Lady of Guadalupe in Mexico were supplied by the Mexican Embassy in Ottawa. Though the twelve million pilgrims attracted annually to the Guadalupe shrine is without doubt impressive, we should remember that this shrine is located on the outskirts of Mexico City, and that people from Mexico City who visit the shrine frequently are counted separately for each visit.

Mary Ann Van Hoof, who claimed to have had visions of the Virgin Mary over a period of several years. The *New York Times* (August 16, 1950) estimated that on one occasion over 100,000 people watched while Van Hoof experienced one of her apparitions. More recently, thousands of Catholics have visited Bayside, New York, to hear Veronica Lueken, who claims to have had visions of the Virgin Mary since 1970. Neither the apparitions at Necedah nor those at Bayside have ever been approved by the Church.

The importance of Marian apparitions in the history of the Mary cult make it appropriate to consider them if we hope to understand that cult fully.

THE TWO CATEGORIES OF MARIAN APPARITIONS

If we approach the study of Marian apparitions (or any set of religious apparitions) on the premise that they are produced by natural causes, then it is evident that they are either *illusions* or *hallucinations*. Although the distinction between these two terms is clear in the psychiatric literature, the terms are often used interchangeably in everyday discourse, and so should be defined. An illusion is the misperception of a physical stimulus whose existence can be verified by independent observers (such as clinical psychiatrists). Thus, if a subject reported seeing the Virgin Mary above a bush, and other observers present did not see the Virgin Mary, but did see a light of some sort in the region of the bush, we would say the subject was probably experiencing an illusion. A hallucination is quite different. Although there are phenomenological issues which insure that any definition of this term will be controversial (Straus, 1962; Rabkin, 1970), most investigators require two conditions before infering the presence of a hallucination. First, the subject must perceive a stimulus and believe that it really exists (that is, is not imaginary). Second, independent observers must be unable to detect a stimulus of any sort that corresponds, however loosely, to that perceived by the subject. Thus, if our subject saw the Virgin Mary above a bush, really believed that she was there, and other observers present saw nothing unusual above that bush, then we would conclude that the subject was probably experiencing a hallucination.

The literature on Marian apparitions appears to show that although most such apparitions are likely to have been hallucinations, there are a few that were probably illusions. For instance, the twelve Marian apparitions that have attracted the most attention during the nineteenth and twentieth centuries would seem to have been those at Paris (to Catharine Labouré) in 1830; at LaSalette, France in 1846; at Lourdes, France in 1858; at Pontmain, France in 1871; at Knock, Ireland in 1879; at Fatima, Portugal in 1917; at Beauraing, Belgium in 1932-1933; at Banneaux, Belgium in 1933; at Necedah, Wisconsin in the early 1950s; at Garabandal, Spain in the early 1960s; at Zeitoun, Egypt in the late 1960s; and at Bayside, New York from the early 1970s to the present. In all these cases save one, there were observers present during one or more of the apparitions who did not see the Virgin Mary. The one exception involved the apparitions to Catharine Labouré in 1830, which occurred when Catharine was alone.

In three cases—at Pontmain, Knock, and Zeitoun—these other observers did, however, report seeing something. At Pontmain the adults who did not see the Virgin did see a cluster of three very bright stars in the region of the apparition, which were not there the following night (Walsh, 1904d: 106). At Knock, at least one witness later reported having seen a white light beside the church next to which the Virgin appeared a few hours later (Purcell, 1961: 151). Finally, a social scientist present at Zeitoun during one of the Virgin's appearances there reports that she did not see the Virgin, but did see a white light in the area where the people around her said they were seeing the Virgin (Nelson, 1973: 6). In these three cases then, because other observers did detect an unusual visual stimulus in the region of the apparition, it seems likely that the apparitions were illusions rather than hallucinations.[3]

In labeling these apparitions as "hallucinations" or "illusions," I do not mean to imply that the seers involved were mentally ill. That hallucinations and illusions often occur to nonpsychotic individuals is well established in the clinical literature (Bliss and Clark, 1962; Eisenberg, 1962; Aug and Ables, 1971). Of particular relevance is Kroll and Bachrach's (1982) study of 134 religious visions from the Middle Ages in Europe. Their major finding was that if we put aside the fact of the vision itself, then only four of the 134 medieval seers seemed to

---

[3] These three Marian illusions are discussed in detail in Chapter Nine.

show any traits that might reasonably be regarded as indicative of mental illness.

Confidence in this initial classification of Marian apparitions into the two categories of hallucination and illusion, is strengthened by the fact that this classification correlates well with other patterns. Consider again the twelve most popular apparitions, each of which is listed in Table 6-1. The fourth column gives for each of these apparitions the number of seers who only saw the Virgin, and the fifth gives the number who both saw *and* heard her. There are several things to note here. First, it is usually the case either that the Virgin is only seen or that she is both seen and heard. She is never seen by some, and both seen and heard by others. The one exception involves Fatima, where two seers (Lucia and Jacinta) both saw and heard the Virgin, whereas one (Francisco) only saw her. Second, in those cases where the Virgin is only seen, the number of seers is invariably much larger than when she is both seen and heard, in which case the usual number of seers is

TABLE 6-1

Selected Characteristics of Twelve Popular Apparitions That Occurred during the Nineteenth and Twentieth Centuries

Date of Apparition	Location	Any Evidence of Unusual Visual Stimulus in Region of Apparition?	Number of Seers Who	
			Only Saw the Virgin	Both Saw and Heard the Virgin
1830	Paris, France	no	0	1
1846	LaSalette, France	no	0	2
1858	Lourdes, France	no	0	1
1871	Pontmain, France	yes	6	0
1879	Knock, Ireland	yes	14	0
1917	Fatima, Portugal	no	1	2
1932-1933	Beauraing, Belgium	no	0	4-5
1933	Banneux, Belgium	no	0	1
Early 1950s	Necedah, Wisconsin★	no	0	1
1961-1965	Garabandal, Spain★	no	0	1-4
1968-1971	Zeitoun, Egypt★	yes	thousands	0
Early 1970s	Bayside, New York★	no	0	1

★ Apparition(s) have not been approved by the Church.

one or two. When the Virgin is only seen, the number of seers ranges from the six who saw her at Pontmain, through fourteen at Knock, to literally thousands at Zeitoun.

Overall, then, the data summarized in Table 6-1 suggest two patterns. First when an apparition is probably a hallucination, since there is no evidence of an unusual visual stimulus in the region of the apparition, then the number of seers is likely to be small, and all are likely to both see and hear the Virgin. Examples include the apparitions at Paris, LaSalette, Lourdes, Fatima, Beauraing, Banneux, Necedah, Garabandal, and Bayside. Second, when an apparition is probably an illusion, since there is evidence of an unusual visual stimulus in the region of the apparition, then the number of seers will be relatively large, and the seers will only see the Virgin. Examples include the apparitions at Pontmain, Knock, and Zeitoun. These patterns are not difficult to explain.

If, indeed, the Marian apparitions at Pontmain, Knock, and Zeitoun really did involve the misperception of an ambiguous visual stimulus, then we would expect the number of seers to be relatively large, since there was, after all, really something there to see; but since the stimulus was purely visual, we would expect the illusion itself to be purely visual. On the other hand, if the other cases were true hallucinations, we would expect the number of seers to be small, because the hallucination of an image that is not there is a far more unlikely event than the simple misperception of an ambiguous stimulus. Since auditory hallucinations are, in fact, more common (and thus, presumably, easier to produce) than visual hallucinations,[4] it seems likely that once an individual does begin hallucinating a visual image, then he or she will not find it difficult to start hallucinating auditory perceptions, as well.

The processes that give rise to hallucinations are almost certainly different from those that give rise to illusions, and so we will discuss the two types of apparition separately. We will deal chiefly with Marian hallucinations, since these appear to be more common than illusions. Chapter Nine, however, will consider some of the empirical patterns that seem associated with the probable illusions at Pontmain,

[4] For a concise overview of the empirical patterns associated with auditory and visual hallucinations, see Minn (1980). More detailed information about hallucinations and their associated characteristics can be found in the various articles on hallucinations which are cited in the text of this chapter and the next two chapters.

Knock, and Zeitoun, and will discuss a few general hypotheses concerning the genesis of such illusions.

Having made the distinction between hallucinations and illusions, I should point out that the same person can experience both. In fact, in at least three well-known cases, it seems likely that a set of Marian hallucinations was preceded by an illusion. The first case involves the apparition of the Virgin to twelve-year-old Mariette Beco at Banneux, Belgium, in 1933.

Mariette's first apparition occurred on the evening of January 15, 1933, while she was waiting for her younger brother to return home. In looking out a window, Mariette saw in the front of her house a beautiful young woman with a "most gracious smile." Mariette became convinced that it was the Virgin Mary. She tried to run outside to be closer to the apparition, but was prevented from doing so by her mother. Over the course of the next month, Mariette experienced several more apparitions of the Virgin, usually outside her house.

Witnesses were present during each of Mariette's apparitions, and except in the first instance, there is no indication that these witnesses saw anything unusual in the region of the apparition. This, together with the fact that in all but the first instance, Mariette both saw and heard the Virgin suggests that she was having true hallucinations. The one exception, the very first occurrence, was the only one in which Mariette stated specifically that she only saw the Virgin. But more importantly for our purposes, when Mariette first saw the beautiful young woman, she called to her mother and asked her to look, too. Her mother jokingly suggested that perhaps Mariette was seeing the Virgin Mary (and thus it was clearly she who planted that suggestion in Mariette's head), but agreed to look. Mariette's mother did not see a young woman, but she did report seeing a "white light" about the size of a human being (Maloy, 1961: 246). Not knowing what it was, she was frightened, and refused to allow Mariette to go outside. The fact that on this occasion an observer who did not see the Virgin did see a physical stimulus suggests that this first apparition, unlike those that followed, was an illusion.

The second case of a Marian hallucination that was probably preceded by an illusion (though not a Marian illusion) involves Lucia, the central seer at Fatima. In 1917 thousands of observers were present on most occasions when Lucia and Jacinta reported both seeing and hearing the Virgin, and these observers generally saw nothing in the region of the apparition itself. These, then, were probably hallucinations, and they will be discussed in detail in Chapter Eight. When Lucia was interviewed, however, she reported having experienced apparitions on two earlier occasions, in 1915 and 1916. These earlier apparitions, she said, involved St. Michael the Archangel rather than the Virgin Mary. The first apparition is of interest here.

In her first *Memoir*, written in 1935, Lucia (Santos, 1976: 60) states that the 1915 apparition occurred when she and two other girls were tending their sheep. Right after having eaten their lunch, she tells us, they saw a figure hovering in the air above a tree. Lucia first decribes this figure as looking "like a statue made of snow, rendered almost transparent by the rays of the sun." A few sentences later she describes it as looking like "a person wrapped up in a sheet." In her fourth *Memoir*, written in 1941, she describes it as a "cloud in human form, whiter than snow and almost transparent" (1976: 150). The figure hovered in the air while the three girls prayed, and then vanished. At the time, neither Lucia nor either of her companions identified the figure as being an angel or any other sort of supernatural being. Only after the apparition of 1916, when Lucia both saw and heard an "Angel of Peace" who identified himself as such, did she conclude that the 1915 apparition had likewise involved the "Angel of Peace."

Two things are significant about the 1915 apparition. First, if Lucia's account is accurate it was also seen by her two companions, since she tells us specifically that they asked her what the figure was. Second, the figure, whatever it was, did not speak. These two facts suggest that the 1915 apparition was an illusion—a suggestion that gains plausibility from data supplied in Walsh's devotional (but by no means uncritical) account of the Fatima apparitions. Walsh (1954: 22n) relates a report that he obtained from a Portuguese writer, who in turn had it from a woman who had lived in the Fatima area. Long before this woman had heard of the Fatima apparitions (that is, before 1917), her daughter had brought home a story about how she and some of her companions had seen "a white man without any head floating in the air." In other words, there does seem to be some basis for saying that there was something "white" in the air in the region around Fatima around 1915. In the case of Lucia, this whiteness was later interpreted as an angel; in the case of the woman's daughter, it became a man without a head. Quite possibly, in the minds of others whose stories have not been preserved, this whiteness became a whole range of other things.

The third set of Marian hallucinations probably preceded by an illusion were the apparitions at the village of Medjugorje in Hercegovina, Yugoslavia.[5] In June 1981, the Virgin Mary began appearing to a group of six children whose ages at the time of the first apparitions ranged from ten to seventeen years. The first few apparitions took place on a small hill near the village, but when the authorities prevented access to the hill, the Virgin began appearing to the children in a variety of locations, including fields, woods, and their homes. Eventually, the children were asked if they could have their apparitions in the parish church, and this has been the favored location ever since. Every evening, after praying the rosary in the main section of the church, the children (whose numbers dropped from six to five in 1983) enter a small room opposite the sacristy of the church, and wait for the Virgin Mary. Virtually every day, the Virgin Mary does in fact appear. These apparitions were still in progress in 1985, and had not yet been approved by the Church.

From the start, one or more of the Medjugorje seers reported both seeing and hearing the Virgin. Since other observers present heard nothing, it seems clear that at least the auditory components of these apparitions (assuming sincerity on the part of the seers) were hallucinations. On the other hand, these other observers did report seeing something unusual. On the occasion of the very first apparition, when one of the young seers asked a nearby male (whose age is not known) to look where the Madonna was, he reported seeing "something completely white, turning" (Kraljević, 1984: 8). Two days later, near the base of the same hill where the Virgin was first seen, a new appearance was preceded "by a brilliant light that shone on the village and the entire area" (Kraljević, 1984: 15). Finally, in an interview in 1983, a thirty-eight-year-old man reported that about twenty days

[5] My analysis of the Medjugorje apparitions is based entirely upon the account of those apparitions given by Kraljević (1984). This book (which seems to be a devotional account, Kraljević's disclaimers notwithstanding) is especially useful because it presents interviews with several of the seers involved and with several of the non-seers who have been present during these apparitions.

after the first apparition, at around eleven in the evening, he and several others had followed the children to the hill where the apparitions had first occurred. While there, he and everyone else present saw a very bright light coming toward them (Kraljević, 1983: 154).

Since the "bright light" has been seen only near the hill where the apparitions first occurred, and has not—for instance—been reported in the church where almost all the later apparitions have occurred, it seems probable that there was some unusual visual stimulus in the region of that hill. In other words, the first few apparitions at Medjugorje, or at least the visual component of these first few apparitions, were probably illusions. Once the local community accepted the reality of the apparitions, however (which seems to have occurred relatively rapidly), the children began having true hallucinations on an almost daily basis.

MULTIPLE SEERS

Although there are few people who both see and hear the Virgin Mary in the case of hallucinations, it is not uncommon for there to be more than one (see Table 6-1). In fact, it is easy to establish that the report of a Marian apparition, if accepted by most people in a local community, does provoke imitations. The best-documented example concerns the events surrounding the apparitions of the Virgin to Bernadette Soubirous of Lourdes in 1858. Bernadette herself (whose apparitions will be discussed in the next chapter) saw the Virgin Mary on eighteen different occasions between February 11 and July 16, 1858. But almost immediately after the reports of her first apparitions began to circulate in the Lourdes area, others began seeing apparitions in the same grotto. Thurston's (1927: 297) analysis of the records of the Church investigation suggests to him that there could have been as many as thirty to forty "false visionaries" at Lourdes in 1858. Some of these are described in Estrade's (1946 [1899]: 104-113) early devotional account of the Lourdes apparitions. One child saw in the grotto a Madonna with scepter and crown, another saw St. Joseph with a lily, others saw St. Peter, St. Paul, or some other saint. An eleven-year-old boy saw a "lady covered with gold and decked out with fur-belows." Most of the "counterfeit visions" reported by Estrade seem to have been purely visual, but some were auditory: one young girl heard a sound like "a conflict between unclean beasts" (Estrade, 1946: 106) issuing from the rocks in the grotto.

Thurston (1927) amplifies Estrade's account by providing information on some of the other "false visionaries" of Lourdes. Claire-Marie Cazenave, age twenty-two, saw "a white rock and almost at the same moment the form of a woman of medium height, carrying a child on her left arm." Madelaine Cazaux, forty-five years old, saw the figure of a young girl, whereas Honorine Lacroix, "over forty," saw the Virgin as a figure no bigger than a four-year-old child, with blue eyes and flaxen hair. Finally, there was Marie Courrech who, like Bernadette herself, both saw and heard the Virgin (though Marie's apparitions occurred on different occasions from Bernadette's). According to Thurston, Marie Courrech's apparitions were initially taken seriously by a number of Church officials, mainly because the descriptions and messages reported by Marie were similar to those reported earlier by Bernadette.

Apart from the case of Marie Courrech, what was seen by these "false visionaries" was quite different from what Bernadette saw. Nevertheless, the Lourdes data do establish the point that when one seer reports an apparition, and when this report is taken at face value by most members of the local community, the occurrence of other apparitions is not unlikely.

If the simultaneous occurrence of two Marian hallucinations is not unlikely, what conditions affect the likelihood that different seers will have similar hallucinations? The obvious variable here is whether or not the seers are in communication with each other. At Lourdes, there is no evidence that any of the "false visionaries" were in communication with Bernadette while she or they were experiencing their apparitions. It is not surprising that they reported different visions. On the other hand, when multiple seers saw and heard the same apparition at the same time, we *invariably* find that the seers had the opportunity to communicate with each other before reporting their apparitions to others. Thus, the one apparition which occurred at LaSalette occurred when the two young seers were off alone tending their cattle; the first apparition of the Virgin at Fatima occurred when the three seers were alone, tending their sheep; and the first apparition at Beauraing occurred when the four children involved were out, alone, on an evening walk.

As the number of apparitions increases, and the seers attract more attention, it becomes more likely that others will be present on the occasion of any particular apparition. Even so, when seers are interviewed it is usually in each other's presence. Walsh's (1954) account suggests that this was true in the case of the Fatima seers. At Beauraing, Thurston (1934: 11) specifically notes that although the seers were interviewed separately by the authorities, they had usually first been interviewed by their families and neighbors in each other's presence. Given, then, that in all cases involving multiple seers they have had the opportunity to communicate with one another, the fact that some Marian apparitions are seen and heard by more than one person does not seem problematic.

In his discussion of the Beauraing seers, Thurston (1934: 20-22) is at pains to suggest that they did not intentionally coordinate their stories—that they were not deliberately deceiving people. He is probably correct, and the same is probably true for all cases involving multiple seers: they are for the most part sincere. What probably happens is that for some reason, one seer begins hallucinating; this provokes imitation on the part of others present; convinced that they are all seeing something, they conclude that they are seeing the same thing; information is exchanged in an effort to determine what this is; having convinced themselves that they are seeing the same thing, they sort through this information in order to build up a consistent report. The process need not be conscious; in fact, it is probably almost always unconscious. But if all this is a correct view of Marian apparitions involving multiple seers, then it leads to a clear prediction that can be tested.

In those cases where the seer or seers have more than one apparition, the number of onlookers tends to increase over time. This is perhaps most dramatically illustrated in the case of Fatima, where the number of onlookers present at each of the six Fatima apparitions was as follows: May 13, 1917, no onlookers; June 13, 50-60 onlookers; July 13, 5,000; Aug. 19, one; Sept. 13, 25,000; Oct. 13, 70,000. The large numbers are partly due to the fact that the apparitions after the first were announced ahead of time, since the children at Fatima reported that the Virgin would appear on the thirteenth of each month. Only one onlooker was present for the apparition of Aug. 19 because it had not been announced in advance, and did not occur at the Cova da Iria, where all the other apparitions appeared. But although the numbers at Fatima are very large, the same general pattern of increase can be seen in other cases, as well. There had been no one else present when the five seers at Beauraing first saw the Virgin on November 29, 1932, but just over a week later, on the occasion of another apparition, there were about 15,000 onlookers (Sharkey, 1961a: 224).

Since most seers are interviewed immediately after their apparitions, and since the presence of onlookers should reduce the opportunity for an exchange of information, then we would expect to find that the reports of the seers present at the same apparition should begin to diverge over time. This is in fact, what happens.

Consider the case of Fatima again. Even devotional accounts (such as Ryan, 1949: 78) have recognized that there were discrepancies between the reports given by the different seers. Lucia, for instance, definitely saw earrings on the lady; the other two seers did not. Francisco definitely saw a rosary hanging on Mary's right arm; Jacinta was not sure if it was the right or the left; Lucia reports that the lady wore stockings; Jacinta did not see any stockings, and so on. Still, devotional accounts stress that for the most part the seers agreed on the main outlines of what they saw. This is correct, but only for the early occurrences. When we come to the sixth and final apparition, with its 70,000 onlookers, we find some very striking divergences between the reports given by the three seers, a fact that has already been noted in critical commentaries on the Fatima apparitions (Rahner, 1963: 34n). Thus Lucia saw two images of Mary, one as she is portrayed on holy cards dedicated to Our Lady of Sorrows, and another as she is portrayed on those illustrating Our Lady of Mt. Carmel. Lucia also saw a half-figure representation of Jesus Christ. Neither Jacinta nor Francisco saw any of these three images.

On the other hand, Lucia, Francisco, and Jacinta did all report seeing an image of the Holy Family, that is, a group including Joseph, Mary, and the infant Jesus. Why did all the seers see this particular image, rather than one of the others seen by Lucia? Probably because during the course of the sixth apparition, Lucia was heard to say, "St. Joseph is going to bless us" (Walsh 1954: 145). This was the only thing that Lucia said aloud during that apparition. Lucia, in other words, communicated to her co-seers the fact that she was seeing St. Joseph. Given the Marian emphasis of the preceding apparitions and the reference to St. Joseph, it is not surprising that Francisco and Jacinta might hallucinate (like Lucia) an image of the Holy Family, since this was probably the most common iconographic situation in which the children had previously encountered Mary and Joseph together. But Lucia did not give her companions any clues to suggest that she was seeing Our Lady of Sorrows or Our Lady of Mt. Carmel, and thus there was no reason for Jacinta or Francisco to begin hallucinating either of these two images.

Perhaps the most dramatic example of how the reports of multiple seers begin to diverge over time occurs in connection with the Beauraing apparitions. Initially, the reports of the Beauraing seers were similar, probably because they had plenty of opportunity to communicate with each other. Not only were the seers usually interviewed in each other's presence, but the five seers came from only two families. Even so, as the apparitions continued, their reports began to diverge. Thurston (1934: 12-13), for instance, has already pointed out that during the later apparitions one or two of the five usually did not see, let alone hear, the apparition manifest to the others. On the occasion of the last apparition, on January 3, 1933, when several thousand onlookers were present, the children were interviewed immediately after the apparition itself, so opportunities for the exchange of information were limited. Table 6-2 indicates what each of the five seers heard the Virgin say during this last apparition. Obviously they all heard something different. It seems likely that it was the fact that

TABLE 6-2

The Divergent Messages Heard by the Five Seers at Beauraing during Their Last Apparition of the Virgin Mary

Name of Seer	What the Seer Heard the Virgin Mary Say
Gilberte Degeimbre (9 years)	"This is between you and me, and I ask you not to mention it to anyone. . . . (Mary tells Gilberte a secret). . . . Good-by."
Gilberte Voisin (13 years)	"I will convert sinners."
Albert Voisin (11 years)	". . . (tells Albert a secret) . . . Good-by."
Andree Degeimbre (14 years)	"I am the Mother of God, the Queen of Heaven, pray always."
Fernande Voisin (15 years)	"Do you love my son? . . . Do you love me? . . . Then sacrifice yourself for me. . . . Good-by."

SOURCE: Maloy (1961: 226-228).

their reports were beginning to diverge that provided the Beauraing seers with the unconscious clue that led them to stop having their hallucinations.

DEVELOPING A SAMPLE OF MARIAN APPARITIONS

Even granting that a single Marian hallucination might easily provoke similar hallucinations in others, we still need to explain that first occurrence. But before developing such an explanation, it will be useful to uncover some of the empirical patterns associated with Marian apparitions, and for this we need to develop a fairly large and representative sample.

Billet's (1973) article listing 210 Marian apparitions might seem a useful starting point, since it is the longest such list available. Unfortunately, in a number of cases, Billet tells us only that an apparition occurred in a certain location, and nothing else. Even in his best-described cases, Billet gives us only the location of the apparition and the name and age of the seer(s) involved. Billet also counted as an apparition any occasion on which the Virgin Mary was seen, regardless of whether or not she was also heard. This means that many of the apparitions in his sample are probably illusions—especially since in many cases Billet tells us that the apparition was seen by "a crowd" or by several people. Finally, Billet's sample of apparitions is drawn from a fairly restricted time period, 1928-1971.

A far better sample can be developed using Walsh's four-volume *The Apparitions and Shrines of Heaven's Bright Queen* (1904). Walsh was a devout adherent of the Mary cult, but his work is still useful for several reasons. First, he described Marian apparitions from the earliest times to the present. Second, most of his essays on particular apparitions provide enough information to allow us to distinguish between hallucinations and illusions, and they provide us with a substantial amount of background information on the seers involved. Finally, though Walsh's work is biased in favor of "approved" apparitions, he does deal with a significant number that have not been approved by the Church.

Walsh begins his own analysis by considering apparitions that took place during the first few centuries of the Christian era. The number of apparitions that occurred prior to about 1100 is not large, however, and the discussion surrounding these early apparitions seems to be based on reports that are not contemporaneous with the events being described. For these reasons, and because Europe was not fully Christianized until around 1100, the present analysis will consider only those apparitions that occured between A.D. 1100 and 1896, the date of the last apparition considered by Walsh.

Walsh discusses eighty different Marian apparitions from this period. These include a variety of quite different events, and in order to maximize the probability that the apparitions in my sample are true hallucinations, I will consider only those that meet the following criteria: first, the seer was in a waking state; second, the seer both saw and heard the Virgin Mary; and third, the image of Mary seen was not provided by a statue or a picture in the region of the apparition. In other words, I exclude those apparitions that occurred when the seer was asleep, since these are best regarded as dreams, and those in which the seer only saw Mary or in which the apparition involved a statue or picture of Mary that talked, since all these are best regarded as illusions.

Selecting cases according to these criteria produces a list of fifty Marian apparitions. In a number of these cases, Mary was seen and heard by several different people, but I will be concerned here only with the central seer associated with each of these fifty apparitions. The central seer is the person who first reports that he or she has seen and heard the Virgin Mary. All else being equal, this is the person most likely to have had the initial hallucination that gave rise to the apparition. On the other hand, all the Marian apparitions experienced by a central seer, even if these apparitions occurred over a number of years, will be analysed here (see Appendix I).

How representative is this final sample of the whole corpus of Marian hallucinations? We have no information, of course, about the whole corpus, but we do have another sample, Billet's list of apparitions. I shall assume that those apparitions listed by Billet which are most likely to have been true hallucinations (rather than illusions) are those which Billet says were seen by only one seer. It turns out that exactly half of the apparitions on his list (105 of 210) are of this sort. In all of those 105 cases, Billet provides information on the location of the apparition involved, and in 92 cases, the sex of the seer involved is either specified by Billet or can reasonably be inferred from the name that he supplies. In other words, we can compare a sample of Marian hallucinations derived from Billet to my own sample at least with regard to geographical location and sex of seer.

The data on geographical distribution is presented in Table 6-3. Although the relatively small number of cases from each country means that any conclusions must be considered tentative, the distributions are remarkably similar: in both samples Italy accounts for the largest share, then France, and then the German/Austrian states. Collectively, these three areas account for almost exactly two-thirds of all apparitions in both samples. This similarity is all the more striking in that my sample includes only apparitions prior to 1900, whereas the sample derived from Billet's list includes only apparitions over the period 1928-1971; moreover, whereas my sample is weighted in favor of approved apparitions, Billet's sample is composed entirely of unapproved apparitions.

With regard to the sex of the seer, however, the two samples diverge. In my sample, twenty-nine were male and twenty-one female; in the sample derived from Billet, considering only those ninety-two cases in which the sex of the seer can be determined, twenty-nine are male and sixty-three are female. In other words, my sample suggests that Marian hallucinations are slightly more likely to occur to males than to females, whereas the sample derived from Billet suggests that

TABLE 6-3
Location of Marian Apparitions

Location of Apparitions	My Sample*		Sample Derivable from Billet (1971)†	
Italy	15	(30%)	43	(41%)
France	11	(22%)	10	(9%)
German/Austrian states	5	(10%)	12	(12%)
Spain	4	(8%)	—	—
England	4	(8%)	—	—
Poland	1	(2%)	2	(2%)
All other European locations	3	(6%)	19	(18%)
All Non-European locations	7	(14%)	19	(18%)
Total	50	(100%)	105	(100%)

* All apparitions in this sample occurred between 1100 and 1900.
† All apparitions in this sample occurred between 1927 and 1971 and involved only one seer.

females are about twice as likely to have a Marian hallucination as males. There is in this case, however, a third standard against which both samples can be compared, since there is clinical evidence to suggest that hallucinations are just as likely to occur to males as to females (Jaffe, 1966; Portell, 1970), and that when a difference is found (Bender, 1954: 45), males are slightly more likely than females to experience hallucinations. Studies dealing with hallucinations in general, in other words, find much the same pattern with regard to sex as I find in my sample.

THE EXPLANATION OF MARIAN APPARITIONS:
THE EFFECT OF RELIGIOUS WORLDVIEW

In trying to explain Marian hallucinations, I see no reason not to assume that they are produced by the same sorts of things that produce hallucinations in general. In general, hallucinations have been related to epilepsy (Horowitz and Adams, 1970), brain damage (Weinstein, 1970), disturbances in the mechanism regulating sleep (Feinberg, 1970), sleep loss (Williams, Morris, and Lubin, 1962), sensory deprivation (Zuckerman, 1970; Solomon and Mendelson, 1962; Vernon and McGill, 1962), the ingestion of various substances (Siegal and Jarvik, 1975), and to a variety of social factors, including social deprivation, neglect, and loneliness (Jaffe, 1966; Bender, 1970). It seems likely, then, that any or all of these factors would predispose some Catholics more than others toward having a hallucination. But we still need to explain why some of them have specifically Marian hallucinations. Part of the answer, I think, is provided by the data on geographical distribution (Table 6-3). The occurence of Marian hallucinations does not correspond closely to the strength of the Mary cult. Although Italy, a region where the Mary cult is strong, does account for the largest proportion of all Marian apparitions, Spain is not, in either sample, associated with many such apparitions.

The only consistent pattern that emerges from the data in Table 6-3 is that the regions most associated with Marian apparitions (Italy, France, Austria, and the Catholic areas of Germany) are those in which Catholicism has been the predominant religion for centuries. Such a finding seems consistent with the clinical finding that subjects having religious hallucinations are likely to come from families who believe that direct communication with supernatural beings is both possible and likely (Aug and Ables, 1971). Thus, Marian hallucinations are going to be more common in those situations where the prevailing religious world view legitimates a belief in the reality of such hallucinations. We are talking here about a religious world view or climate, not simple numbers. Thus, although the number of Catholics in, say, the United States has been only slightly less than the number of Catholics in, say, Italy (at least in this century), the religious climate of the two countries has obviously been different. In Italy, the prevailing religious world view is Catholic; in the United States, it is non-Catholic.

But the presence of a religious world view that legitimates a belief in the reality of Marian hallucinations is obviously only a necessary condition for the occurrence of such apparitions on a large scale; it is clearly not sufficient. Historical circumstance within a traditionally Catholic area can easily insure that the predilection of the population toward religious hallucination is checked. This, in fact, is what seems to have happened in Spain.

In his work on local religion in post-sixteenth-century Spain, for instance, Christian (1981a: 70-80) notes that most Marian shrines in Spain were associated with miraculous images rather than apparitions. These images were usually statues or paintings supposed to have exhibited some unusual characteristic, that is, they bled, sweated, talked, suddenly appeared out of nowhere, and so on, and which over time came to be associated with other miracles. In discussing why miraculous images were more likely to be associated with Marian shrines than were apparitions, Christian starts with a simple observation: "When images were found, the image was there to show. With apparitions, nothing was left to show, so that some proof was needed. How were the people and the authorities to believe the seers, particularly when they were so often marginal figures like shepherds and children" (Christian, 1981a: 18). This common-sense observation suggests to Christian why there were so few Marian apparitions reported from Spain.

Most Marian shrines were built in the countryside, and Christian (1981a: 90-92) sees the building of such shrines as an attempt by rural groups to attain a measure of religious autonomy from central Church authorities, who were mainly associated with urban centers. But precisely because the establishment of such shrines was a bid for autonomy, Church authorities would resist them except where the evidence of divine intervention was clear and incontrovertible. This is why "miraculous images" that could be seen by everyone were more likely to result in the establishment of a shrine than apparitions seen by only one or two individuals. It also explains why, at least after the Reformation, individuals who reported an apparition, Marian or otherwise, put themselves in a certain amount of danger with respect to the Inquisition (Christian, 1981a: 90). In Spain, then, despite a religious world view that legitimated belief in Marian apparitions, essentially political processes insured that such apparitions were infrequent.

THE EXPLANATION OF MARIAN APPARITIONS:
THE ROLE OF IMITATION

Sometime early in the sixteenth century, near the village of Garaison in the French department of Haute-Pyrénées, the Virgin Mary appeared to a twelve-year-old shepherdess named Aglèse de Sagasan. Over a century later, in 1664, the Virgin appeared to a sixteen-year-old shepherdess named Benoite Rencursel near the village of Laus in the department of Hautes Alpes. In 1846, the Virgin appeared to two young children (an eleven-year-old boy and a fifteen-year-old girl) while the two children were tending their cows near the village of LaSalette in the Dauphiné. A few years later, in 1858, the Virgin Mary appeared to Bernadette Soubirous in a grotto near the town of Lourdes in France; although Bernadette was not acting as a shepherdess at the time, she had been one in the recent past. Finally, in 1917, the Virgin appeared to three young children (aged seven, eight, and ten) who were tending their sheep near the village of Fatima, Portugal.

There appears, then, to be a centuries-old tradition of the Virgin Mary appearing to young shepherds and particularly to young shepherdesses. The simplest way to explain this is to argue that when the story of a particular apparition becomes well known in a region, this tends to provoke imitations. Thus we might expect that as stories about the Virgin Mary appearing to a young shepherd becomes well known in a Catholic region, more and more young shepherds and shepherdesses in that region should be predisposed to experience an apparition of the Virgin Mary themselves.

This hypothesis, of course, assumes that the seer (or seers) in one case knew about one or more of the earlier apparitions. In the cases just mentioned, this seems a reasonable assumption, even if it cannot be documented directly. The first four—the apparitions at Garaison, Laus, LaSalette, and Lourdes—all occurred in France, and became the focus of well-known Marian shrines in that country (Gillett, 1952). It thus does not seem unlikely that the apparitions at, say, Garaison and Laus would have been familiar to the seers, say, at LaSalette.

The case of Lourdes is especially interesting because here we have some direct evidence that bears on the imitation hypothesis. In 1857 (the year before the apparitions), a local priest and a local schoolmaster met Bernadette Soubirous in the countryside as she was driving her sheep. According to the schoolmaster's later report, the priest was sufficiently impressed by Bernadette's piety that he very explicitly compared her to the seers at LaSalette. In Estrade's (1946 [1899]: 15) account of the incident, the priest said that Bernadette was exactly as he had always imagined the "children of LaSalette" to have been. In Neame's (1967: 68) account of the same incident, the priest more specifically compared the fourteen-year-old Bernadette Soubirous to Melanie Mathieu, the fifteen-year-old seer at LaSalette. Neame himself pointed out that if the priest's remark was so well remembered as to have been noted down after Bernadette's apparitions, then it is quite possible that Bernadette might have been told of the remark before the event. If so, the fact that she experienced a series of Marian apparitions within a few months after being explicitly compared to another young shepherdess who had experienced a Marian apparition would seem to support the imitation hypothesis.

Fatima, of course, is located in Portugal, and thus might not seem to be part of the otherwise French tradition. Nevertheless, during the latter half of the nineteenth century, Lourdes had become a Marian shrine with an international reputation, and the story of Lourdes had diffused throughout the Catholic world. We know for a fact that the story of Lourdes was known in Fatima, if only because the parish priest at Fatima initially suggested that the strong similarities between Lucia's account of her apparition and the story of Lourdes might mean that Lucia modeled her account upon the Lourdes' story

(O'Connell, 1948: 43-44)—though Lucia denied having heard the story of Lourdes before her own apparition.

Imitation was not, of course, the only factor, or even the major factor, that triggered the apparitions we have been discussing. In succeeding chapters we will investigate the apparitions at both Lourdes and Fatima carefully, and in each case find that there were a number of processes that converged to trigger the experience of a Marian hallucination. But imitation was one of those processes, and it is one of the processes operating in a great many other Marian apparitions, as well.

In the examples so far considered, an apparition became more likely when a potential seer perceived a similarity between himself or herself and the individuals involved in some earlier, well-publicized, apparition. But imitation can operate in another way as well, as when a seer perceives a strong similarity between his or her own personal opinions and the particular message associated with a given apparition. Such seems to have been the case with "imitations" triggered by the Fatima apparitions.

Contemporary devotional accounts give the impression that the central message at Fatima was delivered on July 13, 1917: pray the rosary for the conversion of Russia. This is always interpreted to mean pray the rosary so that Russia might be converted from godless Communism to Catholicism (or, at least, Christianity). Under this interpretation, the Virgin Mary proved herself at Fatima, for the first time, to be a staunch anti-Communist. I say "under this interpretation," since it seems clear that a condemnation of Communism was not originally a part of the Virgin's message at the 1917 apparitions. Early accounts of the Fatima apparitions indicate that what the Virgin requested was that people should pray for the conversion of the *world*. There are two accounts of how this message was changed. In a document written in 1929 (and included in her *Memoirs*; Santos, 1976: 199-200), Lucia tells us that the Virgin appeared to her in that year (1929) and told her that the time had now come to reveal a secret message that she (Mary) had given to Lucia in 1917. That "secret message," of course, was that people should pray specifically for the conversion of Russia. On the other hand, in answer to questions posed to her by an interviewer in 1947, Lucia said that the more specific request that Russia (not the world) be consecrated to the Immaculate Heart of Mary was transmitted to Lucia by the Virgin in an apparition that took place in 1927.

In any event, however and whenever "the pray for Russia" request came to Lucia, it seems clear that this element was added to the Fatima message sometime after 1927. This makes far more sense than the devotional suggestion that such a request was relayed in July 1917—as of that date, the Communists had not yet taken power in Russia. Furthermore, in 1927 the socialist government of Portugal (usually labeled as a "communist" government in devotional accounts of Fatima; see Haffert, 1950) was overthrown in a coup d'état. This would certainly have encouraged the public expression of anti-Communist sentiments on the part of devout Portuguese Catholics like Lucia.

Still, whatever really happened in 1917, the fact is that since 1927 those who accept Lucia's account of the Fatima apparitions have been convinced that in 1917 the Virgin Mary came out strongly against the rise of Communism in Russia. Given the strong anti-Communism that developed in the United States in the postwar period and the strong antagonism against the Soviet Union that accompanied it, it is not surprising to find similarities between the Fatima apparitions and the two most important sets of Marian apparitions to have occurred in the United States since World War II: those experienced by Mary Ann Hoof of Necedah, Wisconsin, in 1950-1970, and those of Mrs. Veronica Lueken of Bayside, New York, between 1970 and the present.

At least during the first few years of Mary Ann Van Hoof's apparitions, the shrine erected on the Van Hoof farm at Necedah drew thousands upon thousands of Catholics. On August 15, 1950, for instance, about 100,000 people were present at an apparition. Judging from Van Hoof's (1971) own account, the crowds began to drop off dramatically about 1953, but the cult was still functioning in the 1970s. The number of Catholics attracted to Bayside to be with Veronica Lueken during her apparitions is more difficult to determine, but various news reports give the impression that thousands of pilgrims visit Bayside annually. More importantly, perhaps, there are a number of groups that promote devotion to the Virgin Mary who is appearing at Bayside under the title of Our Lady of Roses. These groups routinely sponsor newspapers and lectures explaining the nature of the Bayside apparitions throughout the United States and Canada.

The similarities between the apparitions at Fatima and those at Necedah are numerous and obvious. Mary Ann van Hoof clearly saw her experience as being similar to that which occurred at Fatima. Over and over again, she reported the Virgin Mary as saying that people have ignored the messages that she gave "at Fatima and at Lipa." The latter is a reference to the apparitions experienced by a young Carmelite nun in 1948 in the Philippine city of Lipa; the Lipa seer, in turn, stated explicitly that her message was a reiteration of the message given at Fatima (Haffert, 1950: 149-151). Van Hoof's identification with Fatima is also seen in the fact that the statue of Mary first given a place of honor at the Necedah shrine in 1950 was a statue of Our Lady of Fatima (Van Hoof, 1971: xvi).

But the most important similarity between the Fatima and Necedah apparitions lies in the content of the message associated with each. Although the messages and revelations relayed by Van Hoof (especially the later ones) tend to be long and rambling, and not always very coherent, there is one constant theme: pray the rosary to convert Russia and so avoid the impending war with Russia. According to Mrs. Van Hoof's revelations, the Korean War (which had begun just before her first Marian apparition) was only the beginning of this impending war, which would quickly spread to the Pacific coast of the United States. A great number of Van Hoof's revelations were concerned with the people in the United States working on Russia's behalf, with the nature of the coming war (she talks often of the "H-bombs" that will be dropped on the United States), and with the devastation that this war will cause.

In the context of the anti-Communist sentiment that washed over the United States in the early 1950s, and given the fact that most American Catholics of the time believed that the Virgin Mary had appeared at Fatima in 1917 to warn against the rise and spread of the Communist menace, it would have seemed quite natural to many of them that the Virgin Mary would once again appear to issue her warning against Communism. This, I suggest, was one of the factors that predisposed a devout Catholic, Mary Ann Van Hoof, to experience an apparition whose message was closely modeled upon that associated with the Fatima apparitions.

Support for the Necedah cult declined dramatically during the 1960s, as Van Hoof herself mentions several times in her 1971 book. The cult remained sufficiently active during the 1970s that Church authorities felt compelled to censure those involved with it in 1972,

1975, and 1979 (see Foy, 1977: 315; 1980: 134), but it never regained the following it had had in the 1950s. But in 1970, just as the Necedah cult began to die out, Mrs Veronica Lueken of Bayside, New York, first began to experience her apparitions of the Virgin Mary. This apparent coincidence is especially interesting since the messages relayed by Lueken seem remarkably similar to those relayed by Van Hoof. There is, for instance, the same emphasis upon the world having ignored the warning given at Fatima, the same concern with an impending war with Russia, with Russia's plans for world domination, with an enemy that is burrowing from within the United States, with the need to pray the rosary, and so on.

It is possible, of course, that the similarity between the Necedah and Bayside apparitions derives simply from the anti-Communism of each seer that led her to imitate unconsciously the Fatima experience. But one element in Veronica Lueken's apparitions suggests that she may have been influenced by the Necedah apparitions more directly. Consider for instance, the following message, taken from an ad published in 1984 by a group trying to promote support for the Bayside cult:

> Do not take lightly the reports of ships out on the sea and submarines. They are there, my child and my children, and they are not out for a joy ride. It is part of the master plan for the takeover of the United States and Canada.

This passage, colloquialisms and all, is supposed to be a message given to Lueken by the Virgin Mary herself. It is underlined in the original ad, and is the only passage so underlined. Why the great concern with "ships and submarines," rather than, say, missiles or bombers?

If we go back to Van Hoof's (1971) account of the "messages and revelations" given to her by the Virgin, we will find twenty-five separate entries for "subs" in the index, one of the largest entries there. In the text itself, most of these references to "subs" are reports given to Van Hoof (whether by the Virgin Mary or some other source is not always clear) indicating the location of submarines in the oceans of the world. Even then, Van Hoof's own book, which is only an edited compilation of her messages and revelations, does not do justice to her apparent concern with submarines. In the fourth volume of his devotional account of the Necedah cult, Swan (1959: 201-218) devotes an entire chapter to Van Hoof's pronouncements on the activities of "subs and jets." He presents seventy-one "sub reports" and ten "jet reports" that Van Hoof issued in a single one-year period (October 1956 to September 1957). In a typical "sub report," Van Hoof would pinpoint the location of anywhere from five to fifteen different submarines ("two subs near Portugal," "one sub near Havana," "three subs near Sicily," and so on). Van Hoof took these reports seriously, as did Swan and most likely a good many other members of the Necedah cult.

To understand fully Van Hoof's fascination with submarines, we would have to know the associations with which she surrounded them, and this information is unavailable. But the common fascination with submarines raises the possibility that the Necedah and Bayside apparitions may be similar not simply because each is modeled upon Fatima, but also because the Bayside apparitions were modeled directly upon those in Necedah.

So far we have been considering cases in which a Marian apparition provokes later imitations. But perhaps the most important way in which imitation affects Marian apparitions occurs at a far more general level. Thus Marian apparitions in the present are likely to occur most often in those regions where they have occurred in the past. This seems the most parsimonious way to account for Italy's continuing predominance with respect to Marian apparitions. Not only has the Mary cult been firmly established in Italy since at least the early Middle Ages, but in Italy reports of Marian apparitions were never suppressed. There is thus a long tradition of Marian apparitions there—fifteen apparitions, or 30 percent of the sample derived from Walsh's (1904) work occurred there (Table 6-3). If an established tradition of Marian apparitions provokes imitation, we would expect Italy's predominance to continue into the present, and it does. Of apparitions that occurred between 1927 and 1975, we find that Italy still accounts for the largest share (43 or 41 percent; see Table 6-3). The imitation hypothesis suggests, then, that Italy's predominance is also likely to be maintained in the future.

THE EXPLANATION OF MARIAN APPARITIONS:
A PSYCHOANALYTIC APPROACH

In the one analysis in which Freud (1961a [1923]) considered a religious hallucination in any detail, he advanced two hypotheses: first, that the occurrence of such a hallucination serves as a mechanism for the discharge of excess sexual energy, and second, that the content of the apparition was shaped by the seer's desire to gratify an unconscious wish. In this last section we shall see how these two hypotheses can each shed some light on the phenomena of Marian apparitions. As a start, it will be useful to present a summary of Freud's analysis.

Freud was concerned with the apparitions experienced by Christoph Haizmann in the late 1600s. Haizmann was a painter who executed very detailed pictures of his various apparitions, copies of which were available to Freud. These pictures, together with the extensive documentation of the apparitions gathered by Church authorities in the early 1700s and extracts from Haizmann's own diary, provided Freud with his data.

Haizmann had nearly a dozen separate apparitions—possibly more—and a few of these included the Virgin Mary. The central character in the first nine apparitions, however, the ones that most concerned Freud, was the Devil. By considering the characteristics that Haizmann, in his paintings and diary, attributed to the Devil in these apparitions, Freud came to the conclusion that the Devil was a projection of Haizmann's image of his father, who had recently died. More specifically, Freud argued that Haizmann's image of the Devil was shaped by his unconscious *hostility* toward his father, a hostility that had been formed during the Oedipal period and that had long since been repressed.

But hostile attitudes toward the father are, in Freud's general theory, formed in almost all males during the Oedipal period. Why should these impulses have given rise to an apparition in Haizmann's case? Freud's answer, developed in the later sections of his essay, is that Haizmann was a man driven by a strong libidinal impulse to enjoy the pleasures of the material world (he wanted desperately to dress well, to associate with beautiful women, and so on). This strong libidinal drive conflicted with a deep commitment to an ascetic life, acquired as the result of the peculiarities of Haizmann's upbringing. It was the fact that Haizmann's particularly strong libidinal drive was blocked by his great commitment to asceticism that gave rise to the apparitions.

It seems clear, then, that Freud's view of apparitions was the same as his earlier (Freud 1959 [1907]) view of obsessive religious practices, namely that these religious phenomena are sublimations of sexual or aggressive impulses that, for whatever reason, are blocked and cannot be expressed directly. In this view, the function of the apparition (or religious obsession) is to drain off some of the excess generated by the repressed impulse.

Freud goes on to describe in detail the mechanics of the process whereby a blocked impulse gives rise to an apparition, and in so doing, he explains why apparitions come to have a particular content. In his own words, "a damned-up libido which cannot in reality be satisfied succeeds, *with the help of a regression to old fixations*, in finding discharge through the repressed unconscious" (Freud, 1961a: 105, emphasis added). This restatement of his general hypothesis regarding the origin of neuroses argues that a sexual or aggressive impulse that is blocked will reactivate one or more of the sexual and agressive impulses formed during the Oedipal period, which later came to be repressed. In the case of Haizmann, for instance, his strong desire for material comfort, when blocked, reactivated his repressed hostility toward his father. That this unconscious hostility was reactivated, rather than some other "infantile" impulse, was mainly due to the fact that this hostility had already been activated to some degree by his father's recent death.

If Marian apparitions are produced by a process similar to that described by Freud in the case of Haizmann, we should be able to find some evidence linking them to the sublimation of repressed sexual impulses. And if we approach the study of Marian apparition with such a hypothesis in mind, supportive evidence is easy to find. For instance, in those thirty cases in Walsh that are not included in my sample (usually because Mary appears but does not speak), we quite often come across an associated description of a female seer's encounter with Jesus that is rife with sexual imagery. It is difficult not to think of sexual sublimation when a female seer, in addition to her Marian apparition, reports one in which Christ inserts a phallic-shaped object directly into her body, as when the Blessed Ossana reports that her Divine Spouse, Jesus Christ, plunged a "long and terrible nail" directly into her heart, or when the Blessed Catherine of Raconigi reports that her Divine Spouse, also Jesus Christ, plunges his arm (a long and narrow part of his body) into her body so that he can grasp her heart and "wash" it (Walsh, 1904b: 314, 321). Likewise, St. Teresa of Avila, in addition to her Marian apparitions, reported one in which a very beautiful male angel approached her with a long golden dagger ("at whose extremity was a slight spark of flame"), and who subsequently plunged that dagger into her heart and into her entrails

(Walsh, 1906c: 32). In other instances, the phallic imagery is absent, but the reported apparitions nevertheless have a decidedly erotic cast, as when St. Rose of Lima reports an apparition in which the crucified (and thus, presumably, nearly naked) Christ appears to her and tells her to kiss the wound in his side, which she does, and is thereby refreshed (Walsh, 1906c: 127).

Then, too, the hypothesis of sexual sublimation seems consistent with the fact that so many seers went to great lengths to inflict pain on themselves immediately prior to having an apparition. Who can fail to see some evidence of sexual tension, for instance, when the Blessed Benventuta Bojani, at twelve years, girded herself with a rope which, as she grew, "became buried in her flesh, causing her intense pain" (Walsh, 1906c: 148); or when St. Catherine of Siena after taking a vow of chastity, girded herself "with a chain of iron, so hard and terrible that it sunk deep into her flesh and seared it as if it were red-hot" (Walsh, 1906c: 193).

But the presentation of anecdotal evidence drawn from a very small number of cases cannot decide the matter. Besides, our concern here is only with Marian apparitions, and not with apparitions of Jesus Christ. In looking over the personal histories of the fifty central seers who had apparitions of Mary, is there any systematic pattern which suggests that these Marian apparitions are derived from repressed sexual impulses? Yes. The vast majority of our central seers were sexually mature individuals who apparently lacked regular sexual partners. Of those forty-five seers for whom such information is available, forty percent were clerics of some sort (priests, nuns, brothers), 20 percent were unmarried adolescents, and 18 percent were unmarried adults (Table 6-4). Although being a cleric or an unmarried adolescent is not a sure guarantee of celibacy in this or any other society, the fact that nearly eighty percent of our seers were sexually mature individuals who lacked any obvious sexual partners, and the fact that only a very small percentage (4 percent) of these seers were married at the time of their apparitions, seem at least consistent with Freud's general argument.

But Freud also argued that repressed sexual impulses would activate "infantile fixations," which would shape the content of the resulting apparitions. Since we are dealing here with Marian apparitions, it seems reasonable to suppose that such apparitions result when sexual repression activates those infantile desires that give rise to Marian devotion in the first place. I argued in Chapter Three that

TABLE 6-4

The Celibacy Status of the Central Seers in My Sample

Central Seer, at Time of First Apparition	Number in Each Category	Percentage in Each Category*
Cleric	18	40%
Unmarried		
child (1-10 years)	8	18%
adolescent (11-18 years)	9	20%
adult (19 years or older)	8	18%
Married	2	4%
Insufficient Information	5	—
Total	50	100% (N = 45)

* Excluding "Insufficient information."

for males, Marian devotion derives from a son's repressed sexual desire for the mother, whereas for females, such devotion derives from a daughter's desire for sexual intercourse with, and a child from, her father.

But if these infantile wishes do shape the content of Marian hallucinations, then the fact that these wishes are different for males and females means that we can predict some differences between the types of Marian apparition experienced by each. For instance, the son's infantile wish is not simply to have sexual access to the mother, but to have *exclusive* sexual access to the mother. It is this desire for exclusivity that generates hostility toward the father and a desire to eliminate him. One reasonable derivation from this argument would be that male seers would tend, in their apparitions, to disassociate Mary from any obvious father figures. In the case of female seers, on the other hand, the whole point of the apparition is to provide the young girl with a way of identifying with Mary and thus vicariously enjoying her own Oedipal fantasy, which is to have sexual intercourse with the father. This leads us to expect that the apparitions experienced by female seers would include father figures.

In using the data from the sample to test these predictions, I counted a father figure as being present in the apparitions if Mary appeared in the company of any adult male such as the adult Jesus Christ, St. Francis, St. Dominic, or any other adult male saint. On the other hand, the infant Christ, who often accompanies Mary in the apparitions in our sample, was not counted as a father figure; nor, obviously, was a father-figure counted present when Mary appeared only in the company of female saints.

The data in Table 6-5 suggest that, although the correlation is far from perfect, the female seers in our sample were more likely than males to have Marian apparitions that included adult males. The observations in this table are probably not independent, since it is highly likely that the occurrence of later apparitions was influenced by widespread knowledge of earlier ones. Nevertheless, to allow comparison of the data in Table 6-5 with other studies, if the cases were independent, then the result would be both strong and statistically significant (phi = .35, p = .005, using Fisher's Exact Test, one-tailed).

CONCLUSION

In summary, then, once we make the distinction between Marian illusions and Marian hallucinations (and restrict ourselves for the moment to the latter), it appears that Marian apparitions are produced by

TABLE 6-5

Relationship between Sex of Central Seer and Likelihood of Including an Adult Male in a Marian Apparition

Sex of Central Seer	Adult Male in a Marian Apparition?		
	No	Yes	
Male	93% (N = 25)	7% (N = 2)	100% (N = 27)
Female	50% (N = 10)	50% (N = 10)	100% (N = 20)

NOTE: Three seers were eliminated from the sample because the sex or age of the individual(s) who appeared with Mary was not clearly specified; two of these seers were male, the other female.

a variety of factors. These include the organic factors that predispose individuals to experience hallucinations in general, the presence of a religious world view that legitimates the belief that the Virgin Mary often makes earthly appearances, and the tendency to imitate previous Marian apparitions. There is also some evidence to suggest that Marian hallucinations result when sexual outlets are blocked, and that the content of Marian hallucinations is shaped in part by repressed Oedipal wishes. It is this last—psychoanalytic—argument that I want to explore further, since it provides a foundation upon which we can erect an even more complete understanding of Marian apparitions.

So far I have argued that the content of a Marian apparition is shaped by *Oedipal* wishes that are reactivated by a buildup of excess sexual energy. But Freud's general theory of hallucinations, like his general theory of dreams, requires only that the content of hallucinations and dreams be shaped by *infantile* wishes. Although Oedipal wishes are infantile wishes, the reverse is by no means true, especially since Freud often stretched the term "infantile" to include early adolescence. Thus it is entirely consistent with Freudian theory to suggest that hallucinations might be shaped both by Oedipal desires and by other desires formed during the infantile period. Moreover, Freud also argued in connection with the study of dreams that the infantile desire which gives rise to a dream is often activated by a desire or wish formed during adulthood, and that this adult desire or wish often influences the content of the dream, as well. In his well-known analysis of his own "Uncle Josef" dream, for instance, Freud (1953 [1900]: 136-142, 191-195) argued that the dream ultimately reflected his infantile desire to become a Cabinet member in the Austrian government, but that this infantile desire had been activated by a more recent desire to be promoted to a higher professorial rank within his university department. Presumably, a similar process would operate in connection with hallucinations.

Freud's argument, in other words, leads us to expect that the content of various Marian hallucinations might have been shaped not simply by Oedipal desires but also by other infantile desires and by desires formed during adulthood. Since such desires are likely to vary from seer to seer, a full account of the content of any particular apparition must involve investigation of the experiences of the seer having that apparition. Doing this for each of the fifty seers in my sample would be impossible; for one thing, the information is not always available. But in the next two chapters, I will consider the five Marian apparitions that seem to have been most influential in the modern world. In each case, we will find that the content of the apparition does appear to have been influenced by some of the idiosyncratic wishes and desires that characterize the particular seer.

THE VIRGIN AT PARIS, LaSALETTE
AND LOURDES

The three most important Marian apparitions in the nineteenth century all occurred in France, justifying the sense of many French Catholics—then and now—that Mary was, to borrow Boutry's phrase, "la grande consolatrice de la France au XIXe siècle."[1] These were the apparitions at Paris in 1830, LaSalette in 1846 and, of course, at Lourdes in 1858. These were by no means the only places in France that Mary chose to visit during the nineteenth century; Boutry (1982) lists nineteen other relatively well-known Marian apparitions in other areas of France between 1830 and 1896. Nevertheless, the apparitions at Paris, LaSalette, and Lourdes are particularly important because they influenced the course of Marian devotion not just in France but in the rest of the Catholic world, as well.

The "Miraculous Medal," for instance, minted to commemorate the apparitions of the Virgin at Paris in 1830, has easily become—after the rosary and the Brown Scapular—the most popular of all Marian cult objects. Hundreds of millions of these medals have now been distributed, and the wearing of these medals has been credited with thousands of miraculous cures. Because the image of Mary on this medal was an image of "Mary Immaculate," the great popularity of this medal in the 1830s and 1840s undoubtedly influenced the decision to proclaim a belief in Mary's Immaculate Conception an official dogma of the Church in 1854. Devotions oriented around the medal have also proven popular. By the 1960s, for instance, the "Miraculous Medal Perpetual Novena" was being observed in thousands of Catholic churches throughout the world (Dirvin, 1967: 895).

Similarly, the shrine erected at Lourdes to commemorate the ap-

[1] Most of the discussion in this chapter which deals with the apparitions at LaSalette and Lourdes is taken from Carroll (1985), and is reprinted here with permission of the Society for the Scientific Study of Religion, which holds the copyright. The material in this chapter which deals with the apparitions to Catherine Labouré is presented here for the first time.

paritions in 1858 has become, next to the shrine dedicated to Our Lady of Guadalupe in Mexico, the most important Marian shrine in the world. It now attracts four and a half million visitors a year from a variety of different countries, and water from the spring at Lourdes has been credited with thousands of miraculous cures, of which fifty-eight have been officially recognized by the Church as true miracles. In 1907, Pope Pius X acknowledged the universal appeal of Our Lady of Lourdes by authorizing a special Mass to be said in honor of Mary under that title on February 11 each year.

These days, the apparition at LaSalette is less well known than those at Paris or Lourdes, but in the mid-nineteenth century, the shrine at LaSalette enjoyed more or less the same international reputation as that now enjoyed, say, by Lourdes or Fatima.

Not only did these three sets of apparitions all occur in France during a relatively short period of time, they share at least one additional characteristic: in all three cases, the central seer did not initially identify the woman seen as the Virgin Mary. In all three cases, then, our first task is not to determine why the seer might hallucinate an image of the Virgin but to determine whose image was hallucinated. For reasons that will become clear, it will be easier to develop the discussion if we consider the cases of LaSalette and Lourdes first, and then return to the case of Paris.

THE LADY OF LASALETTE

Our first case involves the apparition that occurred on a hillside near the village of LaSalette, France, on September 19, 1846. According to devotional accounts,[2] this apparition was seen by two children, a girl named Melanie Mathieu, nearly fifteen at the time, and a boy named Maximin Giraud, who was eleven. Each child had been hired by a local farmer to herd cattle, and on that day the children had decided to herd the cattle together. Although the families of both children lived in the nearby town of Corps, Melanie and Mathieu had met for the first time only a few days earlier. Herding was for Melanie a routine

---

[2] By "devotional account" I mean a description that posits a supernatural origin for the apparitions being described. Some of the more well-known devotional accounts of the apparition at LaSalette include Cox (1956: 1-68), Kennedy (1961), Northcote (1875), Stern (1980), and Ullathorne (1942[1854]). For a bibliography of works relating to LaSalette, see Stern (1975).

activity, since she had been hired out to local farmers since she was nine. It was, however, a quite novel experience for Maximin, since he had been hired out, apparently for the first time, only within the preceding week.

According to the report given by the children, they took a nap that afternoon. When they awoke, they found their cattle gone. In searching for the cattle (which they found) they came upon a bright light that seemed to be hovering above a boulder on a nearby hillside. Upon closer inspection, they perceived in the midst of this bright light a lady who was seated on the boulder, crying. The lady then arose and addressed the children. She initially spoke in standard French, but after delivering what turned out to be about half of her eventual message, she perceived that the children were having difficulty understanding her, and so switched to the local patois.

The message delivered by the woman at LaSalette has quite properly been described as "apocalyptic" (see Turner and Turner, 1982: 156-164). She warned of the terrible punishments that would soon befall France as the result of the sinful ways into which the people had fallen. The following passages are typical:

> If the harvest is spoilt, you yourselves are the only cause of it. I made you feel this last year in the potatoes [referring to the potato famine], but you took no account of it; on the contrary . . . you swore, and you took the name of my son in vain. . . . There will come a great famine; and before the famine the children under the age of seven will be seized with a trembling, and will fall in the hands of those that hold them; the rest will do penance by the famine. The walnuts will become bad, the grapes will rot. . . .
> (Northcote, 1875: 237-238)

According to the lady, the bad habits that would provoke such terrible punishments included swearing, not going to church regularly, meat-eating during Lent, and so on. Only if people abandoned such habits and turned to prayer would these disasters be avoided. During the course of her speech, the lady also confided to Melanie a secret not heard by Maximin and to Maximin a secret not heard by Melanie.

It is important to note that at no point did the lady identify herself as the Virgin Mary, nor did the children identify her as such in their initial reports of the incident. When they first came off the hillside, the first person they met was the farmer who employed Maximin, and

Maximin related to him the account of what had occurred. Maximin later went to the house of Melanie's employer, where he related his story to the "grandmère" of the house. It was this woman who first suggested that the lady seen on the hillside was the Virgin Mary (Cox, 1956: 4-5). The next morning, the two children were brought before the parish priest, and he too suggested that the lady was in fact the Virgin Mary.

Although this devotional account suggests that the lady of LaSalette was seen simultaneously by Melanie and Maximin, there are several reasons for believing that the initial hallucination was Maximin's. First, it was Maximin who gave the first report of the apparition to a third party after the children had come off the hillside. Second, since later investigation indicated that Melanie knew no French and that Maximin knew at least some (Hidec, 1969: 8-9), Maximin is the more likely originator of an hallucinated image who spoke French during the first half of her message. Third, the lady made at least one very specific reference to an event in Maximin's life when she asked the children if they had ever seen wheat that was spoilt. When the children replied "no," the lady addressed Maximin in particular, and said:

> You have seen it my child, once when you were with your father at Coin. The owner of a piece of ground there told your father to go and see his wheat that was spoilt. You went, both of you, and you took two or three ears of wheat in your hands; you rubbed them, and they crumbled into dust. . . . [Later] your father gave you a piece of bread, and said "Take this my child; let us eat it this year whilst we can get it; I don't know who will be able to eat any next year if the wheat goes on like that." (Northcote, 1875: 239)

By contrast, although the lady dwelt at length and in detail upon this incident from Maximin's life, she did not refer to any specific incident from Melanie's life, and this too makes it likely that Maximin was the original seer.

Labeling Maximin as the "original seer" does not in itself imply that Melanie did not experience a hallucination, too. The material reviewed in the last chapter suggests very clearly that the occurrence of one hallucination can easily provoke imitation, especially if the seers involved are alone. I assume, then, that Maximin's hallucination did induce a similar hallucination in Melanie, just as Lucia's hallucination at Fatima in 1917 induced similar hallucinations in Jacinta and Francisco. The point is only that since the initial hallucination was Maximin's, we must look to the events in his life in order to account for the content of the hallucination at LaSalette.

Given that Maximin was probably the central seer at LaSalette, it seems worth noting that he showed some reluctance to identify the lady with the Virgin Mary. In 1850, he had a well-publicized interview with the Curé d'Ars, a well-known French cleric of the time, for instance. Among other things, the curé explicitly asked Maximin if he had seen the Virgin Mary at LaSalette. Maximin replied simply, "I do not know whether it was the Blessed Virgin. I saw something . . . a lady" (quoted in Northcote, 1875: 293; see also Kennedy, 1961: 105). This was four years after the apparition itself, at a time when the identification of the lady of LaSalette as the Virgin Mary was taken for granted by a wide variety of Catholics. But if the lady in Maximin's hallucination was not the Virgin Mary, who was she? The answer, I suggest, is not difficult to uncover.

Consider the following passage, which occurs early in the speech given by the lady, and which preceded the list of calamities that would befall France:

> If my people do not submit themselves, I must let the hand of my Son fall upon them; it is so strong, so heavy, that I can keep it up no longer. How long a time I have suffered for you! (Northcote, 1875: 236)

On the assumption that the lady is the Virgin Mary, then the Son referred to in this passage is obviously Jesus Christ (which is why it is always capitalized in devotional accounts). To the devout, therefore, the meaning of this passage is clear: Mary has until now restrained her Divine Son from punishing sinners, but will not be able to continue doing so much longer. But if the lady in the original apparition is not assumed to be the Virgin Mary, other interpretations of this passage are possible. In fact, there is some evidence that Maximin did initially give this passage a different interpretation. Consider the following passage in Ullathorne's (1942 [1854]: 44) early and still authoritative account of LaSalette:

> . . . when the beautiful lady spoke of the heavy arm of her Son, he (Maximin) thought she meant that her Son had been beating

her; for, as he at a later time explained, "he did not then know that the Lady was the Blessed Virgin."

(Many modern devotional accounts do not mention that Maximin originally interpreted what he saw and heard as a mother who complained of being beaten by her son.)

To the devout, who assume that the lady at LaSalette was indeed the Virgin Mary, Maximin's initial impression here makes no sense, and so must be a misinterpretation. But if, in fact, the apparition at La-Salette was Maximin's hallucination, then what we probably have here is a description of that hallucination as it was first reported to Melanie by Maximin on the hillside. It appears that what Maximin first saw and heard was a mother who complained of being beaten by her son. Only later, after the apparition had been discussed with others, did it come to be defined as an apparition of the Virgin Mary.

But once we consider the possibility that the lady at LaSalette was a mother who had been beaten by her son, our attention is immediately drawn to a remark that does appear in almost all the devotional accounts. It was uttered by Maximin when he and Melanie first caught sight of the lady. Melanie, apparently, was visibly frightened and dropped her staff, "but the boy [Maximin] told her to pick it up again, adding that he should take care of his [staff], for that if *it* (meaning the figure) offered to do them any harm, he would give it a good blow" (Northcote, 1875: 236; see also Cox, 1956: 17). Maximin, in other words, very clearly expressed a willingness to deliver a beating to the lady. This, together with the observation that the original hallucination was probably of a mother beaten by her son, leads to the conclusion that the son in question was Maximin himself. In other words, Maximin hallucinated an image of a mother whom he himself had beaten. What could have given rise to such a hallucination?

In explaining it, I am going to be guided by Freud's belief that hallucinations, like dreams, represent an attempt to gratify an unconscious wish or desire, usually one formed during childhood. The most straightforward interpretation suggested by the wish–fulfillment hypothesis is that Maximin's hallucination was an attempt to gratify his desire to deliver a beating to his own mother. Does this make sense, given what we know about Maximin's family background? It makes perfect sense. Maximin's natural mother had died in 1837, when Maximin was two years old, and his father had married again almost immediately (Stern, 1980: 18). It seems that Maximin was very much abused by his stepmother (Hidec, 1969: 8). The ill-feeling between the two was sufficiently strong for it to be included even in most of the devotional accounts of LaSalette (Cox, 1956: 12; Kennedy, 1961: 91). I am suggesting, then, that Maximin's hallucination was an attempt to gratify an unconscious wish to harm his stepmother, which derived from the intense hostility he felt as a result of the abuse he had suffered at her hands. In support of this interpretation, we should note that a recurrent finding in the clinical study of childhood hallucinations is that the children who have these hallucinations have usually, like Maximin Giraud, been neglected or abused by one or both parents (see Bender, 1954: 16-50; Eisenberg, 1962; Esman, 1962; Bender, 1970).

Admittedly, such after-the-fact psychodynamic explanations are notoriously easy to construct and next to impossible to falsify. Critics are often quite justified in saying that they are little more than "just so" stories tailor-made to fit whatever data happens to be at hand. Nevertheless, such explanations can often provide the sort of intelligibility discussed at the beginning of this book, and we can evaluate them in the same way we evaluated various theories about the origins of the Mary cult, by determining the degree to which they allow us to order into a coherent pattern a wide range of observations that would otherwise seem disparate.

With all this in mind, what aspects of the LaSalette apparition become intelligible on the hypothesis that the original hallucination was shaped by Maximin's unconscious desire to beat his stepmother? As a start, it provides us with a prosaic explanation for a distinctive feature of that apparition, the fact that the lady was crying: she was crying because she had been beaten. Then, too, there is some evidence that Maximin's stepmother withheld food from the boy, and that for this reason Maximin often went hungry (Hidec: 1969: 9). It therefore seems worth emphasizing that the punishment most emphasized by the lady at LaSalette was famine. The lady, in other words, threatened to withhold food from France "unless the people were good" in the same way that Maximin's stepmother withheld food from him.

But most importantly, perhaps, the hypothesis offered here allows us to account for the general sense of "harshness" that pervades the message of LaSalette. This harshness derives partly from the fact that the bulk of the lady's message is concerned with punishment, with spelling out in detail the terrible calamities that would befall France. But even when specifying the things that will bring about this punishment (and thus, by implication, the things that must be done to avoid it), there is a seeming bitterness about the lady's tone, as in the following passages:

> I have given you six days to labor in, I have reserved the seventh for myself; yet they will not give it to me. . . .

> Only a few old women go to Mass, the others work on Sundays during the summer; and in the winter, when they know not what to do, the youths go to Mass only to make mockery of religion. In Lent they go to the shambles (meat market) like dogs. . . . (Northcote, 1875: 237-238)

The harshness and seeming bitterness evident in these passages are in marked contrast with the tone of gentle reassurance that characterizes most other apparitions of the Virgin Mary. As we shall see, for instance, it would be difficult to think of the girl who spoke to Bernadette Soubirous at Lourdes comparing people, even sinners, to dogs. It is this harsh and bitter quality of the LaSalette message that has led even a Catholic commentator like Thurston (1933: 530; 1934: 119), who fully accepts the authenticity of, say, Lourdes, to characterize the LaSalette apparition as "bizarre." Under the hypothesis being offered here, however, this bitterness derives very simply from the fact that the lady of LaSalette was modeled upon Maximin's perception of his highly punitive stepmother.

Finally, one of the earliest English-language accounts of the message delivered by the lady of LaSalette appeared in the *Gentleman's Magazine* in 1854. The anonymous writer tells us that his account is taken directly from a pamphlet he picked up while traveling in Europe. The lady's message that appears in this 1854 account is substantially the same as it is in later accounts—except for one detail. In the 1854 account, when the lady lists the bad habits that will bring about divine retribution, she includes the following: "they [the people] put stones in their pockets, to throw at girls when they go to church" (Anon., 1854: 12). This particular bad habit seems relatively minor and strangely out of place in the midst of the lady's complaints about people who take God's name in vain, who don't go to Mass, and so on—and this is probably why it is not mentioned in most devotional accounts of LaSalette. Nevertheless, though throwing stones at girls when they go to church might not seem like the sort of thing that would provoke the Lord to loose famine upon France, it is precisely what a mischievous eleven-year-old boy might do, and so be severely punished by an unfriendly stepmother.

OUR LADY OF LOURDES

The apparitions that are almost certain to be most familiar to the readers of this book are those that occurred at Lourdes in 1858. Apart from a number of devotional accounts, we have in the case of Lourdes several first-rate critical accounts; I have relied heavily upon Neame (1967), in particular.[3]

The essential facts surrounding the Lourdes apparitions are easy to summarize. On February 11, 1858, a young girl (fourteen at the time) named Bernadette Soubirous reported seeing a vision of a young girl in the grotto of Massabieille, which is near the town of Lourdes. Bernadette called the girl "Aquero," which simply means "that" or "her" in Bigourdan, the French dialect spoken in the Lourdes area. In all, Bernadette saw Aquero on eighteen different occasions in the period between February 11 and July 16, 1858.

In contrast to the lady at LaSalette (who talked for about half an hour), Aquero did not say much to Bernadette. Although she did speak on seven different occasions, her whole message consists of twelve sentences. Most of these are simple requests for some type of devotion from Bernadette or others: "Will you be so kind as to come here for fifteen days?" "Penitence, penitence, penitence," "I wish people to come here in procession," and so on. But the most famous of all Aquero's statements was her last, which she uttered on March 25, 1858: "I am the Immaculate Conception." It is this, of course, that in the minds of the devout makes it certain that Aquero was the Virgin Mary.

Bernadette herself, however, was at first quite unwilling to identify Aquero with the Virgin. As early as the third apparition, Bernadette was asked if Aquero was the Virgin Mary (Neame, 1967: 88), and when Bernadette was first interviewed by the local priest, Father

---

[3] Devotional accounts of the apparitions at Lourdes include Cox (1956: 69-132), Estrade (1946 [1899]), Keyes (1961), and Lasserre (1872).

Peyramale, he made it clear that many people in Lourdes had already concluded that she had seen the Virgin and asked her if it was so (Lasserre, 1872: 121-122). Bernadette was almost certainly asked the same question on many occasions that have gone unrecorded. Nevertheless, she consistently answered by saying that she did not know who Aquero was, and, in particular, did not know if she was the Virgin Mary. Bernadette did not identify Aquero with the Virgin until March 25, nearly six weeks after the apparitions had commenced, and even then only indirectly, since the identification was made only by reporting Aquero's statement, "I am the Immaculate Conception." Yet if the Aquero in Bernadette's initial hallucination was not the Virgin Mary, who might she have been? As in the case of LaSalette, we might expect to find a clue by examining Bernadette's description of Aquero.

One of Aquero's most striking features, one that most dramatically distinguishes her from the lady of LaSalette, is her age: Aquero was most definitely a girl, not a woman. Bernadette was quite insistent that Aquero was about the same age and height as herself. Bernadette (and thus Aquero) was fourteen years old at the time, though she looked even younger, and was about 4 feet 6 inches tall. As Neame (1967: 222-224) has rightly emphasized, this is a feature of the Lourdes apparitions that their popularizers have tried to suppress. In the classic account of Lourdes, for instance, J. B. Estrade (who was a minor official in Lourdes in 1858, and who interviewed most of the participants involved, including Bernadette) described Aquero as "about sixteen or seventeen" (Estrade, 1946 [1899]: 26). Lasserre (1872: 29) made Aquero twenty. The statue originally placed in the grotto to commemorate the apparitions portrays a woman in her thirties, and, in any event, the statue is about a foot and a half too tall. Bernadette herself very clearly indicated that this statue did not resemble Aquero in the least (Neame, 1967: 228).

Bernadette's insistence that Aquero was about the same age and height as herself suggests that she felt a strong association between herself and the girl she saw. This strong association is one of the things that must be accounted for by any adequate explanation of Bernadette's hallucination.

One of the things that makes it difficult to picture Aquero as a young girl "like Bernadette" is the fact that Bernadette seems clearly to have behaved toward Aquero as if the latter were a reassuring mother. Consider Bernadette's description of the very first appearance of Aquero:

> there came out of the interior of the grotto a golden-colored cloud, and soon after a lady, young and beautiful . . . and (she) placed herself at the entrance of the opening above the bush. She looked at me immediately, smiled at me and signed me to advance, as if she had been my mother. All fear had left me but I seemed to know no longer where I was. (quoted in Estrade, 1946: 26)

This sense of Aquero as a reassuring mother figure comes through virtually all of Bernadette's accounts of the various apparitions, and it is probably the one thing that most distinguishes the tone of the Lourdes apparition from that of the LaSalette appearances. And when Bernadette visited the grotto of Massabieille for the last time (in 1866) just prior to entering the religious life, she cried out, "My mother, my mother! How can I leave you?" and promptly fainted (Estrade, 1946: 204). In short, though there are grounds for arguing that Bernadette did associate Aquero with herself, it also seems clear that she saw Aquero as an idealized mother figure. Given all this, could Aquero have been based upon Bernadette's own mother, just as the woman at LaSalette was based upon Maximin's stepmother? The problem is that Bernadette had three mothers.

Bernadette's natural mother was Louise Castérot. Louise had married François Soubirous in 1843, and they had six children, of whom Bernadette (born in 1844) was the eldest. But when Bernadette was about eight months old, Louise's bodice caught fire from an overturned candle and she was severely burned, with the result that she could no longer nurse Bernadette. She was also expecting her second child. For these reasons, Bernadette was sent to the nearby village of Bartrès to be nursed by a farmer's wife named Marie Aravant, who had recently lost her own child. Bernadette remained at the Aravant household in Bartrès for the next year and a half, and was then returned to her family in Lourdes. We are told, however, that Bernadette remained in contact with her foster parents over the years, and went to Bartrès for an extended visit at least twice every year as she was growing up (von Matt and Trochu, 1957: 5-6).

Both of Bernadette's natural parents seem to have been fairly irresponsible individuals, who had a hard time holding on to money, and who spent a large portion of what they did have on drink. François Soubirous, for instance, had been a miller by trade and had been given charge of a mill run by the Castérot family when he married Louise. His slovenly business practices, however, resulted in the loss of the mill in 1854. He tried—and failed—to reestablish himself with another mill, and made do with a series of casual jobs. In 1857, François was even arrested for theft. Around this time, the Soubirous family moved into a building that had been a jail, but was now too dilapidated for that purpose. The building was infested with lice, and overlooked an inner courtyard containing a stinking dung heap that had been left to rot.

Bernadette herself, on the other hand, was spared much of her family's misery. In 1855 or 1856 (the exact year is uncertain), Louise Soubirous's older sister, Bernarde Castérot Nicolau, offered to raise Bernadette. Bernarde Nicolau was a woman of some substance in the community (she owned a bar, and the business was well managed), and she was Bernadette's godmother. The Soubirous agreed to this arrangement; it did, after all, mean one fewer mouth to feed. Bernadette stayed with her aunt for at least one year, and possibly as long as two (Neame, 1967: 64).

Bernadette moved back to her family sometime in 1857. Later in that same year, however, shortly after the Soubirous had moved into the former jail, Bernadette was once more sent off, this time to live again in Bartrès with her foster parents. They needed someone to help with the work on their farm, and had asked for Bernadette for this purpose. Bernadette returned to Lourdes (and to the lice-infested and stinking Soubirous home) in January 1858. Her visions commenced a few weeks later.

Over the course of her early life, then, Bernadette had three mothers: her natural mother, her foster mother, and her godmother. Was any of these the model for Aquero? In fact, several independent lines of reasoning lead us to believe that Aquero was modeled upon Bernadette's godmother, Bernarde Nicolau.

First, Bernadette seems to have associated Aquero with a sense of warmth and reassurance. This would eliminate Marie Aravant as a possible model, for after Bernadette had entered the religious life, she revealed to a confidante that she had felt very much unloved, rejected, and abused by Marie Aravant, at least during that last stay at Bartrès just before the apparitions (Petitot, 1955: 4).

Bernadette's relationship with her natural mother is more difficult to evaluate. Devotional accounts, of course, suggest that Louise Soubirous loved her daughter dearly. Still, there are some hints that this relationship might have been more strained than such accounts suggest. For instance, Louise Soubirous's remarks to Bernadette, when she came upon her after the second apparition, have been preserved: "So you want to make us the laughing stock of all who know us; I'll give it to you with your hypocritical airs and your stories of the lady" (Estrade, 1946: 32-33). On this same occasion Louise was about to beat Bernadette with a switch, and was prevented from doing so by her sister, Bernarde Nicolau, who was also present. Even so, Louise forbade Bernadette to go to the grotto again.

Bernadette's relationship with her godmother, on the other hand, seems to have been uniformly positive. Bernarde was a woman of some substance, and so, in a purely material sense, the one or two years spent in her godmother's household were probably the most comfortable that Bernadette had ever experienced. Then there is the fact that Bernarde, in contrast to her sister, was consistently supportive of Bernadette when she reported her visions; it was she who prevented a beating after the second apparition. More generally, Neame (1967: 90) has argued that the strong support of Bernarde Nicolau was what first legitimized Bernadette's visions in the eyes of the general public.

Although Louise Soubirous's harsh words for her daughter after the second apparition might possibly have been atypical of their relationship, the weight of the evidence does suggest that if Aquero was surrounded with warmth and reassurance then she was more likely modeled upon Bernarde Nicolau than Louise Soubirous.

There are additional reasons, as well, for believing that Aquero was Bernarde. Consider an incident that is reported in almost all devotional accounts of Lourdes, but which is invariably passed over lightly. Bernadette described Aquero as wearing a white robe girded at the waist by a blue ribbon whose ends hung down the side of the robe, and a white veil. Such a costume was well known to the people of Lourdes: it was worn on ceremonial occasions by the women who belonged to the "Children of Mary," a Marian sodality that had been formed in the 1830s to promote devotion to the Miraculous Medal.

When Antoinette Peyret, a member of the Children of Mary, first heard Bernadette's description of Aquero, it occurred to her that

Aquero might be an apparition of Elise Latapie, the 28-year-old president of that sodality who had died only a few months previously. Elise Latapie had had a reputation for holiness, and that Elise might be Aquero seemed plausible, at least to Antoinette. Antoinette confided her suspicion to her employer, Madame Milhet, and together the two of them went to Bernadette's house. There they secured permission from Bernadette's mother for Bernadette to visit the grotto again. The two of them accompanied Bernadette to the grotto, where Bernadette saw Aquero for the third time, and heard her speak for the first time. Afterwards, however, Bernadette made it clear that Aquero did not look at all like Elise Latapie. At this point, most devotional accounts let the matter drop.

What no one seems to have asked is whether Aquero might have been modeled upon some member of the Children of Mary other than Elise Latapie, someone that Bernadette herself might have known quite well. Did, for instance, any of Bernadette's three "mothers" belong to the Children of Mary? As far as I can tell, only Bernarde Nicolau did (Neame, 1967: 90). To the devout people of Lourdes in 1858, of course, a truly authentic apparition must be an appearance of a supernatural being, such as the Virgin Mary or the deceased Elise Latapie; the possibility that the apparition might be modeled upon a living person like Bernarde would not even be considered. Yet if the apparitions are considered as hallucinations, the fact that Aquero wore the ceremonial dress associated with the Children of Mary becomes one more reason for believing that Aquero was modeled upon Bernadette's godmother, Bernarde Nicolau, who was a prominent member of that sodality.

There is a final reason for believing that Aquero was modeled on Bernarde, and it is less a piece of evidence than a way of explaining the fact that Bernadette seems to have established in her own mind a strong sense of equivalence between Aquero and herself. If Aquero was modeled upon Bernarde, then this strong sense of equivalence would make sense if there was some basis for believing that Bernadette felt a strong sense of equivalence between herself and her godmother. There is: the two have exactly the same name. Not only is Bernadette simply a diminutive of Bernarde, Bernadette and her godmother in fact shared the same baptismal name: Marie-Bernarde (Bernadette's name after entering the convent was Sister Marie-Bernarde). Nor was this accidental, since Bernadette was her aunt's namesake. I suggest that this identity of names established in Bernadette's mind an equivalence between herself and her godmother.

In the end, then, Bernadette's hallucination of Aquero was probably a composite. Parts of the hallucinations (Aquero's dress and the sense of warmth and reassurance) were elements directly associated with Bernadette's godmother, whereas other parts (notably, Bernadette's insistence that Aquero was about the same age and height as herself) resulted from the fact that Bernadette had established an equivalence between herself and her godmother, since both shared the same name. But whether the association is direct or indirect, the evidence suggests that Aquero *did* represent Bernarde Nicolau.

What would have provoked such a hallucination? In January 1858, Bernadette had just returned from Bartrès, where by her own testimony she had felt unloved and rejected. She found herself living in a lice-infested household, where the window in her own room overlooked a dung heap. She knew from past experience that good meals in the Soubirous household would be hard to come by. In this situation, it is not unreasonable to suggest that the young Bernadette might have longed for those years when she had lived in relative comfort with her godmother, a woman with whom she had an especially warm relationship. The hallucination of Aquero, modeled as she was upon Bernarde, can therefore be seen as an attempt to gratify Bernadette's desire to be living once more in comfort with her loving godmother, rather than in poverty with her natural parents.

As before, the adequacy of this interpretation can be judged only by considering how many details of the apparitions this interpretation can account for. Let us consider the best-known feature of the Lourdes apparitions: the fact that Aquero said, "I am the Immaculate Conception."

Devotional accounts point out that the doctrine of the Immaculate Conception was not formally promulgated until 1854, making it unlikely that someone as ill-educated as Bernadette Soubirous would know of that doctrine in that year. That Bernadette did nevertheless report the statement is therefore seen as evidence that her apparition was authentic. Such an account ignores two things. First, the Feast of the Immaculate Conception had been celebrated under that title on December 8 for at least 150 years prior to 1858; furthermore, in the Pyrenees, it was the day of obligatory church attendance (Neame, 1967: 197-198). This alone would have made it likely that Bernadette would have heard the phrase "the Immaculate Conception." Just as importantly, perhaps, Bernadette was likely to have heard about the Immaculate Conception in connection with the Miraculous Medal. In the apparitions experienced by Catherine Labouré in 1830-1831, the Virgin Mary herself had commanded that this medal be struck and that a sodality be formed to promote the wearing of the medal. For reasons that will be explained later, the formal title of this medal was "Medal of the Immaculate Conception," and the sodality formed was the Children of Mary, the same sodality of which Bernadette's aunt was a member.

That the image on this medal, and the medal's association with the Immaculate Conception, were well known in nineteenth-century France is made clear—appropriately enough—in an early treatise on hallucinations by Brierre de Boismont. In the following passage he is describing the appearance of a seventeen-year-old French girl named Alexandrine Lanois during one of her "ecstasies":

> Her head was slightly inclined to the left, and leaned forward; her arms hung down at a short distance from her body; the hands were reversed, the palms turned outwards; the left limb was somewhat inflexed and the lower part of the body slightly inclined.
>
> In fact, she presented very faithfully the attitude of an image or statue of the Immaculate Conception, which was very common throughout our country [France], and being classic, was, I believe, known everywhere. (Brierre de Boismont, 1855: 222)

Later, this same girl reported coming upon "a lady habited in white" whom she recognized as the Virgin Mary and who conversed with her at length. Brierre de Boismont's book was originally published in 1846, so the events occurred long before the apparitions at Lourdes.

That Bernadette (like the now-forgotten Alexandrine Lanois) was familiar with the Miraculous Medal, and that the image on this medal influenced her apparition (just as it obviously influenced Alexandrine's ecstasy), is established by Bernadette's own testimony. In describing Aquero as she appeared on the occasion of the sixteenth apparition (during which Aquero identified herself as the Immaculate Conception), Bernadette said: "The lady was standing above the rosetree, in a position very similar to that shown on the miraculous medal" (Estrade, 1946: 97). The fact that Aquero stood just like the image of the Virgin Mary on the "Medal of the Immaculate Conception," just prior to identifying herself as the Immaculate Conception, suggests that the image on this medal, as well as the association of this medal with the Immaculate Conception, helped to shape Bernadette's image of Aquero.

What, then, did Bernadette's association of Aquero with the "Immaculate Conception" represent? Aquero made her "I am the Immaculate Conception" speech on the morning of March 25, 1858. On the afternoon of the same day, Bernadette described her experience to J. B. Estrade, who is very clear in saying (1946: 99) that although Bernadette did know that the phrase was associated with the Virgin Mary, she did not know the meaning of the doctrine of the Immaculate Conception itself. In part, then, Bernadette's identification of Aquero with the Immaculate Conception probably reflects Bernadette's capitulation to the suggestion (which had been made to her often enough) that Aquero was the Virgin Mary. On the other hand, the suggestion that Aquero was modeled upon Bernarde Nicolau provides us with another, complementary interpretation of this identification.

Since Aquero, like Bernadette, spoke Bigourdan, what she actually said was "Que soy er'Immaculada Concepciou." As Neame (1967: 197) has pointed out, both "immaculada" and "concepciou" were quite ordinary Bigourdan words: "immaculada" meant "unspotted or untainted," while "concepciou" meant "conception as a lady conceives babies." The words, in other words, meant about what they now mean in English. What imagery would have been conjured up in Bernadette's mind when she heard the phrase "immaculate conception"?

To determine that, try the following experiment, which I have tried with students many times. Ask a group of non-Catholics (or Catholics without much training in their religion) to explain the doctrine of the Immaculate Conception. The overwhelming majority will say that it refers to the Virgin Birth, that is, to the fact that Mary had not had sexual intercourse prior to giving birth to Jesus Christ. This is of course incorrect: the doctrine of the Immaculate Conception is the belief that Mary herself was conceived without taint of original sin. Nevertheless, that most people think that it refers to the Virgin Birth is in itself sufficient evidence to suggest that the term "immaculate conception" conjures up an image of a woman who gives birth without the aid of a natural father.

Given that Bernadette was generally ill-educated, and given that her biographers consistently describe her as excessively modest (see, for instance, Petitot, 1955: 7-8), it is likely that she was not particularly enlightened about sexual matters. In the mind of such a person, a woman who gives birth to a child without aid of a natural father could easily be taken as more or less synonymous with a woman who gives birth to a child without aid of a *husband*. This means, then, that Bernadette could easily have associated the phrase "immaculate conception" with an unmarried woman who gives birth to a child. As the reader will have guessed, Bernadette's Aunt Bernarde was just such a woman. Bernarde, in fact, gave birth to two illegitimate children.

Bernarde Castérot's first child was the result of an illicit union with Martin Tarbes, the owner of a local bar (Neames, 1967: 63). Sometime after the child's birth, however, Martin and Bernarde did marry, and when Martin died Bernarde inherited his bar. It was this that provided the material basis for the elevated social position that Bernarde was to attain. Later Bernarde had another child by a second admirer (Neame, 1967: 64). His last name was Nicolau, and this union too was later legalized. These illegitimate births occurred when Bernadette herself was quite young, but they would almost certainly have been talked about—however discreetly—over the years. In the young Bernadette's mind, then, it is very likely that she thought of her godmother Bernarde as a woman who had "conceived immaculately" not once, but twice. That Bernarde in each case had given birth to a son, just like the Virgin Mary, would only serve to strengthen the association between Bernarde and "immaculate conception."

Pressed to associate Aquero with the Virgin Mary, and given that Aquero was really based upon Bernarde, Bernadette would quite naturally be inclined to associate Aquero with the one Marian label that she already associated with Bernarde: the Immaculate Conception.

CATHERINE LABOURÉ AND THE MIRACULOUS MEDAL

It is now time to consider the first of the great Marian apparitions to take place in nineteenth-century France.[4] These were experienced by Catherine Labouré between July 1830 and January 1831. At the same time, Catherine was twenty-four years old (and thus substantially

---

[4] The most comprehensive English-language account of Catherine Labouré and her apparitions is Dirvin (1958); Dirvin (1961) is a shortened version of this book.

older than the seers at LaSalette and Lourdes), and had only recently entered the novitiate of the Sisters of Charity of St. Vincent de Paul, at 140 rue du Bac in Paris. Catherine later reported that during her first few months at the novitiate she had often seen a red blob-like image which she interpreted as the "heart of St. Vincent." During those early months she had also experienced at least one apparition involving Christ himself. The most well-known of Catherine's apparitions, however, were the ones involving Mary, and these commenced on July 18, 1830.

According to her own account, Catherine was awakened on the night of July 18 by a small boy whom she later identified as her guardian angel. The boy led her through the halls of the novitiate until they came to the chapel. After waiting for what seemed a long time, the Virgin Mary herself entered the chapel and sat upon a chair on the altar steps. Catherine approached the Virgin, knelt, and placed her hand upon the Virgin's lap. For the next two hours or so, Mary talked to Catherine about the Sisters of Charity and about the dangers that would soon befall France. The image of the Virgin then faded and Catherine was led back to her room by the boy.

In the early evening of November 27, during the meditation period practiced at the novitiate, the Virgin Mary again appeared to Catherine. On this occasion Mary told Catherine to have a medal struck in her (Mary's) honor. The words "O Mary, conceived without sin, pray for us who have recourse to thee" then appeared around the figure of Mary, and Catherine was told that this scene should be represented upon the face of the medal. This scene then "flipped around" to reveal the design that should appear on the reverse of the medal: a single large M surmounted by a cross resting upon a bar, all of which was to be set above two human hearts. One of the hearts was to be pierced with thorns and the other by a sword. Mary promised that those who wore the medal would receive an abundance of graces. The Virgin appeared to Catherine at least five more times, the last apparition occurring sometime in January 1831, and on each occasion reiterated her request that such a medal be struck.

Catherine herself reported her apparitions only to her confessor, Father Aladel. Although initially skeptical, Father Aladel became convinced that the apparitions were genuine, and petitioned the archbishop of Paris to allow the minting of the medal. The petition was granted, and the medal began to be minted in 1832. Although Church

The Miraculous Medal
Photo courtesy of the Archives of The Catholic University of America.

authorities let it be known that the design for the medal had been introduced by the Virgin Mary during the course of an apparition in 1830, they did not reveal the identity of the seer until 1876, just six months before Catherine Labouré's death. In any event, the wearing of the medal proved immensely popular almost immediately, and it quickly became known as the "Miraculous Medal" by virtue of the large number of cures associated with it. Literally hundreds of millions of these Miraculous Medals have been minted since 1832.

Because the image of Mary on the Miraculous Medal influenced Bernadette Soubirous's apparitions at Lourdes, it is worth noting that the image on that medal was not that seen by Catherine Labouré. In her description of the November 27 apparition, Catherine explicitly said that the Virgin held out in front of her "a golden ball surmounted with a little golden cross, which represented the world" (Dirvin, 1961: 77). No such golden ball appears on the Miraculous Medal; when designing it, Church authorities decided to use the image of Mary with outstretched hands pointing downward that is traditionally associated with Mary's Immaculate Conception. It seems clear that Church authorities modified the version suggested by Catherine so as to produce a medal that could be used to promote popular devotion to the Immaculate Conception. The original title of the medal was "Medal of the Immaculate Conception," and its widespread popularity undoubtedly did pave the way for the proclamation of the belief in the Immaculate Conception as dogma in 1854.

If we examine carefully Catherine's very first apparition, the one least likely to have been contaminated by her discussions with her confessor, we find that Catherine Labouré—just like Maximin Giraud at LaSalette and Bernadette Soubirous at Lourdes—did not initially identify the woman she saw as the Virgin Mary. On the contrary, she very clearly indicated that at first the woman reminded her of someone else, as the following passage makes clear: "a lady was sitting down in a chair on the altar steps at the Gospel side—just like St. Anne, only it wasn't the face of St. Anne. I doubted if it was the Virgin Mary" (Catherine Labouré, quoted in Dirvin, 1961: 70). Catherine then goes on to say, however, that the lady was identified as the Virgin by the "boy" who had led her to the chapel, and that she accepted this identification. Nevertheless, the passage makes it clear that Catherine first associated the woman she saw with St. Anne.

Whether Catherine shifted her identification of the woman from St.

Anne to the Virgin Mary immediately (as she suggests), or later, possibly after discussion with others, is a question that cannot now be answered. But the fact that Catherine includes this initial identification of the woman in her account of the apparition, even though this detail bears no obvious relevance to the rest of the apparition as it came to be interpreted, suggests to me that Catherine's original hallucination was an hallucination of St. Anne, and this needs to be explained.

The proximate cause of why Catherine saw St. Anne seems obvious. Several accounts (Walsh, 1904a: 281; Dirvin, 1961: 63n) mention that there was a picture of St. Anne hanging in the chapel very near the spot where Catherine saw the woman. These same accounts mention that the St. Anne in this picture was wearing a dress of the same color as the woman seen by Catherine sitting in the chapel. All this makes it almost certain that Catherine's hallucination was in part modeled upon this picture.

But this is only part of the answer. There were, undoubtedly, pictures and statues of other saints in the convent. Why did Catherine's unconscious seize upon St. Anne? In the Christian tradition, St. Anne is the mother of the Virgin Mary. The New Testament does not mention her, and most of what is "known" about her derives from an apocryphal work called the *Protoevangelium of James*. Even in that work the legend surrounding St. Anne is thin: she was married to Joachim, she was past child-bearing age, an angel appeared to her and announced that she would bear a child, that child was born, and was, of course, the Virgin Mary. The sparseness that characterizes the story of St. Anne works in our favor here, since it severely limits the psychological associations with which a devout Catholic like Catherine Labouré would have surrounded the concept "St. Anne." In fact, it seems clear that the strongest such association would have been that between "St. Anne" and the label "mother of the Virgin Mary," or possibly the more general label "mother."

Under the hypothesis that hallucinations, like dreams, reflect the attempted gratification of unconscious wishes, especially unconscious infantile wishes, we might predict that Catherine's hallucination of an idealized mother figure like St. Anne was an attempt to reestablish the presence of the warm and loving mother who had been lost when Catherine was quite young. Does this make sense in light of what we know about Catherine's early experience? Yes, since the young Catherine Labouré lost not one mother, but two.

Catherine Labouré was born in the village of Fain-les-moutiers, France, near Dijon, in 1806. All accounts of her life suggest that although her relationship with her father was relatively cool, her ties to her mother were especially close. Catherine appears to have been greatly saddened when her mother died in 1815, when she herself was only nine years old. Almost immediately, however, her mother's sister offered to raise Catherine, Catherine's father agreed, and Catherine went to the nearby village of St. Rémy to live with her aunt. Dirvin's (1958: 18-23) account of Catherine's stay in St. Rémy suggests that she was well cared for there, and that she developed a warm relationship with both her aunt and her uncle. But after only two years, Catherine was recalled home by her father. It seems that Catherine's older sister had entered a convent, and her father wanted Catherine to run his household. Given all this, there is indeed a basis for saying that the young Catherine Labouré lost a loving mother twice: at age nine and then again at age twelve, and that Catherine Labouré's later hallucination of St. Anne was primarily an attempt to reestablish the presence of one or both of them. What still needs to be explained, of course, is why the hallucination occurred when Catherine was twenty-four years old. As we saw earlier, the Marian hallucinations experienced by both Maximin Giraud and Bernadette Soubirous were shaped by infantile desires and wishes that had been formed in the recent past. In Catherine's case, however, we need to explain why a sense of maternal loss experienced when Catherine was quite young should have given rise to an hallucination when she was an adult.

Here again, Freud's own work would seem useful. In the case of Christoph Haizmann's apparition, Freud (1961a [1923]) argued that although Haizmann's apparition of the Devil was shaped primarily by unconscious infantile memories, the proximate cause had been a recent event in the seer's life that had activated those memories.

In Catherine's case, there is no mystery about the recent events that might have reactivated her early memories of maternal loss. First, it seems clear that she went to bed on the night of July 18, 1830, in a state of great emotional intensity. Not only was the next day the feast day of St. Vincent de Paul, the founder of the Sisters of Charity, but this year the celebration of that feast day was especially important, since St. Vincent's relics had only recently been moved from the Cathedral of Notre Dame to the newly erected mother church of the Vincentian fathers. Also, as a feast-day gift, each of the sisters had been given a piece of a surplice once worn by St. Vincent; Catherine tore hers in two and swallowed one of the halves (Dirvin, 1958: 80-81). The emotional intensity experienced on this occasion by a person as devout as Catherine would almost certainly have worked to activate any number of usually repressed memories.

More importantly, perhaps, Catherine had recently experienced a loss that would have seemed similar to her early maternal losses. Prior to entering the Sisters of Charity, Catherine had spent a year living with her brother and sister-in-law, and had developed a very warm and close relationship with her sister-in-law, Jeanne Labouré. It was Jeanne who had tried (with little success) to tutor Catherine in the catechism, and it was she who had intervened with Catherine's father when Catherine had wanted to become a nun. Finally, it was Jeanne who had provided Catherine with the dowry and the trousseau that was required of all who wanted to enter the Sisters of Charity.

Initially, Catherine had served as a postulant in a convent at Châtillon, where her sister-in-law lived, and so the sense of separation from Jeanne would not have been great. With her move to Paris, however, Catherine's sense of separation from Jeanne must have been intensified. The fact that Jeanne had acted as a mother-surrogate for Catherine would in itself insure that this separation from Jeanne would have activated in Catherine her early memories of maternal loss. Further, Catherine's association of Jeanne with her two earlier mothers would only have been strengthened by the fact that Jeanne was her natural mother's cousin, and by the fact that all three women—Jeanne, Catherine's natural mother, and Catherine's maternal aunt—shared the same maiden name (Gontard: see Dirvin, 1958: 47).

In summary, then, given the similarities between Catherine's sister-in-law and the two mothers that Catherine had lost early in life, I suggest that Catherine's move from Châtillon to Paris would have reactivated in Catherine her early memories of maternal loss, and that her hallucination of St. Anne, which occurred within a few months of her arrival at Paris, was a response to these memories.

We must now ask if the interpretation developed here allows us to explain any features of Catherine Labouré's apparitions that would otherwise seem puzzling. Consider, for instance, the design of the Miraculous Medal. There is nothing problematic about the image of Mary that appears on the front of that medal. As already mentioned, that image is the traditional image of Mary Immaculate, and was used not because it reflected what Catherine saw but because Church authorities wanted to promote devotion to the Immaculate Conception.

The design on the back of the medal, however, was more clearly determined by Catherine's report of the design revealed to her during the course of her apparition: a large M surmounted by a cross resting upon a bar, and set above two hearts, one of which is pierced by thorns and the other by a sword. What does this design represent?

To the devout, of course, the answer is obvious: the M stands for Marie/Mary, the cross for Jesus Christ, and the hearts represent the hearts of Mary and Jesus, respectively. The meaning of the design, however, was not entirely obvious to Father Aladel, and he directed Catherine to ask the Virgin Mary what written text should accompany the design on the back in order to make its meaning clearer. At this point, it would have been a simple matter for Catherine to report back with a phrase that elucidated the devotional interpretation of the design. She did not do this. On the contrary, she said only, "The M and the two hearts express enough" (Dirvin, 1958: 98). Catherine's response suggests two things: that the central elements in the design are the M and the two hearts (rather than the cross upon a bar); and that there was some resistance on Catherine's part to elucidating the meaning of the design. This in turn suggests that it was intimately bound up with the unconscious infantile memories that gave rise to the design in her mind.

If Catherine's hallucination was shaped primarily by her infantile memories of the loss of two mothers, her natural mother and her aunt, it seems clear that this can of itself account for the two pierced hearts, given that in modern Western tradition the heart is the organ most associated with the emotions. Two lost mothers, two hearts, each pierced in a different manner. But what about the M? It, too, should be associated with the memory of these two lost mothers. It would be trivial to point out that the "M" might stand for "mere/mother." Less trivial is the observation that both of Catherine's lost mothers had a name that began with M: her natural mother's name was Madeleine Gontard Labouré and her aunt's name was Marguerite Gontard Labouré. Think about this the other way around. Suppose the hypothesis offered here was correct, and that Catherine Labouré's unconscious did operate to produce an emblem that would reflect her infantile memory of two lost mothers, one named Madeleine, the other Marguerite. In that event, what emblem would express these memories more directly and more parsimoniously than the emblem that does in fact appear on the back of the Miraculous Medal? As Catherine herself said, "The M and the two hearts express enough."

THE VIRGIN MARY AT FATIMA
AND PERHAPS AT TEPEYAC

This chapter will consider two more sets of Marian apparitions which—like the three sets discussed in the last chapter—are important because they have greatly influenced the conduct of Marian devotion in the modern world. The first involves the apparitions of the Virgin on a hill called Tepeyac near Mexico City in 1531, and the second, the apparitions of the Virgin at Fatima in 1917. On the surface, it is difficult to imagine two sets of apparitions more dissimilar to one another. The Tepeyac apparitions took place over four hundred years ago, the Fatima apparitions occurred in this century. The Tepeyac apparitions were experienced by a fifty-five-year-old man, those at Fatima by three young children. Tepeyac is in the New World, Fatima in the Old. Yet it is precisely the apparent dissimilarity between these two sets of apparitions—and between these apparitions and those considered in the last chapter—that makes them appealing. There is, after all, always the chance that the analyses in the last chapter succeeded only because we were dealing with apparitions from the same area and from a fairly restricted time period. Extending our analysis to include apparitions as diverse as those at Tepeyac and at Fatima provides an opportunity to establish the generality of the analytic framework.

FATIMA

According to devotional accounts, there were three "waves" of apparitions at Fatima, only the last of which involved the Virgin.[1] First,

[1] The most important of the devotional accounts dealing with the Fatima apparitions is almost certainly that written by Lucia herself (Santos, 1976). Walsh (1954) is also useful, if only because he tempers his acceptance of the supernatural origin of most of what occurred at Fatima with a healthy skepticism about some aspects of those apparitions. Other devotional accounts include Cox (1956: 133-188), McGraith (1961), O'Connell (1948) and Ryan (1949).

in 1915, Lucia Santos (aged eight) and two companions with whom she was tending sheep saw a transparent white cloud in the shape of a man. The image persisted while they ate their lunch, but did not speak. As I have argued, this apparition was probably an illusion of some sort.

The next wave occurred in 1916. This time the seers were Lucia (now nine years old) and her two cousins, Francisco Marto (aged eight) and his sister Jacinta (aged six)—who were not the companions with Lucia in 1915. While tending their sheep, these three, on three separate occasions, saw an angel who identified himself variously as "the Angel of Peace" or "the guardian angel of Portugal" who would "bring peace to that country."

The most elaborate of the angel's apparitions was the third and last. He appeared to the children holding a chalice, above which was suspended a host that dripped blood. After prostrating himself and praying aloud, he took the chalice (which had remained suspended in mid-air while he prayed) and gave the host to Lucia and the chalice itself to Jacinta and Francisco so that they might drink from it. After praying some more, he disappeared.

It is difficult to know how to treat the apparitions of 1916. None of the three children mentioned them to anyone at the time, and their existence came to light only when the children were interviewed in connection with the Marian apparitions of 1917. It is entirely possible, in other words, that the 1916 apparitions were not hallucinations (or illusions) at all, but rather projections onto the past of feelings and concerns that developed in 1917.

But if we take the 1916 apparitions at face value, we must decide who the central seer was. In this case, we have a very extensive set of recollections set down by one of the seers. At the request of Church authorities, Lucia (by then a nun) wrote out four long *Memoirs* in the period 1935 to 1941, and these are now available in English (Santos, 1976). In each case, Lucia was asked to address her memoir to a specific set of questions about all the apparitions at Fatima. There is, however, a great deal of overlap among the four memoirs, and Lucia did not always describe the same incident in the same way. This seems especially true in the case of her descriptions of the apparitions of the angel in 1916.

In her first account of that apparition, which appears in her second memoir (originally written in 1937), Lucia (1976: 61-63) gives the impression that the angel was seen and heard by all three children. Certainly she never says anything to suggest that the angel was not seen and heard by all three. Later, however, Lucia was specifically asked to expand upon her recollections of Francisco, and she did this in her fourth memoir, originally written in 1941. There, Lucia (1976: 121-123) describes the 1916 apparitions of the angel again, and although she says that Francisco saw the angel, she makes it clear that he did not hear it (a pattern that would be repeated in connection with the 1917 apparitions). Since Francisco had to ask Lucia and Jacinta what the Angel had said, it seems certain that either Lucia or Jacinta was the central seer. Which one?

A clue comes in a question about the apparition that Francisco is supposed to have asked several days after the angel's final appearance. According to Lucia (Santos, 1976: 123), Francisco knew that the angel had given Holy Communion to Lucia, but didn't know what the angel had given to him (Francisco) and Jacinta. It was Jacinta who provided Francisco with an answer, making it clear that they had drunk from the chalice and that drinking from the chalice "was Holy Communion too," just as receiving the host was. This incident indicates that Francisco had some difficulty in seeing the apparition as well as in hearing it. But perhaps more important is the fact that it was Jacinta (not Lucia) who answered Francisco's question, and so filled in the details of the apparition for him. Since no passage in Lucia's account of the 1916 apparitions suggests that on other occasions it was Lucia who filled in the details in this way, I conclude (though the evidence is not nearly as clear as I would like) that Jacinta was the central seer for the 1916 apparitions.

What, then, did Jacinta see? As her response to Francisco indicates, she saw an angel distribute Holy Communion to all three children, even though Lucia received it by receiving the host and she and Francisco received it by drinking from the chalice. To anyone familiar with Walsh's devotional account of Fatima, this should strike a responsive chord. Walsh (1954: 28-27) indicates that just before the 1916 apparitions, Jacinta had wanted desperately to receive her First Holy Communion. She was only six at the time, and so far younger than most of those who received their First Communion. But Jacinta knew that Lucia had been allowed to receive her First Communion at age six, and she wanted to do likewise. (Given the apparent pride with which Lucia, even in later life, regarded the fact that she had been allowed to

receive Communion at six, it seems likely that the young Lucia probably never let her companions forget just how special she had been; see
Santos, 1976: 54-57.) In any event, Jacinta pressured her mother into
allowing her to take the catechism classes given by the local priest for
those wishing to receive First Communion. She was devastated,
Walsh tells us, when the priest told her that she was too young, and
besides, did not know her catechism well enough. It was shortly after
this that the three children saw the angel.

We can therefore regard the apparition of the angel as a hallucination that in a very direct way gratified the wish of a grieving six-year-
old child. True, during the course of the apparition only Lucia had received Communion in the regular way (just as in real life, only Lucia
had received Communion at all), but, as Jacinta insisted in describing
the incident to Francisco, she too (along with him) had received Holy
Communion, though in a different way.

Now we come to the most important set of apparitions, those that
occurred in 1917. On May 17 of that year, Lucia (now ten), Francisco
(now nine) and Jacinta (now seven) decided to tend their sheep on a
plot of land owned by Lucia's father. The land was in a place called the
Cova da Iria. (Cova means dell or hollow; Iria is proper name corresponding to Irene.) While on a hillside near the Cova da Iria, the children saw what they took to be lightning. Thinking a thunderstorm
imminent, they hurried down the hillside. Halfway down they saw
standing before them, on a small bush, a lady dressed in white. She
was "more brilliant than the sun" and "radiated a light more intense
than a crystal glass filled with sparkling water" (Santos, 1976: 156).

The lady told the children not to be afraid. When Lucia asked her
where she was from, she replied that she was from heaven. When Lucia then asked, "What do you want of me?" (and in her account Lucia
very definitely says "me," not "us"), the lady responded that she
wanted the children to come to the Cova on the thirteenth day of the
next six months, and that she would appear to them on each occasion.
Lucia then asked the lady some more questions. Would Jacinta and
Francisco both go to heaven? Yes, the lady replied, but Francisco
would have to say many rosaries. What about two friends who had
recently died, were they in heaven, too? The lady said that one was in
heaven, one in purgatory. She then told the children that they would
have to suffer for the conversion of sinners, instructed them to pray
the rosary, and then disappeared.

The children, at least according to Lucia's account, promised to keep the news of the apparition to themselves. Seven-year-old Jacinta, however, found that impossible, and seems to have told her family almost immediately after arriving home that she and the others had seen the Virgin Mary.

The fact that it was Jacinta who first reported the apparition to outsiders would suggest that Jacinta was the central seer. Francisco probably was not, since, as in 1916, he never heard the 1917 apparition; he also had some initial difficulty in seeing it (Ryan, 1949: 56). But there is also a great deal of evidence to suggest that Lucia was the central seer. It was she who initiated the conversation with the lady in the apparition, and it was to Lucia that most of the lady's remarks were addressed, in both the first and succeeding apparitions. Furthermore, most of the information about the various apparitions at the time that they were occurring seems to have been provided by Lucia.

If Lucia was indeed the central seer at Fatima, then her response when first confronted with the suggestion that she had seen the Virgin is informative. It seems that when Jacinta told her family about having seen the Virgin in the Cova da Iria, the report quickly reached the Santos household. (Lucia's father and the mother of Francisco and Jacinta were brother and sister.) Lucia was absent at the time, and it was her older sister who later came upon Lucia and asked her for the first time if she had seen the Virgin. Lucia was upset that the news had leaked out, and said "I don't know if it was Our Lady. It was a very pretty little woman" (Walsh, 1954: 56). Lucia, in other words, like Bernadette Soubirous at Lourdes, showed some initial reluctance to identify the lady in the apparition as the Virgin Mary.

I should make clear that in that first apparition, the lady did not identify herself as Mary, did not associate herself with a Marian title, and did not associate herself with Jesus or anyone else in the Christian pantheon. The explicit association with Mary came only with the second and succeeding apparitions. At the second apparition (on June 13, 1917), the lady talked of her "Immaculate Heart" ("The Immaculate Heart of Mary" being a common Marian title), and specifically said that Jesus wanted to make use of the children so that she (the lady) would be better known and loved. In the third apparition (July 13, 1917), the lady asked that the children pray the rosary in honor of Our Lady of the Rosary, and once again mentioned "my Immaculate Heart." By the time of the sixth and final apparition (October 13,

1917), the lady specifically identified herself as Our Lady of the Rosary.

The fact that Lucia showed some initial reluctance to identify the lady with the Virgin, and the fact that there is nothing in Lucia's description of that first occasion to suggest that the lady was the Virgin Mary, suggest that Lucia's first apparition was a hallucination of someone else. On the other hand, the inclusion of references to the Virgin in the second and succeeding occasions suggests that sometime between the first and the second apparitions Lucia did accept the suggestion (which appears to have been made originally by Jacinta) that the lady was the Virgin Mary. But if not the Virgin Mary, who was it that Lucia saw in the first apparition?

Clinical studies of hallucinations in very young children indicate that they are usually modeled upon some figure in the child's family background (Bender, 1954: 16-50). This would lead us to expect that the lady whom Lucia first saw was modeled on someone in her own family. And in that very first apparition, Lucia did link the lady to a member of her family. This occurred when Lucia asked the lady about the girls who had died recently. Most devotional accounts present a misleading view of what was said here. It is often implied, for instance, that the dead girls were about the same age as Jacinta, Francisco, and Lucia. Ryan (1949: 56) reports that they were friends of Lucia (who was ten at the time), McGraith (1961: 183) says that they were Lucia's playmates, and O'Connell (1948: 31) names one of the dead children as "little Maria das Neves." In fact, the two girls that Lucia asked about were not really children at all. In her own account, Lucia (Santos, 1976: 158) tells us that one of the girls had been about sixteen years old when she died, and the other around eighteen or twenty. What is most interesting from our point of view, however, is that these were girls who used to come to Lucia's home in order to learn weaving from Lucia's eldest sister (Santos, 1976: 158). In other words, Lucia asked the lady about two older girls whom she clearly associated with her oldest sister. This suggests that the initial hallucination of the lady was a hallucination of that sister, and the "little woman" whom Lucia saw was probably modeled for the most part upon Maria Santos, who was twenty-two years old in 1917.

To understand why such an interpretation makes sense, we need to know something about Lucia's family background. Lucia's father, like the father of Bernadette Soubirous, seems to have been an irresponsible individual with a heavy dependence upon alcohol. Lucia's mother, on the other hand, whose name was Maria Rosa, emerges from both Lucia's account and the various devotional accounts of Fatima as a hard-working person on whom fell the responsibility for sustaining the Santos family. One consequence seems to be that Lucia, as the youngest of seven children (six of whom were daughters), was raised more by her older sisters than by her mother. Thus, Lucia (Santos, 1976: 22) tells us, it was not uncommon for the neighbors to drop off their young children at the Santos household before going to work, and for Lucia and the other young children to be cared for by her sisters. Then, too, in recalling her childhood, Lucia (1976: 52-56) singles out only two things as having been especially important to her prior to the 1917 apparitions, and in both cases, it is her sisters, not her mother, who figure prominently. First, Lucia tells us, she had a passion for dancing, and it was her sisters who dressed her up in finery, who brought her to these dances, and who supervised her while there. Her mother, she tells us, attended these dances, as well, but was usually in charge of the cooking or some such activity. The second thing of importance in Lucia's childhood was her First Holy Communion, and she describes this event at length. But here again, it is her sisters, not her mother, whom she most associates with the great day. Thus, she informs us with apparent pride, it was her sisters who stayed up the entire night making her white Communion dress, who brought her to the church, and who took her to her appointed place in the line of first communicants (Santos, 1976: 56-57).

In short, although it would be wrong to imply that Lucia's attitude toward her mother was unfriendly, it does seem reasonable to say that her sisters had acted as mother-surrogates while Lucia was young, and that as a result Lucia had developed a very warm and very intense relationship with her sisters. It is only against such a backdrop that we can fully understand the importance of the events that immediately preceded Lucia's first apparition.

These events are well described by Lucia herself (Santos, 1976: 64-65). First, a new parish priest arrived and promptly forbade any more community dances. Given her passion for dancing, Lucia was devastated. Second, Lucia's father lost some of his land, something that Lucia charitably attributed to his having fallen into bad company where his "weakness" got the better of him. Third, Lucia's two eldest sisters left home to get married. Finally, to make ends meet, Maria Rosa sent

Lucia's two remaining sisters out to work as servants. The only ones remaining at home, Lucia tells us, were herself, her mother, and her brother (she makes no mention of her father). In describing how her mother would often talk of her now-empty home, and then burst into tears, Lucia writes: "It was one of the saddest scenes that I have ever witnessed. What with longing for my sisters, and seeing my mother so miserable, I felt that my heart was breaking" (Santos, 1976: 65).

And so what happened next? What happened, if I am right, is that ten-year-old Lucia hallucinated an image of a "little woman" modeled upon her older sisters, notably her oldest sister, who had recently left home, and for whom Lucia—by her own testimony—longed. That first hallucination, in other words, can be viewed as a fairly straightforward attempt to reestablish the presence of a loved mother figure (or mother figures) whom Lucia had recently lost. That is why there is no reference to the Virgin Mary in the first apparition, why Lucia associated the lady with her oldest sister (by asking the question about the two girls who used to work with her), and why Lucia showed some initial reluctance to identify the "little woman" as the Virgin Mary. One advantage of this interpretation is that it allows us to explain an important feature of the Fatima apparitions, namely, why the lady who appeared to Lucia ultimately identified herself as "Our Lady of the Rosary."

I have already indicated that sometime between the first apparition, on May 13, 1917, and the second apparition, on June 13, 1917, Lucia seems to have accepted the suggestion made by Jacinta (and almost certainly others) that she was seeing and hearing the Virgin Mary. If the initial hallucination was indeed modeled mainly upon her oldest sister, then the fact that her sister's name was Maria probably made it that much easier to accept such a suggestion. But the Virgin Mary is known to Catholics under a bewildering variety of titles. Mary is the Star of the Sea, The Immaculate Conception, Our Lady of Good Counsel, Our Lady Help of Christians, Our Lady of Perpetual Help, Our Lady of Mt. Carmel, Our Lady of the Snows, Our Lady Refuge of Sinners, Our Lady of Sorrows, Our Lady of Ransom, Our Lady of the Rosary, Our Lady of the Miraculous Medal—to say nothing of the many titles (Our Lady of Lourdes, of Guadalupe, and so on), that associate Mary with a particular location. We know that Lucia was familiar with some of these. She tells us (Santos, 1976: 168), for instance, that during her last apparition (on October 13, 1917) she saw

Mary first as Our Lady of Sorrows and then saw her again as Our Lady of Mt. Carmel.

But the Marian title that figures most prominently in Lucia's account of her experiences is clearly Our Lady of the Rosary. Thus, in the July apparition the lady told Lucia to pray the rosary in honor of Our Lady of the Rosary, and in the August apparition told her to use any money left at the Cova da Iria to finance a *festa* in honor of Our Lady of the Rosary. Finally, during the last apparition (in October) the lady specifically identified herself as Our Lady of the Rosary. Why the association of the lady seen by Lucia with this particular Marian title rather than some other?

At one level, the answer is obvious to anyone who reads Lucia's description of her early childhood, since she tells us (Santos, 1976: 55–56) that of all the statues in her parish Church representing Mary, the one representing Mary as Our Lady of the Rosary was her favorite. Lucia was especially attached to this particular statue because the altar dedicated to the statue was cared for by her sisters, and it was for this reason, Lucia tells us, that she usually went to that statue, rather than some other, to pray.

In summary then, Lucia's initial hallucination was probably an attempt to reestablish the presence of the warm mother figures whom she had recently lost, due to the fact that her four older sisters had all recently moved out of the Santos household.[2] But the connotations associated with her sisters continued to shape Lucia's hallucination even after she had accepted the suggestion that the lady was the Virgin Mary. Thus the Mary that Lucia hallucinated became the one Mary that Lucia most associated with her sisters, Our Lady of the Rosary.

[2] In the case of three well-known sets of Marian apparitions, then—involving Bernadette Soubirous at Lourdes, Catherine Labouré at Paris, and Lucia Santos at Fatima—I have argued that the initial hallucination was an attempt to reestablish the presence of a reassuring mother figure who had for some reason been lost. I suspect that this is an extremely common pattern. In the case of the Marian apparitions at Medjugorje, Yugoslavia, for instance, the first person to see the Virgin was a sixteen-year-old girl named Ivanka Ivankovic. It hardly seems coincidental that Ivanka's mother had died only two months prior to the outbreak of the apparitions, that she had by all accounts been devastated by her mother's death, and that her father was living in Germany as a migrant worker (Kraljević, 1984: 152). Ivanka was also the first of the Medjugorje seers to talk to the Virgin, and the first thing she asked about was her mother. (She was told that her mother was safe in heaven with Mary; Kraljević, 1984: 13, 144.) Here again, in other words, there are solid reasons for believing that a Marian apparition was at least initially an attempt to reestablish the presence of a reassuring mother. This, then, is probably one of the first hypotheses that should be considered when investigating the background of any particular seer involved with a Marian apparition.

OUR LADY OF GUADALUPE

Accepting devotional accounts at face value,[3] we know with precision the date and time of the first apparition of Our Lady of Guadalupe: it occurred at daybreak on the morning of December 9, 1531. On that morning, a Christianized Indian named Juan Diego was hurrying to attend Mass in a village some distance from his own. In the course of his trip, he passed a hill called Tepeyac, located about five miles north of Tenochitlán (which grew to become modern Mexico City). As he passed Tepeyac, he heard singing coming from the top of the hill, and then a woman's voice calling his name. In response, he climbed to the top of Tepeyac and came face to face with a very beautiful Indian girl who appeared to be about fourteen years old.

After asking Juan where he was going, and after learning that he was going to Mass, the girl identified herself as the Virgin Mary. She then told Juan that she wanted a shrine built on Tepeyac in her honor, and that at this shrine she would minister to Indians like himself. Juan was then instructed to make the Virgin's request known to the bishop in Tenochitlán.

Juan went to the residence of the bishop, Don Fray de Zumárraga. Zumárraga listened to Juan's story with politeness, but no real interest. Later that same day, Juan returned to Tepeyac and found the Virgin waiting. He reported Zumárraga's lack of interest, and the Virgin told Juan to try again to convince the bishop. Accordingly, Juan returned to the bishop's residence on the next day (Sunday), but Zumárraga was still unconvinced. Juan again reported his failure to the Virgin at Tepeyac, and the Virgin told Juan to try a third time to convince Zumárraga. This time, however, he was to come to Tepeyac before going to Tenochitlán, and she would provide him with a sign to be used in convincing the bishop.

The next day, however, Juan did not return to Tepeyac. His uncle, Juan Bernardino, had become deathly ill, and Juan Diego did not want to leave his side. On Tuesday, Juan Diego did decide to go to Mass, but because he did not want to be sent to Tenochitlán, he went around

---

[3] Devotional accounts of the Tepeyac apparitions include Eliot (1961), Johnston (1981), and Keyes (1941). Most of the early documents relating to the Guadalupe cult at Tepeyac have been brought together, in English translation, by Demarest and Taylor (1954).

Tepeyac. Nevertheless, when he was in the vicinity of the hill, he saw the Virgin coming down to meet him. When she arrived, she said "Am I not here who am your Mother?" (Eliot, 1961: 49), and told him that since he was under her protection, his uncle's health would be restored.

The Virgin then directed Juan to go to the top of Tepeyac and to pick some roses that he would find growing there, even though it was not the season for roses. Juan did as he was told, found and picked the roses (which, of course, were growing on the top of Tepeyac, just as the Virgin had said), and carried them back to the Virgin cradled in his *tilma*, a type of Aztec cape worn in front. The Virgin then arranged the flowers in his *tilma*, and tied the bottom corners of the *tilma* around Juan's neck so that the flowers would not fall out.

Juan hurried with his flowery bundle to see Zumárraga. When he was brought into the bishop's presence, he let the end of his *tilma* fall forward. The roses dropped to the floor, and there—on the front of the cloak—was an image of the Virgin that Juan Diego had seen. Zumárraga was convinced immediately of the miraculous origin of this image, and so of the reality of Juan's apparitions.

The next day, when Juan returned home, he found that his uncle was completely cured. It seems that the previous morning Juan Bernardino had himself been visited by the Virgin. She had cured him and told him about the picture that she had sent with Juan Diego. She had also specifically requested that this image be venerated under the title of "Our Lady of Guadalupe." Thus ends the devotional account.

The great stumbling block to anyone searching for the psychological origins of the Tepeyac apparitions is the fact that there are no accounts of these apparitions that date from the period of the apparitions themselves. There are, for instance, no references to any apparitions occurring at Tepeyac in the writings of Bishop Zumárraga, even though he was supposed to have been a central participant in the drama. The earliest known account of the apparitions at Tepeyac was published in 1648 by Miguel Sánchez. The following year, in 1649, a second account was published by Luis Lazo de la Vega, and a third, by Luis Becerra Tanco, was published in 1675. These three early accounts are the basis for all modern devotional accounts of the Tepeyac apparitions. (All three of these early accounts, translated into English, are given in Demarest and Taylor, 1956.)

The inability to provide documentary evidence dating from about

1531 cannot be emphasized too strongly, since it is usually glossed over even in scholarly investigations of the Guadalupe cult. Kurtz (1982), for example, presents a detailed analysis which argues that the Tepeyac apparitions, or at least the popularity of these apparitions, was a response to a number of tensions that operated in Mexico between the time of the Conquest (c. 1519-1521) and 1531, the date of the apparitions themselves. But such an argument is undermined if the tradition of the Tepeyac did not develop until, say, the late 1500s or the early 1600s—a possibility that is as consistent with the documentary record as Kurtz's assumption that the tradition did develop in 1531.

None of this is to deny that there was a shrine dedicated to "Our Lady of Guadalupe" at Tepeyac in about 1530. To understand this apparent anomaly, it is necessary to review the history of the Tepeyac shrine, and here I rely entirely upon Lafaye (1976). First, there is no doubt but that Tepeyac had a religious history that predated the Christian period. There are several early commentaries by Spanish observers that make it clear that the preeminent female deity in the Aztec pantheon was a mother goddess named Tonantzin, and that Tonantzin's most important shrine was located atop Tepeyac. It was from amid the ruins of this shrine, then, that Juan Diego heard his voice.

These early commentaries also make it clear that sometime shortly after the Conquest, a Christian shrine was erected at Tepeyac and was dedicated to Our Lady of Guadalupe. One of the most important of these early sources is the record of an investigation launched by Church authorities in 1556 (Lafaye, 1976: 238-242), in response to a sermon preached by a leading Franciscan, Fray Francisco de Bustamante, who had argued that the Indians worshiping at Tepeyac were still worshiping Tonantzin under the guise of Our Lady of Guadalupe. This investigation makes no mention of any apparitions having occurred at Tepeyac.

Who, then, was the "Our Lady of Guadalupe" enshrined at Tepeyac? She was the Mary who had appeared to a poor shepherd near the Guadalupe River in the Estremadura region of Spain sometime during the fourteenth century. She had led the shepherd to a miraculous image of herself (a statue), and the shrine established to house this statue had become one of the most popular of all the Marian shrines in Spain. Daughter-shrines dedicated to "Our Lady of Guadalupe"

appeared throughout the New World as a result of Spanish coloniza-
tion, and the original shrine at Tepeyac was almost certainly one of
them (Lafaye, 1976: 216-230). Many of the Conquistadors were from
Estremadura, and would have been particularly attached to the "Guadalupe" shrine there. Cortés himself was born in a village in Estremadura quite near the shrine, and we know that he supported the Estremadura Guadalupe shrine generously (Smith, 1983: 66).

If the Tepeyac shrine was a daughter-shrine, we would expect that
the image of Mary venerated there would have been a replica of the
statue of Mary housed in the Guadalupe shrine in Estremadura, and
there is some evidence that this was so, at least initially. One of the
earliest references to the image venerated at Tepeyac appears in a letter
written by the Spanish viceroy in 1575, who said, "They gave the image the name of Our Lady of Guadalupe saying that she resembled the
image of the monastery of Guadalupe of Spain" (Lafaye, 1976: 233).
The original Tepeyac image is thus more likely to have been a replica
of the statue housed at the Spanish Guadalupe shrine than the now familiar image on cloth.

Another important bit of information relating to the original image
at Tepeyac appears in an account written in 1582 by Miles Philips, an
English sailor who had been captured in Mexico by the Spanish in
1568 (see Demarest and Taylor, 1956: 218-221). The Philips account
is the first reference to the Guadalupe shrine written in English. In describing how he and his fellow captives were marched from Vera Cruz
(where they were captured) to Mexico City, Philips tells us that as
they neared Mexico City they came to "a very fair church, called Our
Lady's Church." In this church, he tells us, there was "an image of
Our Lady, of silver and gilt, being as high and as large as a tall
woman," whom the Spanish venerated under the title of "Nuestra
Señora de Guadalupe." In a footnote commenting on this passage,
Demarest and Taylor (1956: 220n), who accept the story of the Tepeyac apparitions at face value, state, "Obviously, Miles Philips did
not notice the Holy Image, and mistook a silver and gilt statue for it."
A simpler explanation, however, is that Miles Philips described what
was, in 1568, the principal image venerated at Tepeyac. In fact, Lafaye's analysis of the documentary references to the Guadalupe shrine
at Tepeyac convinces him that the image on cloth now venerated there
placed the original statue sometime after 1575.

Taken all together then, the patterns documented by Lafaye seem consistent with the following account: the original Christian shrine at Tepeyac was a daughter-shrine dedicated to Our Lady of Guadalupe of Estremadura in Spain. Sometime toward the end of the sixteenth century or the beginning of the seventeenth century, various attempts were made to "Indianize" this shrine and make it more autonomous. This involved, in part, replacing the replica of the Spanish statue of Our Lady of Guadalupe with an image on cloth which portrayed Mary as an Indian. More importantly, given our concerns here, the Tepeyac "Our Lady of Guadalupe" was cut loose from the original apparition legend, and associated with a new legend in which Mary appeared in the New World and in which she appeared to an Indian, not a Spanish herdsman. But if the story of the Tepeyac apparitions is just an Indianized account of the original story associated with Our Lady of Guadalupe, we should find some similarities between the two stories—and we do.

Although Lafaye (1976: 219-220) presents a brief version of the original apparition legend, a far more complete account is given by Christian (1981b: 89-92). According to that legend, some simple herdsmen were tending their cows near the Guadalupe River in Estremadura, when one of them went looking for a missing cow. Climbing a high hill, he came upon the cow, and it appeared to be dead. He started to butcher it, and had actually made the first incision, when the cow suddenly sprang to life. The man was scared, but at that moment the Virgin Mary appeared. She told the herdsman to bring others to this place and to dig at the exact spot where she had appeared. There, she said, they would find a statue of her. This statue was to be housed in a shrine built for this purpose. Those in charge of the shrine were to be instructed to feed the poor at least once a day.

The herdsman hurried back to his companions. Although initially skeptical, they were convinced of this story when they saw the cow that had been brought back to life, with the marks made by the herdsman when he had begun to butcher it. The herdsman returned home, only to find his wife weeping for a son who had died. He then consecrated his dead son to the service of the shrine to be built for the "Virgin of Guadalupe," and the young man promptly returned to life.

Finally, the man went to the clergy and told them what had occurred. Men were sent to dig at the site of the apparition. They came upon a cave in which they found, as promised, a statue of the Virgin. A small sanctuary was immediately erected to house the statue. Over the years, this sanctuary became associated with any number of miraculous cures. The herdsman, his wife, and their children became the guardians of the sanctuary, and passed the job along to their descendants.

Lafaye (1976: 294-296) has already pointed to the obvious similarities between the two "Guadalupe" accounts: in both cases the apparition occurred on a hill and appeared to a married man of relatively low status; in both cases the Virgin requested that a shrine be built in order to house an image of herself; in both cases a close relative of the seer (the herdsman's son, Juan Diego's uncle) was saved from death by the Virgin's intervention; and, of course, in both cases the Virgin was called "Our Lady of Guadalupe."

Christian's (1981b) work makes it clear that some of these elements (such as the low status of the seer and the association of the apparition with an image) were common to a great many Spanish apparitions of the late medieval and the Renaissance period. But this in no way detracts from the suggestion—implicit in Lafaye—that the story surrounding the Guadalupe apparition in Tepeyac was modeled upon that in Estremadura. There is one "marker" in particular that points to the Old World origin of the Tepeyac story: according to devotional accounts, the roses picked by Juan Diego were Castilian roses, not normally found in Mexico (Eliot, 1961: 50; Johnston, 1981: 34). This reference to Castilian roses makes sense if the Tepeyac story was based upon the Estremadura story, since the Guadalupe shrine in Estremadura was greatly favored by the Castilian monarchy, and was easily the most popular Marian shrine in Castile during this period (Christian, 1981b: 88).

The absence of any documentary reference to a tradition of an apparition associated with Tepeyac until 1648, and the fact that the tradition, once it appeared, showed such striking similarities to the original Guadalupe story, means that we do not need to assume that the Tepeyac story was based upon the hallucinatory experiences of some seer. The evidence is, however, consistent with the suggestion that the story arose as part of the effort to Indianize the shrine dedicated to Our Lady of Guadalupe at Tepeyac, and that it was constructed simply by Indianizing the original Guadalupe legend.

Having said that, of course, there seems little point in including an analysis of the Tepeyac apparitions in a book concerned with the psychological processes that give rise to the hallucinations (or illusions) on which Marian apparitions are based. I have included it because there are a number of elements in the Tepeyac story that do not appear in the original Guadalupe story, and that do not seem typical of Marian apparitions in Spain or even in general. This raises the suspicion that perhaps the story reflects the merger of two accounts: the original Guadalupe legend (as Lafaye suggests) and someone's actual hallucinations. This does not mean that we must believe that such hallucinations, if they occurred, took place precisely in 1531 to someone called "Juan Diego." It is enough if a report of someone's hallucinations was available during the period (c. 1575-1648) when the story of the Tepeyac apparitions was taking its present form. The best way to retrieve an account of these experiences, if such existed, is to look at those elements in the Tepeyac story that do not appear in the original Guadalupe legend.

One of the dramatic differences between the two stories has to do with the family background of the seer involved. In the original legend we are told that the herdsman had a living wife and children; in the Tepeyac story, devotional accounts make it clear that Juan Diego was a widower and that he and his wife had no children (Keyes, 1941: 25; Demarest and Taylor, 1956: 116; Eliot, 1961: 40; Johnston, 1981: 25). If we conclude from this that the Tepeyac seer (whom I shall call Juan Diego for convenience) was indeed a widower with no children, than an obvious hypothesis suggests itself—Juan Diego's hallucination was a hallucination of his dead wife.

There is, in fact, one bit of evidence that directly supports this hypothesis. In her devotional account of the Tepeyac apparition, Eliot (1961: 42) mentions that the earliest accounts of this apparition indicate that Juan addressed the Virgin using various *diminutive* forms of address. Certainly the use of diminutives by Juan Diego does occur in de la Vega's 1649 account (Demarest and Taylor, 1956: 41-48). Eliot tries to explain this by suggesting that "probably Aztecs of Juan's servant caste habitually used them [diminutives] towards their superiors." I have been unable to locate any ethnographic material dealing with the use of diminutives among the Aztecs, but Eliot's explanation seems unlikely. It is a widespread linguistic norm that when diminutives are used in conversations between individuals of different social rank, it is the person of superior rank who uses the diminutive form in addressing a person of inferior rank (Brown and Gilman, 1960; Brown, 1965: 92-99). The cross-cultural linguistic pattern, in other words, is exactly the opposite of what Eliot suggests, and there is no basis for believing that the Aztecs would have been an exception to that pattern. But there is a second linguistic norm that is relevant here: when two people are from the same social stratum and share a sense of intimacy, it is not uncommon for them to exchange diminutives.

To understand which linguistic norm was operating in Juan Diego's case, then, we need to know if the Virgin used diminutives in addressing Juan. It turns out that she did. Thus, when calling his name, she called out "Juan! Juan Diego! Juanito! Juan Diegito" (Eliot, 1961: 41; Johnston, 1981: 26). The linguistic evidence therefore suggests very clearly that Juan Diego felt he was addressing someone of the same social stratum as himself, and with whom he shared a sense of intimacy. The most obvious such person would have been his wife.

In fact, the hypothesis that Juan Diego's original hallucination was of his dead wife provides a new perspective on several of the unique elements in the Tepeyac story (apart from the seer's status as a childless widower). At one point in the story, for instance, Juan goes out of his way to avoid contact with the apparition. The devotional rationalization for this, of course, is that he wanted to be with his sick uncle and so did not want to be sent to Bishop Zumárraga again. But if what Juan saw was an image of his dead wife, another—and in some ways simpler—interpretation seems plausible: he avoided the apparition because he thought it was a ghost of his dead wife and was afraid of it. This interpretation would be falsified if it turned out that the Aztecs did not believe in ghosts, or if they considered ghosts to be benign. In fact, neither possibility is true; quite the reverse. In his *General History of the Things of New Spain* (written in the 1560s, and so roughly contemporaneous with the events described here), Fray Bernardino de Sahagun tells us both that Aztecs believed that the ghosts of the dead sometimes appeared to living humans, and that these ghosts were regarded with fear (Sahagun, 1979: 180).

Consider another feature of the Tepeyac apparition: the fact that Juan heard singing from Tepeyac before seeing the Virgin. In most other Marian apparitions, the Virgin Mary—if she announces her coming at all—announces herself with a flash of light; even in the Tepeyac case, the earliest accounts (Henderson, 1983: 37) mention that Juan saw a brilliant light before seeing Mary. But these same early accounts also mention that he heard singing, and this is an element absent from both the original Guadalupe legend and any other account of a Marian apparition that I am familiar with. Sahagun (1979: 180), however, tells us that the Aztecs believed that when ghosts appeared to human beings, they moaned and groaned. If the original hallucination was regarded by the historical Juan to be a ghost of his dead wife, it seems likely that he would have reported that the ghost (like all good Aztec ghosts) moaned and groaned. It is not unlikely that when Juan's story was converted into an account of a Marian apparition (and merged with the original Guadalupe legend), this moaning and groaning (which seems inappropriate to a Marian apparition) would easily be transformed into singing.

Another unusual feature of the Tepeyac story involves the personal contact between Juan and the Virgin. After Juan had gathered the roses, he brought them back to the Virgin, and she then arranged them in his cloak and tied the bottom corners around his neck so the roses would not fall out. I know of no other Marian apparition in which the Virgin herself ties a cloak (or anything else) around the neck of a seer. But tying a cloak around a man's neck *is* an important part of the traditional Aztec marriage ceremony. Sahagun's (1969: 127-133) description of this ceremony indicates that the bride and groom were positioned in front of the hearth in the groom's household. The groom approached the bride and placed a shift on her; the bride's mother then approached the groom and tied a cloak around his neck. The matchmakers then tied a corner of the groom's cloak to the bride's shift, and—after a few more ceremonials—the couple was considered married.

Although in the marriage ceremony it is the top of a cloak that is tied around the husband's neck, whereas in the Tepeyac story the Virgin ties the bottom of Juan's cloak around his neck, the fact remains tying a cloak around a man's neck does appear in the Tepeyac story, does not appear in the original (Estremadura) Gaudalupe legend or in accounts of other Marian apparitions, and does appear in the traditional Aztec marriage ceremony. All this is just one more bit of evidence to suggest that Juan's hallucination was shaped by memories of his dead wife. True, in the marriage ceremony it is the wife's mother, not the wife, who ties the cape around the groom's neck. But the person seen by Juan was defined as a mother: although Juan described her as a young girl, she explicitly told him that she was his mother and that she would protect him. Juan's hallucination, in other words, probably reflected the condensation of several memories associated with his wife on the day that they were married.

Furthermore, if we grant that tying the cloak around Juan's neck does suggest that his hallucination was being shaped specifically by the memories of his marriage to his wife, then we have a basis for explaining why Juan saw a fourteen-year-old girl: Aztec girls were generally married at about sixteen years of age (Vaillant, 1962: 124), and Sahagun's (1969: 130) account suggests that it was not uncommon for girls to marry even earlier. In other words, what Juan saw was probably an idealized image of his wife as she had been when they were married.

In summary, then, a whole range of elements unique to the Tepeyac story—Juan Diego's avoidance of the Virgin, the singing he first heard, the Virgin's tying of the cloak around his neck, the fact that the Virgin was both a fourteen-year-old girl and a "mother"—become explicable on the hypothesis that Juan's hallucination was modeled mainly upon his wife and, in particular, was shaped by memories of his marriage day.

At this point, as in the case of the apparitions to Catherine Labouré, we must now explain the timing of Juan's hallucination. Assuming that traditional accounts are correct, and that Juan's wife had been dead for several years, why did he hallucinate an image of her as a young bride when he himself was in his mid-fifties? Since the answer to such a question can only be discovered by considering those events in Juan's life just prior to the hallucination, and since we have absolutely no information about such events, the task here would seem impossible.

We might try to read some significance into the traditional date of the first Tepeyac apparition, December 9. Was this an important date in Aztec history? Not really. On the contrary, it seems all too conveniently close to a date important in the Christian tradition: the feast of the Immaculate Conception of Mary had traditionally been celebrated on December 8, and the celebration of the Immaculate Conception on this date had been made a universal feast of the Latin Church in 1476 (Holweck, 1910: 680). In New Spain, in fact, the Immaculate Conception was celebrated from December 8 to 17 (Keyes, 1941: 178), a period that subsumes all the dates on which Juan Diego saw the Virgin Mary. It seems likely then that the particular dates (December 9, 10, 12) assigned to Juan Diego's apparitions were added to the Juan Diego story sometime during the period when that story was being merged with the original (Estremadura) Guadalupe tradition. These dates, in other words, were probably just one more way in which poor Juan's hallucination of his dead wife was "Marianized."

There is, however, one incident in the devotional accounts of the Tepeyac story that might point to the incident that triggered Juan's hallucination. These accounts make it clear that when Juan reached the top of Tepeyac, he not only saw the Virgin, but also saw physical objects on the hill with heightened perception. In Eliot's (1961: 42) account, we are told that when Juan looked at the cactus leaves they "gleamed like emeralds, and their spines gold." Likewise, every stone and every plant "was sharply etched on Juan's vision, transparent and jewel-like in colour." Johnston (1981: 26) conveys all this by suggesting that Juan Diego saw the plants and bushes atop Tepeyac as characterized by "a riot of color, as if they were being viewed through the stained glass windows of some magnificent cathedral." These reports are strikingly similar to the reports of subjects who have experienced drug-induced hallucinations, since such people often report the perception of objects in bright, saturated colors (see, for instance, Siegal and Jarvik, 1975: 109). Such drug-induced hallucinations also usually show clear evidence of having been shaped, at least in part, by the subject's memories (Siegal and Jarvik, 1975: 145-148), which is consistent with the hypothesis that Juan's hallucination was shaped by memories of his wedding day.

The suggestion that the historical Juan's Diego hallucination may have been triggered by a hallucinogenic drug is buttressed by the fact that such drugs were, in fact, used by the Aztecs. Thus, both Sahagun (1959: 38-40) and Motolinia (1950: 46), who wrote about 1540, report that the Aztecs ingested mushrooms in order to produce visions. Munn's (1973) account of the use of various hallucinogenic mushrooms by the Mazatec Indians in Oaxaca (whose ancestors were part of the Aztec empire) contains accounts of hallucinatory experiences that seem very similar to the account traditionally attributed to Juan Diego.

Unlike the Marian apparitions considered previously, then, where the apparition in question was probably triggered by a recent social event (Bernadette's return to the Soubirous household; Catherine Labouré's separation from her sister-in-law; Lucia's loss of her sisters), there is some basis for believing that the hallucination experienced by the historical Juan Diego was drug-induced and shaped by memories of his dead wife and their wedding day so many years earlier.

A CONCLUDING DIGRESSION:
THE MIRACULOUS IMAGE OF TEPEYAC

Since the miraculous image on cloth associated with Our Lady of Guadalupe in Mexico continues to attract the attention of so many people (including a variety of non-Catholics: see Smith, 1983), a few remarks about this image seem in order. Lafaye concluded that the original image at Tepeyac was almost certainly a replica of the statue of the Estremadura "Our Lady of Guadalupe," and that this statue was replaced by the present image sometime after 1575 as part of the Indianization of the Tepeyac shrine. The suggestion that the present image was incorporated into a developing tradition about apparitions at Tepeyac seems consistent with results obtained recently from an infrared analysis of that image (Smith, 1983: 90-91). It appears that some of the details of the current image were definitely added after the original painting was completed, and it seems clear that at least some of these added details were designed to make the Virgin in the image seem more similar to the Virgin described by Juan Diego. For example, one of the few precise details about the Virgin's appearance supplied by Juan Diego was that she radiated golden rays, and the "golden rays" on the Guadalupe image are among the details added at a later date.

Furthermore, although it is not usually mentioned in the devotional accounts, Aztec artists in the sixteenth and seventeenth centuries were quite well known for painting religious images on cloth, and these images were routinely hung in Christian churches (Lafaye, 1976: 232-233). It thus seems likely that the image on cloth now associated with Our Lady of Guadalupe was originally just one of many hung in the Tepeyac shrine.

The suggestion that the Tepeyac image was originally painted by some now-unknown Aztec artist even provides a basis for explaining one final feature of the Tepeyac story not usually found in accounts of other Marian apparitions: the association between the creation of the image on Juan Diego's cloak and flowers. The story suggests that the image was produced by contact with the flowers that Juan had picked and that the Virgin arranged in his cloak. This brings to mind Moto-linia's (1950 [c. 1540]: 220) remark that Aztec artists typically made their paints from flowers (which was why, Motolinia tells us, they felt free to suck their brushes clean when changing colors). In other words, the suggestion that the Tepeyac image was produced miracu-lously as a result of contact with flowers might be a simple distortion of the original perception that the image, like most religious images on cloth of the time, had been painted with paints made from flowers.

MARIAN ILLUSIONS

French troops under the young Napoleon invaded Italy in 1796. As the French army moved south, a sudden rash of "miraculous" events broke out in Italy, most of which were associated with Marian images. In Arezzo, for instance, just south of Florence, a terracotta image of Mary began to do strange things. Just what it did depended upon who you talked to. Some people said that the image's face turned luminescent. Others reported that the image opened and closed its eyes. Still others saw sparks and flashes of light shoot from the image's eyes. In Siena, an old and dirty painting, traditionally known as *The Grieving Madonna*, also began to shoot sparks from her eyes. (This particular picture was seized by the French, cleaned, and found to be a picture of Cleopatra; presumably it then stopped shooting sparks.) More generally, images of Mary began crying, sweating blood, radiating sparks, moving about, and so on, all over central Italy. Marian images in the city of Rome itself seem to have been especially active.[1]

Since all the reports were associated with a concrete image of some sort (a statue, a painting, and so on), we are almost certainly dealing here with illusions rather than hallucinations. Nor will many readers be surprised by the observation that such illusions proliferated during Napoleon's invasion of Italy. It seems reasonable to suppose that when civilian populations are faced with danger and destruction, they would seek to reduce their anxiety by reassuring themselves that the forces of the supernatural world are on their side. They would be extremely receptive to the suggestion that a powerful supernatural mediator, such as the Virgin Mary, was giving them a sign that indeed she was on their side. But although all this may seem an obvious explanation of the sudden rash of wonder-working images that sprang

---

[1] A full account of the Marian wonders that accompanied Napoleon's invasion of Italy can be found in Rinaldi (1981), and it is upon that account that my summary here is based.

up in Italy following the Napoleonic invasion, it is an explanation never mentioned in connection with the Marian apparitions at Pontmain, Knock, and Zeitoun, despite the striking similarity between these cases and the Italian ones just described.

A LADY APPEARS AT PONTMAIN

On the evening of January 17, 1871, in the small village of Pontmain, France, Eugene Barbedette (age twelve) was working in his family's barn with his younger brother Joseph (age ten) and their father, Cesar Barbedette.[2] Shortly before 6:00 they were joined by a neighbor, Jeanette Detais, who had come to talk with Cesar. Taking advantage of the break, Eugene went to the barn door to see what the weather was like. He was impressed with the number of stars that seemed clearly visible. Suddenly, looking at the sky just above a neighbor's house, he saw the image of a lady. She wore a long robe with flowing sleeves and was very beautiful. The robe was dark blue and studded with stars. She also wore a long black veil that covered her ears and her hair, and seemed to extend down to the middle of her back. On top of this veil she wore a golden crown.

Eugene stood transfixed, looking at the image, for several minutes. When Jeanette Detais came out of the barn, he asked her if she could see the lady. She could not. His father then came out, and he, too, saw nothing. Finally, young Joseph Barbedette came out and he saw exactly the same image as Eugene. Cesar Barbedette, however, was convinced that there was nothing there, and so insisted that his sons go back into the barn to continue their tasks.

A few minutes later, Eugene again went outside, and again reported seeing the image. This time Cesar Barbedette sent for his wife Victoire. She arrived, but could see nothing. Furthermore, the commotion was beginning to attract the attention of the neighbors, so she gave Eugene a sharp blow on the arm and told him to keep quiet. Eugene and Joseph continued to insist that they saw the lady. Whether simply to keep the children quiet or because she was touched by their sincerity, Victoire suggested that they might be seeing the Virgin Mary, and therefore suggested that they pray five Our Fathers and five

[2] The most comprehensive account of the Pontmain apparition is Richard (1971 [1939]). Other accounts include Galvin (1970), Rogo (1983: 214-218), and W. Walsh (1904d: 99-116).

Hail Marys. After these prayers, Victoire went back into her house for her glasses; putting them on and returning, she still could not see the lady. Neither could the Barbedette maid, who by this time had also come outside. Convinced now that the two boys were just trying to evade their chores, Victoire sent them back into the barn. A few minutes later they were called to dinner.

After dinner, the boys went outside, and still saw the lady suspended in the sky. When Eugene suggested that the lady was about the same size as Sister Vitaline (a nun who taught at the local school), Victoire Barbedette suggested that they should send for this nun. Sister Vitaline arrived, but—like all the other adults—could see nothing. When she returned to the nun's residence, however, she came across two young girls, Françoise Richer (age eleven) and Jeanne-Marie Lebosse (age nine). Sister Vitaline brought these two girls back to the Barbedette barn, and after a short time both girls reported seeing the same image as Eugene and Joseph.

Meanwhile Sister Vitaline had gone off to get one of her colleagues, a Sister Marie Edouard. Although Sister Marie Edouard (when she arrived) saw nothing, she seems to have been absolutely convinced that an apparition of the Virgin Mary was in progress and that for some reason it was visible only to children. She therefore went off to a neighboring household and told its owner to bring his young grandson to the Barbedette barn. This young boy was named Eugene Friteau (age six), and when this child arrived he, too, saw the lady. Eventually, the growing group at the Barbedette household was joined by a mother carrying her two-year-old daughter. This young infant looked in the region of the sky where the image was appearing and cried out "Jesu! Jesu!" The devotional interpretation (Walsh, 1904d: 107) is that this infant did indeed see Mary, but responded by crying aloud the only holy name that it knew, "Jesus."

By now, a little over an hour had passed since Eugene Barbedette had first caught sight of the apparition. The lady had been seen by at least five children (six if you count the infant who shouted "Jesu"), but by none of the fifty or more adults who had congregated near the Barbedette barn. Everyone seems to have accepted the suggestion that the image was an image of Mary. So far the lady had said nothing, but she *had* moved. She seems to have smiled, for instance, and she definitely got larger. Sometime after all five (or six) seers were together, an oval frame appeared around the lady, and set into the sides of this frame were four brackets, each holding an unlit candle.

At this point, Sister Marie Edouard began reciting the Magnificat. This is the prayer recited by the Virgin Mary when she visited her cousin Elizabeth just after the Annunciation; it is recorded in Luke 1: 46-55, and pious tradition has always suggested that it was composed by the Virgin Mary herself.

After the recitation of the Magnificat, the children reported that a large white "writing space" had appeared beneath the Virgin's feet. Slowly the letter M formed in the space, then the Letter A, then I and then S. A few minutes later this first word was followed by others (always one letter at a time), until the message read "mais priez mes enfants" ("but pray my children"). After some more hymns and some more praying on the part of the crowd, a second sentence appeared in the same way: "Dieu vous exaucera en peu de temps" ("God will hear you shortly"). Finally a third sentence: "mon fils se laisse toucher" (usually translated as "my son permits himself to be moved"). The message remained suspended beneath the Virgin for about ten minutes, then disappeared.

There followed a number of changes in the image. The lady's expression turned sorrowful, she sometimes moved her arms to keep time with the hymns being sung, a small red cross appeared on her tunic over her heart, a large cross appeared in her hands, a banner that read "Jesus Christ" appeared above this cross, the large cross disappeared, a small cross appeared over each of the lady's shoulders, and a star lit each of the four candles, one by one. Finally, a white veil seemed to engulf the Virgin from below until she disappeared entirely. Slowly the oval frame, the candles, the white veil, and all else that remained also disappeared. The entire apparition had lasted a little less than three hours.

What are we to make of the apparition at Pontmain? There are solid reasons for believing that it was an illusion rather than a hallucination. It seems that on the evening of the apparition there were three very bright stars in the heavens that were seen by everyone present, and that by the following night these three stars had disappeared (Walsh, 1904d: 106). Whether or not these were really stars or were something else, there was something there for everyone to see, and it was directly associated with the apparition. This was made clear when Eugene Barbedette was trying to get Sister Vitaline to see the lady. He first directed her attention to the three stars, and after establishing that she could see them, he told her that the lady's head was "just in the middle" of those three stars (Richard, 1971: 27).

Devotional accounts, as one might expect, emphasize the unanimity of the seers in describing what they saw, and imply that this unanimity mitigates against the apparitions having been an illusion elicited by those three bright stars. In evaluating this, we must keep in mind that all the seers made their reports in each other's presence. There was thus plenty of opportunity for one seer to take the reports of the others into account before speaking. It also seems to have been true that at least the first four seers had the opportunity to discuss what they were seeing in private before they made their reports to the adults present. When Joseph Barbedette first joined his brother Eugene at the barn door, it appears that the two were alone for several minutes before being joined by their father. Likewise, after Sister Vitaline brought Françoise Richer and Jeanne-Marie Lebosse to the Barbedette barn, she seems to have left them alone with the two boys, Eugene and Joseph, while she herself went to get Sister Marie Edouard. It was only when Sister Vitaline returned that the two young girls told her that they too had seen the Virgin (Richard, 1971: 29-30).

But if the apparition at Pontmain was an illusion, why did it occur when it did? On January 17, 1871, the Franco-Prussian War was in its final stages, and France had by then suffered a series of humiliating defeats. Paris had been under siege since September 1870, and under bombardment since late December. The city's population was starving and on the verge of surrender. Closer to home, the Prussians had arrived on the outskirts of Laval and were expected to enter that city the next day. Laval was the capital of Mayenne, the department in which Pontmain itself was located.

Quite apart from the general anxiety produced by such a situation, the Barbedette family had been experiencing a more personal anxiety. There were, in fact, three Barbedette children: Joseph, Eugene, and an older son named Auguste. Auguste (and thirty-four other males from Pontmain) had gone off to fight the Prussians several months previously. The Barbedettes had been worried constantly about his safety, especially in the weeks just preceding the apparition, since during that time they had heard nothing from Auguste (Richard, 1971: 20). Almost daily, the family had tried to secure Auguste's safekeeping by praying the rosary together and going to the local church to do the Stations of the Cross. In addition, on the day of the apparition itself, Eugene had served at a morning Mass during which the priest had asked the congregation to pray for all the men of Pontmain who were away fighting. Eugene, I might add, was especially attached to Auguste because the latter was his godfather as well as his brother (Walsh, 1904d: 102).

It is only against this background that we can understand the importance of Jeanette Detais' visit to the Barbedette barn, since it appears that it was her visit that triggered the initial illusion seen by Eugene. Jeanette Detais was no ordinary neighbor, but the person responsible for burials in the village of Pontmain (Richard, 1971: 18). I assume that the simple sight of Jeanette Detais would have had the effect of intensifying poor Eugene's anxiety over his elder brother, and it was this intensified anxiety, I suggest, that shaped what Eugene first saw.

Why should an intensified anxiety of this sort have given rise to an image of the Virgin Mary? I don't think that it did. Eugene did not suggest (at least at first) that he had seen the Virgin. That suggestion was first made (possibly in jest) by his mother, and then again (with great seriousness) by Sister Marie Edouard. Even devotional accounts indicate that when Eugene first saw the image he "thought it was the announcement of the death of his brother" (Richard, 1971: 20). The fact that what Eugene first saw was a sign that his brother had died probably accounts for why this sign, the lady, was wearing a long black veil. Though a long black veil is not traditionally a part of Marian iconography, the wearing of black vestments is associated with funerals in France as in the rest of the Western world.

Presumably it was Eugene's report that he was seeing a lady in the region of those three stars that induced a similar perception in the other seers. But faced with the absolute certainty on the part of one of their teachers (Sister Marie Edouard) that the lady must be the Virgin Mary, these other seers interpreted the lady in this way. Even Eugene himself eventually put aside his first interpretation (that the lady was a sign of his brother's death) and accepted the "Virgin Mary" interpretation. For the sake of argument, I am willing to grant that most of the children were sincere, that is, they really perceived the illusion that they reported. Still, at least one of the seers, Jeanne-Marie Lebosse, retracted her testimony in later life (Galvin, 1970: 97), which means that we cannot rule out entirely the possibility that some of the "seers" did not really see the illusion.

We must also keep in mind that the illusion was certainly not seen by most people present. Even devotional accounts are in agreement that none of the adults present saw the apparition. More importantly, perhaps, there is also some evidence that not all the children present did, either. Although Richard (1971: 26-28) tells us only that Sister Vitaline brought back two girls (Françoise Richer and Jeanne-Marie Lebosse), and that both girls saw the apparition, Walsh (1904d: 106) indicates that Sister Vitaline actually brought back three girls and that the third girl (who is unnamed) did not see the apparition. If that is so, there was at least one child present who did not see the apparition. Given that the commotion at the Barbedette barn had attracted a crowd of around fifty adults, it seems virtually certain that there must have been other children present, as well, and the fact that these other children are not mentioned in devotional accounts suggests that they, like the adults present, did not see the apparition.

As the number of seers increased, and as they began discussing the apparition with each other and with those around them, each seer probably began to add details. Certainly the sudden proliferation of so many different crosses (the small red cross on the lady's tunic, the large cross she held in front of her, the small crosses that appeared over each shoulder) seems consistent with the suggestion that different seers were adding different elements as the apparition progressed. Since each seer made his or her report in the presence of all the others, there was plenty of opportunity to make one element "disappear" before adding something new.

Furthermore, at least some of the elements added by the various seers seem to have been suggested to them—however unconsciously—by the adults present. For instance, the first word that was spelled out in the "writing space" was "mais." A pause followed, and then the words "priez mes enfants." But something had happened in the interval between the "mais" and the rest of the message. A man came upon the crowd and said, "You have only to pray! The Prussians are at Laval" (Richard, 1971: 37). Is it a coincidence that the children suddenly saw "pray my children" beneath the Virgin immediately after hearing a man say "You have only to pray"? I think not. More generally, it seems that there was quite a lot of conversation between the child-seers and the adults who had gathered at the Barbedette barn

(Richard, 1971: 77). Most of that conversation has not been preserved: if it had, I suspect that we would be able to pinpoint the unconscious cues that led to the appearance of the other elements that were added to Eugene's initial illusion.

In summary then, the initial apparition at Pontmain was probably an illusion prompted by the joint occurrence of two events: Eugene Barbedette's anxiety over the possible death of his older brother, an anxiety that had just been intensified by Jeanette Detais' visit, and Eugene's perception of what was undeniably an unusual visual stimulus, the "three stars." The initial illusion of a lady was interpreted by Eugene as indicating his brother's death. But as a result of the addition of new seers, and the negotiation (however unconscious) between these seers and the adults around them, the illusion came to be defined as one more likely to relieve the generalized anxiety prevalent among the villagers in Pontmain: an apparition of the Virgin Mary, who told the villagers, by way of a written message, that their loved ones would be safe if they prayed to Jesus Christ.

By happy coincidence, the Prussians decided not to enter Laval the next day, and an armistice ending hostilities was signed on January 28th, just eleven days after the Pontmain apparition. All this, naturally enough, had the effect of enhancing belief in the reality of that apparition. Though the Church usually acts cautiously in the matter of apparitions, the one at Pontmain was embraced by Church authorities, at least in France, with alacrity. In February 1872, just a little over a year after the apparition, the bishop of Laval issued a pastoral letter, read in all the churches of his diocese, in which he professed his own belief in the reality of the apparition and authorized devotion to "Notre Dame d'Esperance de Pontmain" (Walsh, 1904d: 115). That same year construction began on a basilica at Pontmain, and by 1873, over 100,000 pilgrims had visited the shrine there. Although Pontmain has been somewhat eclipsed by other Marian sanctuaries in France, it still attracts over 300,000 visitors a year.

OUR LADY OF KNOCK

Knock is a small village in County Mayo, in the western part of Ireland.[3] Around 7:00 on the evening of August 21, 1879, it was raining

---

[3] Devotional accounts of the Knock apparition include O'Keefe (1949), Purcell (1961), and M. Walsh (1955, 1970).

heavily in Knock, and one of the villagers, a woman named Mary McLoughlin, was on her way to visit the house of a friend, Margaret Beirne. Mary McLoughlin was unmarried and worked as a housekeeper for the local priest, Archdeacon Cavanaugh. On her way to the Beirne household, Mary McLoughlin glanced toward the local church (which seems to have been two or three hundred yards away) and saw two things: a bright light near the southern wall of the church, and three statues near that wall. She was surprised that Archdeacon Cavanaugh had ordered new statues, and even more that they had been left out in the rain. Nevertheless, she did not give the matter any further thought, and did not mention the statues when she arrived at the Beirne household.

Around 8:00, Mary McLoughlin left the Beirne's accompanied by Mary Beirne, Margaret Beirne's sixteen-year-old daughter. It was still raining heavily. According to the testimony given later by Mary Beirne to Church authorities,[4] she and Mary McLoughlin were about three hundred yards from the church when she (Mary Beirne) saw the statues. Mary Beirne insisted that Mary McLoughlin had not mentioned the statues earlier. Approaching closer to the church (in the company of Mary McLoughlin), Mary Beirne recognized the statues to be the Virgin Mary, St. Joseph, and St. John the Evangelist. Furthermore, she realized that they were not statues at all, since they were floating in the air several feet away from the church wall and at least two feet above the ground. In addition, although it does not appear in Mary Beirne's formal deposition, there is at least one report (Purcell, 1961: 153) that suggests that both Mary McLoughlin and Mary Beirne saw the statues moving.

After a few minutes, Mary Beirne went off to tell others in the village what was happening; Mary McLoughlin remained behind (in the rain) to watch the apparition. Reconstructing what happened next from the testimony given by the fourteen witnesses who reported seeing the apparition at Knock, it appears that Mary Beirne went to at least two households. First, she went to her own household, and four of the people there went to see the apparition: Margaret Beirne (Mary Beirne's mother), a younger Margaret Beirne (Mary's sister), Dominick Beirne (Mary's brother), and Catherine Murray (Mary Beirne's

---

[4] The testimony gathered from the Knock seers in 1879 is reprinted in both O'Keefe (1949: 25-41) and M. Walsh (1955: 19-32). Though devotional accounts put a great deal of weight on this testimony, we should keep in mind that the Church authorities who gathered it never bothered to send their report to Rome.

eight-and-a-half-year-old niece, who was visiting at the time). Mary Beirne also went to the house of Mrs. Judith Campbell, who was caring for her sick mother. A seventy-five-year-old woman named Bridget Trench was visiting with Mrs. Campbell at the time, and both women—Judith Campbell and Bridget Trench—went to the scene of the apparition.

Although Mary Beirne also returned to the scene of the apparition, Dominick Beirne (Mary's brother) went to find still more villagers to tell them about what was happening. Whether Dominick did this before going to the apparition site, or whether he went to the site and then left to spread the news is unclear. In any event, the following individuals told the later inquiry that they were contacted by Dominick Beirne and that they subsequently went to the site and saw the apparition: another Dominick Beirne (an older cousin), Patrick Beirne (age sixteen, another relative), Patrick Hill (an adolescent), John Durkhan, and John Curry (age six and a half). All in all then, Mary and Dominick Beirne brought eleven people to the apparition site. A final person, Mrs. Hugh Flately, came upon the scene herself. All fourteen of these people reported seeing the same apparition.

Not everyone contacted that night was willing to endure the rain in order to see what was going on. At one point Mary McLoughlin went to fetch Archdeacon Cavanaugh himself. Whether because he did not pay attention to what she was saying (and devotional accounts favor this interpretation) or because what she told him was not as precise as she later claimed, the archdeacon did not visit the site. Likewise, in her testimony (O'Keefe, 1949: 29), Mary McLoughlin said that when she first sent Mary Beirne off, she specifically instructed Mary to bring back Mary's uncle Brian Beirne and her aunt, Mrs. Brian Beirne. If these two individuals were present in the Beirne family household, they never came to the apparition.

The apparition at Knock was seen, then, by fourteen different people over a period that lasted from roughly 8:00 to 9:30. Devotional accounts emphasize that all fourteen seers gave the same account of what they saw. This is not quite true. Certain of the accounts, for instance, are far more detailed than others. Further, it is clear that at least some individuals saw things others did not. Two of the young boys present saw angels floating around the three figures, and these angels do not seem to have been seen by anyone else (Purcell, 1961: 155). Still, all the seers did agree on the central features of the apparition, three figures hovering a few feet above the ground, and they all agreed that these three figures were the Virgin Mary, St. Joseph, and St. John the Evangelist.

Was the apparition at Knock an illusion or a hallucination? The relatively large number of seers and the fact that none of the figures spoke would suggest that it was an illusion, that it was (in other words) the misperception of some unusual visual stimulus. This stimulus appears to have been a globe of brilliant light. In their testimony to Church authorities most of the seers specifically associated the apparition with such a light: Patrick Hill reported a clear white light that went up and down; Mary McLoughlin reported a white light around the figures; John Curry reported seeing a light; Judith Campbell reported that there was a beautiful light shining around the figures; and so on. But perhaps the most important information comes from a farmer named Patrick Walsh. He was not at the apparition site, but he was about half a mile away on the night of August 21, and he did glance toward the church. According to the testimony that he gave to Church authorities later, he noticed a "large globe of golden light," more brilliant than anything he had seen before, hanging in the air near the church. But it was only on the following day (August 22) that he made inquiries and found out about the apparition.

In the case of Knock, then, as in the case of Lucia's 1915 apparition and the apparition at Pontmain in 1871, we have some basis for believing that there was an unusual visual stimulus of some sort in the region of the apparition. But what was this stimulus? At the time, unfriendly commentators suggested that the apparition had been produced by a magic lantern, and this suggestion is still kept alive in journalistic accounts of Knock (Whale, 1980: 192). Devotional accounts, however, go out of their way to stress that attempts to duplicate the apparition using magic lanterns were clear failures (O'Keefe, 1949: 23; Purcell, 1961: 162-163), and I have no reason to doubt their conclusion. We do not need to posit anything so crude. If Bernadette Soubirous could hallucinate the apparitions at Lourdes, and if three bright stars could elicit the incredibly complex illusion at Pontmain, then certainly it would not be difficult for the seers at Knock to see three figures in the midst of an amorphous globe of light.

In seeking to explain why the globe of light at Knock came to be seen as an apparition of the Virgin Mary, it is difficult to avoid the conclusion that Mary Beirne played a central role in structuring the perception of the other seers. Devotional accounts suggest that it was Mary McLoughlin who first saw the apparition on her way to the Beirne household, but that she did not initially recognize it for what it was. Nevertheless, whatever Mary McLoughlin saw on that first trip, it was not sufficiently impressive to cause her to investigate further, nor even for her to mention it to the Beirnes. The simplest explanation is to assume that, in fact, Mary McLoughlin saw nothing unusual on her way to visit the Beirnes.

It is only later, when Mary McLoughlin left the Beirne household in the company of young Mary Beirne, that the real story of Knock begins, since it is only then that we get a report suggesting that an apparition was in progress. Further, even devotional accounts make it clear that it was Mary Beirne who first called Mary McLoughlin's attention to the "statues," Mary Beirne who first reported seeing the statues move, and who first identified one of the figures as the Virgin Mary. These observations would suggest that it was Mary Beirne who first planted the suggestion that an apparition of the Virgin Mary was in progress. This conclusion is buttressed by a careful examination of the testimony later collected from each seer by Church authorities (O'Keefe, 1949: 25-41).

For instance, one of the figures was identified by all the seers as St. John the Evangelist. How did they know that it was this saint rather than some other? The figures at no point communicated anything to the seers. The rationale for this identification is, in fact, presented very clearly in the testimony given by Mary Beirne (O'Keefe, 1949: 30-33). She knew it was St. John the Evangelist, she tells us, because the figure resembled a statue of St. John the Evangelist that she had once seen in Lecanvey (another village in County Mayo). Just as the statue in Lecanvey held a book in one hand, so did the figure in the apparition; just as the fingers of the statue's right hand were raised as if in preaching, so too were the fingers of the figure in the apparition, and so on. Although other seers reported seeing the "St. John" figure in the apparition just as Mary Beirne saw it, no other witnesses linked this figure to an actual statue that they themselves had seen. This obviously suggests that Mary Beirne's interpretation of what she saw was influenced by her memories of the statue of St. John the Evangelist that she had seen in Lecanvey, and that she communicated this interpretation to the other seers.

Furthermore, if we examine carefully the testimony of each seer, we can even trace out the precise interpersonal paths over which Mary Beirne's initial report of an apparition diffused to the other seers. For example, the first person to whom Mary Beirne passed her interpretation of what was happening was obviously Mary McLoughlin. But when Mary Beirne returned to her family, we know from the testimony of Dominick Beirne (O'Keefe, 1949: 35) that she explicitly told her family that an apparition of the Virgin Mary was in progress at the church. From the testimony of Bridget Trench (O'Keefe, 1949: 37) we know that Mary Beirne also described the apparition when she arrived at the Campbell household. Similarly, from the testimony of the elder Dominick Beirne (O'Keefe, 1949: 41) and Patrick Beirne (O'-Keefe, 1949: 34), we know that they were explicitly told that an apparition was in progress when they were contacted by the younger Dominick Beirne, Mary's brother.

In other words, the evidence suggests clearly that the suggestion that an apparition was in progress was communicated to all the seers (save Mrs. Hugh Flatley, who came upon the scene by herself) either by Mary Beirne herself or by her brother Dominick. Furthermore, except in the case of Mary McLoughlin and Mrs. Hugh Flatley, the other seers at Knock received Mary Beirne's report of what was happening at the church before they arrived at the site. They arrived in other words, expecting (or at least half-expecting) to see the apparition that they promptly saw. Finally, the documentary record also indicates that information was shared among the seers after they had arrived at the apparition site. Bridget Trench tells us that she took one of the figures to be St. John because this is what she heard those around her saying (O'Keefe, 1949: 37), and young Catherine Murray makes a similar remark (O'Keefe, 1949: 38).

Two questions remain that are central to this analysis: why did Mary Beirne experience the particular illusion she did, and why was her report of what was happening so readily accepted by the other seers? At least part of the answer to the first question can be had by focusing upon one of the more unusual features of the Knock apparition, the fact that the Virgin Mary and the two saints were seen hovering in the air, about two feet off the ground.

Generally, when Mary is seen close by during the course of an apparition, she is resting on something (a chair in the case of the apparition to Catherine Labouré, a bush or small tree in the case of Lourdes or Fatima, and so on). Mary is usually not resting on something only when her image is seen at distance (as in the case of Pontmain or the "holy card" images seen by Lucia during the final Fatima apparition). I know of no other well-known Marian apparition, apart from Knock, in which Mary was seen up close and yet hovering a few feet above the ground.

On the other hand, there is one iconographic situation in which Mary regularly appears a few feet above the ground, and this is in traditional depictions of the Assumption of Mary into heaven in bodily form. Although a belief in Mary's Assumption into heaven was not proclaimed dogma until 1950, the Feast of the Assumption is one of the oldest and most important of all Marian feasts, celebrated at least since the seventh century. Moreover, although the doctrine of the Assumption (like the doctrine of the Immaculate Conception) has generated a certain amount of theological controversy over the years, surveys of lay and clerical opinion in the nineteenth century (O'Carroll, 1982: 56) indicate that by that time a belief in the Assumption had become nearly universal among Catholics. Likewise, both scholarly commentators (Holweck, 1907: 6) and devotional guides (Cabrol, n.d.: 1045) have always suggested that the Assumption was the most important of all Marian feasts. Given the importance of the Assumption to the Mary cult, the event has been the subject of innumerable paintings over the centuries, and virtually all of these portray Mary as hovering a few feet above the ground on her way to heaven (see, for instance, Ferguson, 1976: plates 29, 30). That Mary Beirne saw Mary hovering above the ground in this same manner would suggest that her initial illusion might have been shaped by traditional depictions of the Assumption.

Again, although there is no tradition of St. John the Evangelist appearing with Mary during the course of her earthly apparitions, there is only one situation in which Mary is traditionally paired with St. John the Evangelist, and this, again, involves traditional depictions of the Assumption. Because the New Testament (John 19: 26-27) records that Jesus entrusted the care of his mother to "the disciple he loved," and since pious tradition holds that the "beloved disciple" was the Apostle John, it has become an iconographic convention to include St. John the Evangelist in portrayals of Mary's Assumption (Ferguson, 1976: 76).

The similarity between traditional depictions of the Assumption and the apparition at Knock also provides us with a partial explanation for the timing of that apparition. The Feast of the Assumption was celebrated on August 15, six days prior to the apparition on August 21. More significant, however, is the fact that the Feast of the Assumption was to be celebrated again on the next day, August 22. This is made clear in the preamble to the report prepared by Church authorities in 1879 when investigating the apparition. It states that the alleged apparition occurred "on the evening of the 21st August, the vigil of the octave of the Feast of the Assumption of the Blessed Virgin Mary" (O'Keefe, 1949: 25). An octave is an eight-day period during which a particular feast is celebrated. The most important days of an octave are the first, which is usually the feast day itself, and the last or "octave" day. Granting octave status to a feast is a way of recognizing its importance, and for that reason most such feasts have been associated with Christ (Christmas, Epiphany, Easter, the Ascension, Pentecost, Corpus Christi). Only two Marian feasts have been considered important enough to be associated with octaves, the Assumption and the Immaculate Conception, of which the Assumption, at least around the turn of this century, was considered the more important.

Although no previous commentator on the Knock apparition has suggested that the apparition was modeled upon traditional depictions of the Assumption, the evidence suggests that Mary Beirne's initial illusion was at least in part triggered by the ceremonies surrounding the octave of the Assumption and was shaped by her memories of traditional depictions. It is relevant to add that Dominick Beirne, Mary's brother, was the sacristan for the church at Knock, and that Mary sometimes substituted for him in this role. Mary Beirne was accompanying Mary McLoughlin on the evening of August 21 precisely because she was on her way to lock up the church, a duty usually performed by her brother (Purcell, 1961: 151). As sacristan, Dominick—and possibly Mary Beirne herself, if she substituted for her brother on a regular basis—would have been very much involved in setting up the church for the various devotions that took place during the octave of the Assumption.

On the other hand, this feast was celebrated annually at Knock, and yet obviously did not trigger illusions in Mary Beirne every year. There must have been something special about 1879 that made Mary Beirne, and the seers at Knock generally, more susceptible than usual to the experience of a Marian apparition.

Certainly there was no army invading Ireland. There had been extensive crop failures in County Mayo (and in the rest of Ireland) in 1877 and 1878, and some accounts (Rogo, 1983: 219) attribute the Knock apparition to the stress produced by such failures. But there had been crop failures before, and these had not produced Marian apparitions. I know of no apparitions that occurred in connection with the Great Famine of the 1840s, for instance.

Those familiar with modern Irish history, however, will know that 1879 is the year usually taken as marking the effective beginning of the Irish Land War. This was not, of course, a war in the usual sense. It was a political struggle between two groups, Irish tenant farmers and the mainly absentee landlords who owned the land that these farmers worked.

The Land War was provoked by the extraordinary increase in rents that followed upon the crop failures of 1877 and 1878, and by the mass evictions that took place when thousands of tenant farmers were unable to pay these high rents. To counter these mass evictions, Irish farmers formed themselves into political organizations called "land leagues." Though there were some violent clashes between the land leagues and the landlords and their agents, the best-known tactic employed by the leagues was the complete ostracism of landlords who refused to mitigate their demands. One of the first to undergo such ostracism was Captain Charles Boycott, and so the tactic itself came to be called a boycott. The recent, sociologically oriented account by Clark (1979) makes it clear that although there had been some political activity among farmers in 1877 and 1878, such activity escalated dramatically in 1879, and it is only then that the land leagues were formed in any number.

What seems particularly important from our point of view is that County Mayo, and Knock in particular, was especially hard hit by the evictions. Around the time of the apparition, for instance, we know that eighteen families had been evicted from their land (Purcell, 1961: 148-149). I have been unable to determine the total number of families living in the Knock area in 1879, but we do know that the village of Knock itself included only about a dozen homes (O'Keefe, 1949: 11). It thus seems likely that eighteen families would have constituted a significant proportion of the farm families living in and around Knock. We know for a fact that the people of Knock were much concerned about the evictions around this time. In June 1879 a public demonstration had been held at Knock (and several other villages in

County Mayo) to protest the evictions, and on August 16, just five days before the apparition, one of the first of the land leagues in County Mayo had been formed in Castlebar, 17 miles from Knock (Clarke, 1979: 247). I suggest, then, that it was the threat or the experience of eviction that created in the inhabitants of Knock a strong susceptibility to the suggestion that an apparition of the Virgin Mary was in progress on the evening of August 21.

In summary, then, the people at Knock in 1879 were susceptible to the suggestion that an apparition of the Virgin Mary was in progress for the same reason that the people at Pontmain were susceptible to that suggestion: such an apparition would indicate that the forces of the supernatural world were on their side, and this belief in turn would reduce their anxiety over the threatened loss of their property and their livelihood. Faced with an ambiguous visual stimulus (the mysterious "globe of light"), and presented with Mary Beirne's specific suggestion that there were three figures in that light, corresponding to the Virgin Mary, St. Joseph, and St. John the Evangelist, this susceptibility led the seers at Knock to see the same apparition that Mary Beirne saw.

THE VIRGIN APPEARS AT ZEITOUN

We come now to the final set of apparitions to be considered here, the apparitions of the Virgin at Zeitoun, Egypt in 1968-1971.[5] For many members of the Mary cult, this apparition is particularly important because most of the seers were Muslims.[6] Surely, the usual argument goes, if Muslims see the Virgin, this cannot be attributed to anything but an actual appearance of the Virgin Mary. Such a case would seem to be an exception to one of the patterns so far associated with Marian apparitions, namely, that such apparitions are most likely to occur where the prevailing religious world view legitimizes a belief in Mary's role as a powerful supernatural intercessor. This alone necessitates a consideration of the Zeitoun apparitions.

Zeitoun is a district about fifteen miles north of Cairo. On the evening of April 2, 1968, two men leaving the garage in which they

[5] Descriptions of the apparitions at Zeitoun can be found in Nelson (1973), Palmer (1981), and Rogo (1983: 250-257).
[6] Palmer (1981), for instance, lays great stress on the fact that the seers were mainly Muslims.

worked happened to look up toward the dome of a Coptic Christian church, called the Church of the Holy Virgin. They saw there a figure dressed in white, and thought at first that it was a nun who was about to commit suicide. The police were notified. By the time the police arrived, however, a considerable crowd had gathered. The police tried to disperse this crowd by telling them that the "figure" was nothing more than a reflection of the light from some of the street lamps nearby. But at this point the custodian of the Church of the Virgin made the suggestion that the figure was in fact the Virgin Mary (Nelson, 1973: 5), and this suggestion seems to have been accepted almost immediately by most of the assembled seers. As a result, they did not disperse.

After a few minutes, the figure disappeared. Convinced that an apparition of the Virgin Mary had occurred, crowds of Muslims and Coptic Christians continued to gather at the Church over the next few days in the hope that she would return. Finally, on April 9, she did, though again she remained visible for only a few minutes. After the second appearance, she began to appear quite frequently (often two or three times a week), though at irregular and unpredictable intervals. The crowds continued to grow, of course, and by the end of April it was not unusual for nearly 100,000 people to be in attendance.

Though the apparitions seem to have been little reported in the Western Press,[7] they were a major story in the Arab newspapers. As early as May 1968, a committee set up by the Coptic Patriarchate of Egypt concluded that the apparitions were real. By June, the apparitions had been given de facto approval by the Ministry of Tourism, and this ministry began printing and distributing pamphlets dealing with the events.

It is difficult to get a sense of what the Virgin looked like at Zeitoun, since descriptions varied depending upon the particular apparition (they continued into 1971) and the person being interviewed. Sometimes, for instance, the Virgin was seen full figure; sometimes as a bust. Sometimes she was standing more or less stationary above the dome of the church; sometimes she moved about in the sky. Sometimes her hands were folded; sometimes she was seen to bless the crowd. There were, however, a few constants. Everyone agreed that appearances of the Virgin were usually accompanied by "doves of

[7] The only exception to this pattern that I have been able to locate is a fairly extensive account of the Zeitoun apparitions that appeared in the London *Times* on May 6, 1968.

light," which appear to have been spots of light that flew around the dome and the Virgin at very great speeds. Everyone also agreed that the figure of the Virgin was generally very diffuse, and enveloped by a bright light of some sort, also very diffuse. Finally, everyone agreed that the Virgin at Zeitoun did not speak.

The fact that the Virgin at Zeitoun was seen by so many people, and that she did not speak, would in themselves suggest that the apparitions at Zeitoun—like those at Pontmain and Knock—were illusions. In this case, however, we are fortunate in that Cynthia Nelson, a social scientist teaching in Cairo at the time, investigated the Zeitoun apparitions while they were in progress. Nelson's (1973) article is probably the best account of an apparition in progress presently available, and I have relied upon her report heavily.

Of particular importance to us is Nelson's report of what she saw when she visited the site of the apparition at the end of April 1968:

> When I looked to where the crowds were pointing, I too, thought I saw a light . . . as I tried to picture a nunlike figure . . . I could trace the outlines of [such] a figure. But as I thought to myself that this is just an illusion . . . the image of the nun would leave my field of vision.

It is difficult to imagine a more concise account of how an ambiguous visual stimulus can be converted into an image of the Virgin Mary if that is what the seer intends that he or she should see.

But now we must confront the issue raised at the beginning of this discussion: even granting that there was an ambiguous visual stimulus of some sort above the Church of Our Lady at Zeitoun, why would the mainly Muslim seers present choose to interpret this stimulus as an image of the Virgin Mary? Part of the apparent difficulty, I think, is that most Western Christians are ethnocentric in that they assume that the Muslim attitude toward, say, Jesus Christ and the Virgin Mary is probably similar to the Christian attitude toward Mohammed. Since most believing Christians regard Mohammed as a "false prophet," they assume that most Muslims view Jesus and Mary in a similar manner. But in the Muslim world view, Mohammed is simply the final prophet in a long line of prophets that have been chosen by God to spread his message here on earth. Included as prophets of God in the Islamic tradition are such familiar figures as Moses, David, and Jesus.

To Muslims, all these men were prophets, whose messages have been twisted and misinterpreted by their followers.

Because Jesus is recognized as a prophet of God in the Islamic tradition, his mother—the Blessed Virgin Mary—is also singled out for special attention. As Nelson (1973: 9) points out, the Koran mentions specifically that Allah himself chose Mary, that he made her pure, and that he exalted her above all other women.

There is nothing in Muslim theology, of course, that leads to the conclusion that Mary is a powerful intercessor with God, and therefore that prayers directed at Mary would be particularly efficacious. There is nothing, in other words, that lays the basis for a full-fledged Mary cult. But the fact that the Koran specifically mentions that Mary was chosen by God and exalted by him above all other women does lay the theological foundation for the suggestion that Mary might be chosen as a messenger from God—and this is precisely how the Virgin at Zeitoun seems to have been viewed.

The Virgin's apparitions at Zeitoun occurred just ten months after Egypt's disastrous defeat during the Six-Day War in 1967. That defeat plunged Egypt into a state of national despair, and generated a great deal of anxiety about the future. This was occasioned partly, of course, by the fact that the apparently invincible Israeli army had swept up to the eastern edge of the Suez Canal, and was not far from Cairo (or, for that matter, from Zeitoun).

The Egyptian government had acted to reverse this sense of despair in a number of ways. It had, for instance, arrested and tried several army officers and government officials on whom were placed responsibility for the defeat. On March 30, 1968, just a few days before the apparitions at Zeitoun, President Nasser proclaimed what has come to be known as the "March 30 Manifesto," a document that outlined his plans for the future of Egypt in light of the 1967 defeat.

It seems reasonable to suggest that the apparition at Zeitoun was—like the government actions just mentioned—a response to the anxiety generated by the 1967 defeat. The people of Egypt, in other words, were susceptible to any suggestion which indicated that God was on their side, as such a suggestion would reduce their anxiety over the future. The idea that God might send the Virgin Mary as a sign that he was indeed on their side is consistent with the Koran's view of Mary, and so the people of Egypt would have been very receptive to the possibility that an apparition of the Virgin Mary was in progress at Zeitoun.

Such an interpretation seems validated by the finding that virtually all the seers interviewed by Nelson did associate the Virgin at Zeitoun with the 1967 defeat, and did interpret her appearance there as a *bishara kheir*, a sign of good things to come (Nelson 1973: 8). This popular view of the Zeitoun apparitions was also encouraged by a number of official groups. Shortly after the Coptic authorities issued their endorsement of the Zeitoun apparitions, the Coptic patriarch of Egypt suggested at a news conference that the apparitions might be an omen indicating that God would insure an Arab victory against the Israelis in the future (Nelson, 1973: 9).

But even granting that Egyptians might be generally receptive to the idea that God might send an image of Mary as a sign of his favor, why did the apparitions occur specifically at Zeitoun? Remember that the initial identification of the figure at Zeitoun as the Virgin Mary came not from the two garage workers who first saw this figure, but from the Christian custodian of the Church of the Virgin. It is hardly unlikely that a Christian, when confronted with a luminous figure atop a church called the Church of the Virgin, might suggest that this figure is the Virgin Mary.

But perhaps more importantly, Christians were not the only ones who would have been predisposed to see Mary in or around Zeitoun. It is a well-established local tradition, accepted by both Christians and Muslims, that Zeitoun was one of the places visited by the Holy Family when they fled Palestine to Egypt in order to avoid the Slaughter of the Innocents ordered by King Herod. The same local tradition suggests that during this flight, the Virgin rested under a large sycamore tree that still stands near Zeitoun. Because of its association with the Virgin, this sycamore has been considered sacred by most Muslims and Christians in the area, and local women (both Muslim and Christian) have traditionally left votive offerings in that tree if they wanted to bear children and could not (Nelson, 1973: 9).

In summary, then, Muslims in Zeitoun would have been predisposed to see a Marian apparition not only because such an apparition (if interpreted as a sign from God) was consistent with the Koran's treatment of Mary but also because Muslims, like Christians, strongly associated Mary with the Zeitoun area. Given this—together with the undeniable reality of a luminous something atop the Church of the Virgin in Zeitoun, the susceptibility of Egyptians at this time to the suggestion that God would send them a sign of a better future, and the specific suggestion (first proposed by a Christian) that the figure was the Virgin Mary—then it is not really surprising that so many of the seers at Zeitoun were Muslim.

The Zeitoun case is not the only one in which a significant number of Muslims have seen the Virgin Mary. For instance, an Associated Press report in the *Toronto Star* on September 4, 1983, indicated that a nonspeaking image of the Virgin had appeared on a wall in a village near Bethlehem, and had been seen by hundreds of Palestinian Arabs. Though the village in question is mainly Christian, the report implies that a substantial number of the seers were Muslim. In this case, again, the apparition occurred in an area strongly associated with Mary in both Christian and Muslim tradition. It is likely that other reports of Marian apparitions seen by Muslims have appeared in Arabic newspapers over the last thirty years.

CONCLUSION

Anyone who reads accounts of the apparitions at Pontmain, Knock, and Zeitoun must inevitably become curious about the nature of the visual stimulus that elicited the Marian illusion at each of these places. What were those three bright stars at Pontmain? What produced the globe of light near the church at Knock? What was the nature of that luminous figure atop the church at Zeitoun? Some speculation is possible. For instance, given that a heavy rain fell during the entire period of the apparition at Knock, the globe of light may well have been produced by some meteorological process. Generally, however, it seems wisest to say that in all these cases we simply do not know what produced these visual events.

Mysterious lights are the stock in trade of any number of folk traditions, and are also discussed in books dealing with the paranormal (see, for instance, Michell and Rickard, 1977: 26-27). The simplest way to account for these reports is to assume that lights of uncertain origin do occasionally appear (probably for a variety of different reasons), and are interpreted in a number of different ways. Sometimes they are labeled "ball lightening," sometimes "will-o-the-wisps," sometimes "fairy lights," and, of course, sometimes "UFOs." Under

the right set of circumstances, they are sometimes considered apparitions of the Virgin Mary.

It also seems clear that those Marian illusions which come to our
attention are likely to be those in which the physical source of the illusion is difficult to uncover, whereas those which are "obvious" illusions tend to be forgotten. Consider, for instance, two Marian illusions that seem to have been forgotten. The first occurred in January
1920, when a number of people in Noveant (Lorraine), France, reported seeing an image of the Virgin Mary near a churchyard. The
image resembled traditional images of the Virgin, was seen by a number of different people, more or less at the same time each day. The
local priest investigated, however, and found that the image was produced by the shadows cast by two very distant trees. It just happened
that at sunset each day (at least in January), the shadows of these two
trees combined to form an image that did look exactly like traditional
images of the Virgin. Closer to home, a house in San Antonio, Texas,
began to attract a number of observers (some devout, some not) in
September 1983, when an image of the Virgin appeared on an outside
wall. In this case, however, it was clear even to the devout that the image was produced by a porch light reflecting off a car bumper. If the
car was shaken, the image moved; if the porch light was turned off, it
disappeared.[8] The apparition at Noveant did continue to attract a large
number of pilgrims for a while, even after the priest proposed his
"shadow" explanation, but it did not become the basis of a continuing
cult. I have heard no further reports of the apparition at San Antonio.
Presumably, the very obviousness of the physical process producing
these illusions made it unlikely that either would become the focus of
a continuing cult. If a Marian illusion does become the focus of a continuing cult, then, the nature of the visual stimulus that elicited the illusion was presumably not obvious. If these processes were not obvious at the time that they were occurring, they are certainly not
going to be easily identified now.

There is one final point that must be made about Marian illusions,
and it has to do with the number of seers. In Chapter Six, the relatively large number of seers associated with Marian illusions, as compared to Marian hallucinations, was attributed to the fact that in the

---

[8] Reports dealing with the illusion at Noveant were carried in the *New York Times* on January
25 and January 29, 1920. An Associated Press report dealing with the illusion in San Antonio
was carried in the *London Free Press* (London, Ontario) on September 6, 1983.

case of an illusion there is really something there to see. It now appears that this formulation was incomplete. Although the presence of a real visual stimulus creates the potential for the resulting illusion to be seen by a relatively large number of seers, this is not going to happen unless there are a relatively large number of seers present who are predisposed to perceive that illusion. The analysis of the three cases in this chapter suggests that a relatively large number of seers will see a Marian apparition only when, first, they confront an unusual stimulus of some sort; second, they are experiencing great anxiety over the future; third, someone makes the explicit suggestion that an apparition of the Virgin Mary is in progress; and fourth, their religious world view legitimates the belief that an apparition of the Virgin Mary might be a sign from God that He is on their side. It was the concatenation of all these things in the case of Pontmain, Knock, and (especially) Zeitoun that produced the relatively large number of seers associated with these particular apparitions.

CONCLUSION

From the perspective of say, 1960, an adherent of the Mary cult could easily have argued that the preceding century and a half had been a period of great advance in Marian devotion. The nineteenth century had witnessed three of the best-known of all Marian apparitions—those at Paris, LaSalette, and Lourdes—and all three had given rise to important devotional practices. Then too, after nearly a thousand years of theological debate, the Church had finally committed itself irrevocably to a belief in Mary's Immaculate Conception by proclaiming that belief a dogma in 1854. The intensity of Marian devotion could also be seen in the fact that virtually every one of the several dozen new religious orders for women founded during the nineteenth century was dedicated to the Virgin Mary (Laurentin, 1964: 10).

This upsurge in Marian devotion intensified in the twentieth century, when there were more apparitions, the most notable being those at Fatima. The early twentieth century saw the formation of a number of very popular lay organizations, all affecting a military style and all dedicated to winning the world for Mary: The Militia of the Immaculate Conception was founded in 1917, the Legion of Mary in 1921, and the Blue Army in 1947. There was also a dramatic increase in the number of Marian sodalities, that is, local groups whose members were drawn from the same occupational and social strata, which were formed for the purpose of promoting Marian devotion. Writing in the late 1940s, Pope Pius XII (1948: 2) could boast that although the number of local sodalities seeking certification from Rome had never exceeded ten a year before 1900, the number had grown into the thousands per year. Church authorities and Catholic theologians fanned the flames of this increasing devotion to Mary in a variety of ways. Between 1948 and 1958, for instance, there were over 126 Marian Congresses held in various cities around the world, and 1954 was proclaimed the Marian Year by Pius XII. One estimate (Laurentin, 1964:

(219)

11) suggests that by the late 1950s nearly a thousand new books on Mary were being published every year, and this includes only scholarly works, not the thousands of devotional books and pamphlets that must also have been published.

All this changed quite suddenly, mainly as a result of a change in the Church's official attitude toward Mary. This change became evident during the Second Vatican Council in the early 1960s. During the first session of this Council, an attempt was made by pro-Marian bishops to persuade the Council to commit itself to developing a separate document dealing specifically with Mary. To the surprise of many, this attempt failed. During the second session of the Council, other groups proposed instead that Mary be discussed as part of the conciliar document dealing with the Church itself. Though many pro-Marian bishops argued that this might be construed as a slight upon Mary, in fact the proposal passed, if by only 50 votes out of a total of 2,180. The significance of this decision lay in the fact that in tying the discussion of Mary to a discussion of the Church, limits were set to the degree to which Mary could be aggrandized. One commentator at the time (Butler, quoted in Neame, 1967: 262) expressed this by pointing out that if Mary had been discussed in "lonely independence," then "Marian maximalism would find no checks to its extravagant flights."

More important, perhaps, is what the Council said in its statement on Mary (see Abbott, 1966: 85-96). Although no new dogma or doctrine was proclaimed, the emphasis in this document clearly ran counter to the Marian zeal that had been building for a century and a half. In talking about "The Role of the Blessed Virgin in the Economy of Salvation," for instance, the Council rooted its arguments solidly in the New Testament, and pointedly did not make much use of those extra-Biblical traditions that have always been dear to adherents of the Mary cult and offensive to Protestants. Although the Council's discussion of "Devotion to the Virgin Mary in the Church" said nothing to suggest that such devotion was unwarranted, it reiterated that this devotion must be subordinated to the worship of God. We are told that the veneration of Mary should be seen primarily as an aid to the adoration of Christ, that the Mary cult differs essentially from the Christocentric "cult of adoration," and that theologians and "preachers of the divine word" must be careful to "avoid the falsity of exaggeration" with respect to the Mary cult. The Council's statement also notes that although Mary has been given the title of "Mediatrix," this should not be construed as detracting in any way from the fact that there is only one true Mediator between God and humankind, and that is Jesus Christ. In emphasizing the need to subordinate the Mary cult to the Christ cult, and the need to avoid the excesses associated with some forms of Marian devotion, the Council was implicitly suggesting that there were many in the Church who had lost sight of these things. Pope John XIII himself, the person responsible for convening the Council, had in fact made this explicit by pointing out that "the Madonna is not pleased when she is placed up above her son" (quoted in Graef, 1963a: i).

Marian devotion did not, of course, die out in the post-Vatican II era, but it did subside considerably. For instance, although there have been a few Marian congresses since Vatican II, there have not been nearly as many as there had been before. Fewer scholarly books are written about Mary, and those that are tend to be less concerned with providing theological justification for Mary's preeminence in the Christian pantheon than with discussing the need to modify our image of Mary in order to make her more "relevant" to the modern age (for a review of this recent literature, see Cunningham, 1982: 93-104). Of all the lay armies dedicated to conquering the world for Mary, the only one that appears to be still functioning is the Blue Army of Our Lady of Fatima.

There is a certain sense of *déja vu* in this apparently sudden reversal in the fortunes of the Mary cult. Prior to the Reformation, it would have seemed to outside observers that the Mary cult was firmly entrenched in a great many of the societies that eventually embraced Protestantism. In England, for instance, an observer could easily have pointed to the fact that the Marian shrine at Walsingham was the most popular English Christian shrine as evidence of England's commitment to Mary. Yet when the Reformation came, the English had little difficulty in converting "Our Lady of Walsingham" to "The Witch of Walsingham," razing that shrine, and generally purging devotion to Mary from an Anglicanism that otherwise looked very much like Roman Catholicism. What happened to the apparently strong support for the Mary cult? How could it have evaporated so fast?

The answer, or at least the answer suggested here, is that because the Mary cult does have some universal appeal (since devotion to Mary does gratify the Oedipal desires of both sexes), it will flourish whenever it is encouraged by those in power, whether secular or religious. But this appeal is not sufficiently strong to sustain the Mary cult in the absence of such official encouragement. When official support for the cult ceases, for whatever reason, then the cult will die out. The cult thus disappeared in those areas in which Protestantism came to power, and could easily fade away in the modern age should the diminution of the Church's support for the cult, begun at Vatican II, continue unabated.

The analysis in this book suggests that the only exception to this pattern will occur in those areas where the prevailing form of family organization produces in sons a desire for the mother that is especially strong and strongly repressed, as in areas where the father-ineffective family prevails. There the Mary cult is likely to flourish regardless of official encouragement. It is in these same areas, of course, that we are most likely to find those masochistic elements (such as an emphasis upon Christ's Passion) that have always accompanied the Mary cult.

The future of the Mary cult, then, is assured only in those areas— like southern Italy and Spain—where it has always been the most successful, since the father-ineffective family is still common in these regions. Although this book has been concerned mainly with the Mary cult in Europe, it seems clear from the work of Oscar Lewis and others that the father-ineffective family is widespread in Latin America, as well, and so I would expect the Mary cult to remain strong there, too. As for the cult's success in most other areas of the world, this will depend almost entirely upon the position taken by Church authorities.

There is some basis for believing that the Church's position on Mary might be moving back to what it was in the pre-Vatican II period. If this is true, then possibly the Mary cult will experience a modest revival. There seems little doubt, for instance, that John Paul II has a deep personal attachment to Mary. This is not surprising, given John Paul's Polish origins and the strength of the Mary cult in modern Poland. When he was simply Cardinal Wojtyla, his Krakow archdiocese included Jasna Góra, location of the most important of all Marian shrines in Poland. Virtually every important speech made by John Paul since his accession includes a reference to Mary and the need for Marian devotion. In his first two years as pope, John Paul made a point of visiting and delivering major speeches at the shrine of Our Lady of Guadalupe in Mexico, the Shrine of Our Lady of Knock in

Ireland, and of course, the shrine of Our Lady of Czestochowa at Jasna Góra, Poland.

If the pope's personal popularity causes devotion to Mary to be widely endorsed by a cross-section of the Church hierarchy, then we might witness a Marian revival within the Church. But even if this occurs, we must remember that it could just as easily be reversed should one of John Paul's successors chose to emphasize anew a program of Marian restraint. The important point is that the Mary cult will remain strong regardless of Church encouragement only in those areas where the prevailing form of family organization produces in sons the especially strong but strongly repressed desire for the mother that has always been the psychological wellspring of Marian devotion.

Before ending this investigation, I would like to discuss the often-made suggestion that the Catholic image of Mary is likely to undergo a change in the near future, and more specifically, that Catholics should think of Mary less as a supernatural being with a distinct personality and more as some sort of metaphor or symbol. Such a suggestion, for instance, seems implicit in the attempt by Vatican II to establish a metaphorical equivalence between Mary and the Church. Thus, in its statement on Mary, Vatican II tells us that Mary was "the first flowering of the Church, the model of the Church," that the Church like Mary is Virgin, that in Mary the Church has already reached perfection, and so on. Andrew Greeley (1977) has argued that there is a need for the Mary cult, since in worshiping Mary we are really only worshiping the feminine side of God. Cunningham (1982) has made a similar argument by suggesting that in seeking Mary's maternal protection we are seeking an aspect of God normally denied us by the patriarchal view of God that is part of the Western tradition. Rahner (1981: 140-141) has predicted that the Catholicism of the future will be based almost exclusively upon "essential Christian piety," and argues that the same set of spiritual beliefs will underlie all forms of Catholic devotion. This will have the effect of blurring devotional distinctions now considered important. With regard to the Mary cult, for instance, he argues that although Catholics will continue to venerate Mary, they will venerate her as a general symbol of certain Christian virtues, and not under her many, unique titles. In his own words, "we will speak of Jesus but not the Infant of Prague. We will speak of Mary but have less to do with Lourdes and Fatima."

All of this strikes me as highly unlikely. Under the argument presented here, Mary's popularity derives primarily from the fact that she is a mother goddess disassociated from sexuality. Yet the changes just discussed, if they would have any effect at all, would diminish or obscure this unique association of elements. For instance, if Mary is changed so that she is not just a person but also a metaphor for the Church, then—if anything—this should make it harder for sons to see Mary as a straightforward projection of their own flesh-and-blood mothers. Likewise, if Mary becomes simply the feminine side of God, then in venerating Mary are we really venerating a mother goddess disassociated from sexuality, or something far more general and far more all-encompassing? I expect, then, that the Mary who continues to be venerated within the Church will be the same Mary who has, at least since the fifth century, been venerated there, and that suggestions about making Mary a symbol or metaphor represent wishful thinking on the part of liberal theologians for whom traditional Marian devotion is a bit embarrassing.

Rahner's comments, in particular, seem to me to be off the mark. In the eyes of the believer, Mary's decision to appear at particular places at particular times is one of the things that most clearly establishes her as a distinct supernatural personality. Venerating Mary at the shrines associated with these sites, then, becomes a way of affirming Mary's separate identity as a powerful mother goddess. I see no reason for any of this to change. I expect, then, that Marian devotion in the future will be as much centered around Our Lady of Lourdes, Our Lady of Fatima, Our Lady of Guadalupe, and so on as in the past. Nor is there any reason to believe that apparitions of the Virgin Mary, at least in predominantly Catholic areas, will cease, since the processes producing these apparitions are as likely to operate in the future as in the past. I therefore expect that the Queen of Heaven will visit this world in the next thousand years about as often as she has during the past thousand years, and that some of the shrines to be associated with these future apparitions will come to rival Lourdes and Guadalupe.

More generally, there will be a cult devoted to Mary (or Cybele or whatever She comes to be called) as long as there are economic conditions that produce the father-ineffective family. And as long as there is a cult devoted to Her, there will be people who speak with the Goddess face to face.

THE SAMPLE OF FIFTY APPARITIONS USED IN CHAPTER SIX

Name of Central Seer	Site of the Apparition(s)	Reference to Walsh (1906)
1. Unknown	Thetford, England	I, 251–256
2. St. Norbert	Premontre, France	I, 273–278
3. Thomas à Becket	England	I, 281–284
4. B. Hermann Joseph	Cologne, Germany	I, 311–314
5. Alice Craft	Warwickshire, England	I, 325–328
6. St. Dominic	Prouille, France	I, 353–364
7. B. Reginald	Rome, Italy	II, 17–19
8. St. Hyacinth	Kiev, Russia	II, 25–29
9. B. Albert	Padua, Italy	II, 37–40
10. St. Peter Nolasco	Barcelona, Spain	II, 47–52
11. St. Raymond Nonnatus	Catalonia, Spain	II, 53–55
12. Monaldi Bonfilius	Florence, Italy	II, 57–72
13. St. Simon Stock	Cambridge, England	II, 77–87
14. St. Peter Celestine	Aquila, Italy	II, 107–108
15. St. Mechtilde	Heldelfs, Germany	II, 115–124
16. St. Gertrude	Heldelfs, Germany	II, 127–144
17. B. Benvenuta Bojani	Cividale, Austria	II, 147–150
18. Paul of the Wood	Recanati, Italy	II, 151–158
19. St. Clare	Rimini, Italy	II, 161–162
20. St. Angela	Foligno, Italy	II, 163–169
21. St. Nicholas	Tolentine, Italy	II, 171–173
22. Pope John XXII	Avignon, France	II, 175–179
23. St. Bridget	Alvastra, Sweden	II, 181–187
24. St. Catharine	Siena, Italy	II, 189–206
25. B. Mary Mancini	Pisa, Italy	II, 209–211
26. St. Bernadine	Siena, Italy	II, 239–258
27. St. Veronica	Milan, Italy	II, 285–288
28. Thierry Schoere	Alsace, France	II, 309–311
29. Domenica	Florence, Italy	II, 373

Name of Central Seer	Site of the Apparition(s)	Reference to Walsh (1906)
30. Juan Diego	Mexico	III, 13-22
31. St. Teresa	Avila, Spain	III, 27-34
32. St. Stanislaus	Vienna, Austria	III, 41-57
33. St. Alphonsus	Valenica, Spain	III, 59-66
34. St. Aloysius Gonzaga	Italy	III, 91-94
35. Thomas Michaelek	Lezajsk, Poland	III, 101-103
36. Michael de La Fontaine	Peru	III, 105-106
37. St. Rose	Lima, Peru	III, 125-136
38. V. Ursula Benicasa	Naples, Italy	III, 137-145
39. B. John Massias	Lima, Peru	III, 147-149
40. Benoite Rencure	Laus, France	III, 191-200
41. B. Margaret Alaloque	Paray-le-Monial, France	III, 209-231
42. Catherine Lebouré	Paris, France	III, 275-288
43. Unknown	Montana	III, 291-292
44. Pierre-Maximin Giraud	LaSalette, France	III, 305-336
45. Bernadetta Soubirous	Lourdes, France	IV, 17-25
46. Francis M. Shanuboga	Dassapore, India	IV, 35-38
47. Mary Wilson	St. Louis, Missouri	IV, 45-55
48. Mary Kade	Philippsdorf, Bohemia	IV, 59-70
49. Estelle Faguette	Pellevoisin, France	IV, 119-148
50. Jean Madelaine	Tilly-sur-Seulles, France	IV, 205-217

ABBOTT, WALTER M., S.J. (ed.)
1966   *The Documents of Vatican II.* New York: Guild Press.

ALTHEIM, FRANZ
1938   *A History of Roman Religion.* London: Methuen.

ANONYMOUS
1854   "On supposed apparitions of the Virgin Mary; and particularly at LaSalette." *Gentleman's Magazine and Historical Review* 41: 10-17.

APULEIUS, LUCIUS
1928   *The Golden Ass, Being the Metamorphoses of Lucius Apuleius.* W. Adlington, tr. Revised by S. Gasalee. London: William Heinemann.

ARNOBIUS
1886   *The Seven Books of Arnobius Against the Heathen. In The Ante-Nicene Fathers.* Volume 6. Rev. Alexander Roberts and James Donaldson, eds. Buffalo: Christian Literature Company.

ASHE, GEOFFREY
1957   *King Arthur's Avalon.* Revised edition. London: Collins.
1973   *The Finger and the Moon.* London: Heinemann.
1976   *The Virgin.* London: Routledge and Kegan Paul.

ASHE, GEOFFREY (ed.)
1968   *The Quest for Arthur's Britain.* New York: Praeger.

AUG, ROBERT, and BILLIE S. ABLES
1971   "Hallucinations in nonpsychotic children." *Child Psychiatry and Human Development* 1: 152-167.

AUGUSTINE
1887   *The City of God. In Nicene and Post-Nicene Fathers of the Christian Church.* Philip Schaff, ed. 11: 1-511. Buffalo: Christian Literature Company.

BALSDON, J.P.V.D.
1969   *Life and Leisure in Ancient Rome.* London: Bodley Head.
1983   *Roman Women: Their History and Habits.* New York: Harper &
[1962] Row.

BAUS, KARL
1980   "The development of the Church of the Empire within the framework of the Imperial religious policy." *In The Imperial Church from Constantine to the Early Middle Ages.* K. Baus, H.-G. Beck, E. W. Ewig, and H. J. Vogt, eds., pp. 1-89. New York: Seabury Press.

BENDER, LAURETTA

1954 *A Dynamic Psychopathology of Childhood*. Springfield, Ill.: Charles C. Thomas.

1970 "The maturation process and hallucinations in children." *In Origin and Mechanisms of Hallucinations*, Wolfram Keup, ed., pp. 95-101. New York: Plenum Press.

BENET, SULA

1951 *Song, Dance and Customs of Peasant Poland*. New York: Roy Publishers.

BENNET, J. W.

1968 "Paternalism." *In International Encyclopedia of the Social Sciences*. David L. Sills, ed., 11: 472-477. New York: Macmillan.

BENZ, ERNST

1963 *The Eastern Orthodox Church*. Chicago: Aldine.

BILLET, BERNARD

1973 "Le fait des apparitions non reconnues par l'Eglise." *In Vraies et fausses apparitions dans L'église*. B. Billet, J.-M. Alonso, B. Bobrinsky, M. Oraison, and R. Laurentin eds., pp. 5-54. Paris: Editions P. Lethielleux.

BLISS, EUGENE L., and LINCOLN D. CLARK

1962 "Visual hallucinations." *In Hallucinations*. Louis J. West, ed., pp. 92-107. New York: Grune and Stratton.

BLUE ARMY

1982 *Blue Army Manual*. Washington, N.J.: Blue Army of Our Lady of Fatima Headquarters.

BORD, JANET, and COLIN BORD

1982 *Earth Rites: Fertility Practices in Pre-industrial Britain*. London: Granada.

BOURNE, FRANK C.

1966 *A History of the Romans*. Boston: D.C. Heath.

BOUTRY, PHILIPPE

1982 "Marie, la grande consolatrice de la France au XIXᵉ siècle." *L'Histoire* 50 (November): 30-39.

BOXER, C. R.

1975 *Mary and Misogyny: Women in the Iberian Expansion Overseas, 1415-1815*. London: Duckworth.

BRANDES, STANLEY H.

1980 *Metaphors of Masculinity*. Philadelphia: University of Pennsylvania Press.

BRANSTON, BRIAN

1957 *The Lost Gods of England*. London: Thames and Hudson.

BRAUDEL, FERNAND

1973 *The Mediterranean and the Mediterranean World in the Age of*
[*1949*] *Philip II.* Volume 2. New York: Harper & Row.

BRIERRE DE BOISMONT, A.

1855 *A History of Dreams, Visions, Apparitions, Ecstasy, Magnetism*
[*1846*] *and Somnambulism.* Philadelphia: Lindsay and Blakiston.

BROWN, ROGER

1965 *Social Psychology.* New York: Free Press.

BROWN, ROGER, and A. GILMAN

1960 "The pronouns of power and solidarity." *In Style in Language.*
T. A. Sebeok, ed., pp. 253-276. Cambridge: MIT Press.

BULGAKOV, SERGIUS

1935 *The Orthodox Church.* London: Centenary Press.

BURTON, ROGER V., and JOHN W. M. WHITING

1961 "The absent father and cross-sex identity." *Merrill-Palmer Quarterly*
7 (April): 85-95.

CABROL, ABBOT (ed.)

n.d. *The Roman Missal.* 12th edition revised. New York: P. J. Kenedy
and Sons.

CAMPBELL, J. K.

1966 "Honour and the devil." *In Honour and Shame.* J. G. Peristiany, ed.,
pp. 139-170. Chicago: University of Chicago Press.

CARCOPINO, JEROME

1970 *Daily Life in Ancient Rome.* Harmondsworth: Penguin.
[1941]

CARROLL, EAMON R.

1978 "The Virgin." Book review, *Catholic Historical Review* 64: 101-102.

CARROLL, MICHAEL P.

1978 "Freud on homosexuality and the super-ego: some cross-cultural
tests." *Behavior Science Research* 13: 255-271.

1979 "The sex of our gods." *Ethos* 7 (Spring): 37-50.

1982 "The rolling head: towards a revitalized psychoanalytic perspective
on myth." *Journal of Psychoanalytic Anthropology* 5 (Winter): 29-56.

1983 "Visions of the Virgin Mary: the effect of family structures on
Marian apparitions." *Journal for the Scientific Study of Religion* 22
(September): 205-221.

1985 "The Virgin Mary at LaSalette and Lourdes: whom did the children see?" *Journal for the Scientific Study of Religion* 24 (March): 56-
74.

1985a "The trickster feigns death and commits incest: some methodological contributions to the study of myth." *Behavior Science Research*
19 (September): 24-57.

CHAPMAN, JOHN

    1911   "Montanists." *In The Catholic Encyclopedia.* 10: 521-524. New York: Robert Appleton.

CHESHIRE, NEIL

    1975   *The Nature of Psychodynamic Interpretation.* London: John Wiley and Sons.

CHRISTIAN, WILLIAM A., Jr.

    1972   *Person and God in a Spanish Valley.* New York: Academic Press.

    1981a *Local Religion in Sixteenth-Century Spain.* Princeton: Princeton University Press.

    1981b *Apparitions in Late Medieval and Renaissance Spain.* Princeton: Princeton University Press.

CLARK, SAMUEL

    1979   *Social Origins of the Irish Land War.* Princeton: Princeton University Press.

CLARKE, EDITH

    1957   *My Mother Who Fathered Me.* London: Allen and Unwin.

COREN, HARRY Z., and JOEL S. SALDINGER

    1967   "Visual hallucinosis in children: a report of two cases." *The Psychoanalytic Study of the Child* 22: 331-356.

COX, MICHAEL J.

    1956   *Rain for These Roots.* Milwaukee: Bruce Publishing Co.

CROSS, TOM PEETE

    1952   *Motif-Index of Early Irish Literature.* Bloomington: Indiana University Press.

CUNNINGHAM, LAWRENCE

    1982   *Mother of God.* San Francisco: Harper & Row.

DAVIES, NORMA

    1981   *God's Playground: A History of Poland.* Volume 1. Oxford: Clarendon Press.

DAVIS, ELIZABETH GOULD

    1972   *The First Sex.* New York: Penguin.

DELHAY, P.

    1967   "History of celibacy." *In New Catholic Encyclopedia.* 3: 369-374. New York: McGraw-Hill.

DEMAREST, DONALD, and COLEY TAYLOR

    1956   *The Dark Virgin: The Book of Our Lady of Guadalupe.* Freeport, Maine: Coley Taylor.

DENIS-BOULET, NOELLE M.

    1960   *The Christian Calendar.* New York: Hawthorn Publishers.

DIRVIN, JOSEPH I.

1958   *Saint Catherine Labouré of the Miraculous Medal.* New York: Farrar, Straus and Cudahy.

1961   *The Lady of the Miraculous Medal. In A Woman Clothed with the Sun.* John J. Delaney, ed., pp. 63-86. Garden City, N.Y.: Doubleday.

1967   "Miraculous Model." *In New Catholic Encyclopedia.* 9: 894-895. San Francisco: McGraw-Hill.

DU BOULAY, JULIET

1974   *Portrait of a Greek Mountain Village.* Oxford: Clarendon Press.

DUFF, A. M.

1958   *Freedmen in the Early Roman Empire.* Cambridge: Heffer and Sons.

DUNDES, ALAN

1962   "The Earth-Diver: creation of the mythopoeic male." *American Anthropologist* 64 (June): 1,032-1,051.

1980   "The hero pattern and the life of Jesus." *In Interpreting Folklore.* Alan Dundes, ed., pp. 223-261. Bloomington: Indiana University Press.

DURKHEIM, EMILE, and MARCEL MAUSS

1963   *Primitive Classification.* Translated by Rodney Needham. Chicago:
[1903] University of Chicago Press.

EICKELMAN, DALE F.

1981   *The Middle East: An Anthropological Perspective.* Englewood Cliffs, N.J.: Prentice-Hall.

EISENBERG, LEON

1962   "Hallucinations in children." *In Hallucinations.* Louis J. West, ed., pp. 198-207. New York: Grune and Stratton.

EISENSTADT, S. N., and LOUIS RONIGER

1980   "Patron-client relationships as a model of structuring social exchange." *Comparative Studies in Society and History* 22 (January): 42-77.

ELIADE, MARCEA

1958   *Patterns in Comparative Religion.* New York: New American Library.

ELIOT, ETHEL COOK

1961   "Our Lady of Guadalupe in Mexico." *In A Woman Clothed with the Sun.* John J. Delaney, ed., pp. 39-60. Garden City, N.Y.: Doubleday.

EMBER, MELVIN, and CAROL R. EMBER

1971   "The conditions favoring matrilocal versus patrilocal residence." *American Anthropologist* 73 (June): 571-594.

ESMAN, AARON H.
  1962 "Visual hallucinoses in young children." *The Psychoanalytic Study of the Child* 17: 334-343.
ESTRADE, J. B.
  1946 *The Appearances of the Blessed Virgin Mary at the Grotto of Lourdes:*
  [1899] *Personal Souvenirs of an Eye-Witness.* Dublin: Clonmore and Reynolds.
FARNELL, LEWIS RICHARD
  1907 *The Cults of the Greek States.* Volume 3. Oxford: Clarendon.
FEDOTOV, G. P.
  1966 *The Russian Religious Mind.* Volume 2. Cambridge: Harvard University Press.
FEINBERG, I.
  1970 "Hallucinations, dreaming and REM sleep." *In Origin and Mechanisms of Hallucinations.* Wolfram Keup, ed., pp. 125-132. New York: Plenum Press.
FERGUSON, GEORGE
  1976 *Signs and Symbols in Christian Art.* London: Oxford University Press.
FERGUSON, JOHN
  1970 *The Religions of the Roman Empire.* Ithaca, N.Y.: Cornell University Press.
  1980 *Greek and Roman Religion: A Sourcebook.* Park Ridge, N.J.: Noyes Press.
FOY, FELICIAN A. (ed.)
  1977 *Catholic Almanac.* Huntington, Ind.: Our Sunday Visitor.
  1980 *Catholic Almanac.* Huntington, Ind.: Our Sunday Visitor.
FRANK, TENNEY (ed.)
  1938 *An Economic Survey of Ancient Rome.* 5 volumes. Baltimore: Johns Hopkins University Press.
FRAZER, SIR JAMES
  1929 Publii Ovidii Nasonis Fastorum Libri Sex: *the* Fasti *of Ovid.* Volume 3. London: Macmillan.
FREMY, DOMINIQUE, and MICHELE FREMY (eds.)
  1984 "Pelerinage et apparitions." *Quid.* Paris: Editions Robert Laffont, pp. 562-566.
FREUD, SIGMUND
  1953 *The Interpretation of Dreams.* In the *Standard Edition of the Complete*
  [1900] *Psychological Works of Sigmund Freud* (hereafter abbreviated as S.E.) 4: 1-338, 5: 339-627. London: Hogarth Press.
  1955a "A child is being beaten." S.E. 17: 179-204.
  [1919]

1955b *Totem and Taboo.* s.e. 13: 1-164.
[1913]

1959 "Obsessive actions and religious practices." s.e. 9: 117-127.
[1907]

1961a "A seventeenth-century demonological analysis." s.e. 19: 65-105.
[1923]

1961b "The economic problem of masochism." s.e. 19: 157-172.
[1924]

1961c *The Future of an Illusion.* s.e. 21: 3-58.
[1927]

1961d *Civilization and Its Discontents.* s.e. 21: 57-145.
[1930]

1964 *New Introductory Lectures on Psychoanalysis.* s.e. 22: 1-182.
[1932]

FRIEDL, ERNESTINE
1962 *Vasilika: A Village in Modern Greece.* New York: Holt, Rinehart and Winston.

GAGER, JOHN G.
1975 *Kingdom and Community: The Social World of Early Christianity.* Englewood Cliffs, N.J.: Prentice-Hall.

GALVIN, NAIRN
1970 "*Chronicle*: Pontmain and Marian Apparitions." *Marian Library Studies* 2 (December): 95-98.

GEARING, FRED
1968 "Preliminary notes on ritual in village Greece." *In Contributions to Mediterranean Sociology.* J. G. Peristiany, ed., pp. 65-72. Paris: Mouton.

GEISENDORFER, JAMES V. (ed.)
1977 *Directory of Religious Organizations.* Washington, D.C.: McGrath Publishing.

GERHARD, HEINZ P.
1964 *The Icons of the Mother of God.* Vaduz, Liechtenstein: Overseas Publishers.

GIEYSTOR, A.
1979 *History of Poland.* 2nd edition. Warsaw: Polish Scientific Publishers.

GILLETT, H. M.
1952 *Famous Shrines of Our Lady.* Westminster, Md.: Newman Press.

GILMORE, DAVID D.
1982 "Anthropology of the Mediterranean." *In Annual Reviews in Anthropology.* B. Siegel, ed. 11: 175-205. Palo Alto: *Annual Reviews Inc.*

1983 "Sexual ideology in Adalusian oral literature: a comparative view of a Mediterranean complex." *Ethnology* 22 (July): 241-252.

GILMORE , M. M., and D. D. GILMORE

1979 "Machismo: a psychodynamic approach (Spain)." *Journal of Psychological Anthropology* 2 (Spring): 281-300.

GIMBUTAS, MARIJA

1982 *The Goddesses and Gods of Old Europe: 6500-3500 B.C.* Berkeley: University of California Press.

GOUGH, MICHAEL

1973 *The Origins of Christian Art.* London: Thames and Hudson.

GRAEF, HILDA

1963a *Mary, a History of Doctrine and Devotion.* Volume 1. *From the Beginning to the Eve of the Reformation.* New York: Sheed and Ward.

1963b *The Devotion to Our Lady.* New York: Hawthorn Publishers.

1965 *Mary, a History of Doctrine and Devotion.* Volume 2. *From the Reformation to the Present Day.*

GREELEY, ANDREW

1977 *The Mary Myth: On the Femininity of God.* New York: Seabury Press.

GRIMM, HAROLD J.

1973 *The Reformation Era: 1500-1650.* 2nd Edition. New York: Macmillan.

GROSS, FELIKS

1973 Il Paese: *Values and Social Change in an Italian Village.* New York: New York University Press.

HAFFERT, JOHN M.

1950 *Russia Will Be Converted.* New York: AMI International Press.

HAMMOND, N.G.L., and H. H. SCULLARD

1970 *The Oxford Classical Dictionary.* 2nd edition. Oxford: Clarendon Press.

HARDON, JOHN A., S.J.

1975 *The Catholic Catechism.* Garden City, N.Y.: Doubleday.

HAYWOOD, RICHARD M.

1967 *Ancient Rome.* New York: David McKay.

HEICHELHEIM, FRITZ M., and CEDRIC A. YEO

1962 *A History of the Roman People.* Englewood Cliffs, N.J.: Prentice-Hall.

HENDERSON, REV. G. GORDON

1983 "The apparition of Our Lady of Guadalupe: The image, the origin of the pilgrimage." *Marian Studies* 34 (Sept.): 35-47.

HERBERT, JAMES

1983 *Shrine.* London: New English Library.

HERZFELD, MICHAEL
1984   "The horns of a Mediterraneanist dilemma." *American Ethnologist*
11 (August): 439-454.

HEYOB, SHARON KELLY
1975   *The Cult of Isis among Women in the Graeco-Roman World.* Leiden:
Brill.

HIDEC, MAX
1969   Les secrets de La Salette. Paris: Nouvelles Editions Latines.

HILGERS, JOSEPH
1912   "Scapular." *In The Catholic Encyclopedia.* 13: 508-414. New York:
Robert Appleton.

HILLERBAND, HANS J.
1973   *The World of the Reformation.* New York: Charles Scribner's Sons.

HIRN, YRJO
1957   *The Sacred Shrine.* Boston: Beacon Press.
[1912]

HOLM, NILS
1982   "Mysticism and intense experiences." *Journal for the Scientific Study
of Religion* 21 (September): 268-276.

HOLWECK, FREDERICK
1907   "Assumption of the Blessed Virgin Mary." *In The Catholic Encyclopedia.* 2: 6-7. New York: Robert Appleton.
1910   "Immaculate Conception." *In The Catholic Encyclopedia.* 7: 674-
681. New York: Robert Appleton.

HOROWITZ, M., and J. E. ADAMS
1970   "Hallucinations on brain stimulation: evidence for revision of the
Penfield hypothesis." *In Origin and Mechanisms of Hallucinations.*
Wolfram Keup, ed., pp. 23-35. New York: Plenum Press.

HULTKRANTZ, AKE
1961   "Bachofen and the Mother Goddess." *Ethnos* 1-2: 75-85.

HUMPHRIES, ROLFE (tr.)
1968   *Lucretius: The Way Things Are.* Bloomington: Indiana University
Press.

HUTTER, IRMGARD
1971   *Early Christian and Byzantine Art.* New York: Universe Books.

HYDE, WALTER W.
1946   *Paganism to Christianity in the Roman Empire.* Philadelphia: University of Pennsylvania Press.

ISWOLSKY, HELENE
1960   *Christ in Russia.* Milwaukee: Bruce Publishing Company.

JAFFE, STEVEN
1966   "Hallucinations in children at a state hospital." *Psychiatric Quarterly*
40 (January): 88-95.

JAMES, E. O.

1959   *The Cult of the Mother Goddess*. New York: Barnes and Noble.

JARRET, BEDE

1911   "Pilgrimages." *In The Catholic Encyclopedia*. 12: 85-99. New York: Robert Appleton.

JOHNSTON, FRANCIS

1981   *The Wonder of Guadalupe*. Rockford, Ill.: Tan Books.

JOHNSTON, HAROLD W.

1973   *The Private Life of the Romans*. New York: Cooper Square Pub-
[1932]   lishers.

JONES, ERNST

1951a   *Essays in Applied Psychoanalysis*. Volume 2. London: Hogarth Press.

1951b   "The Madonna's conception through the ear." *In Essays*
[1914]   *in Applied Psychoanalysis*, 2: 266-357. London: Hogarth Press.

1951c   "A psycho-analytic study of the Holy Ghost concept."
[1922]   *In Essays in Applied Psychoanalysis*, 2: 358-373. London: Hogarth Press.

1951d   "Psycho-analysis and the Christian Religion." *In Essays in Applied*
[1930]   *Psycho-analysis*, 2: 198-211. London: Hogarth Press.

JUNG, CARL G.

1970a   *Four Archetypes: Mother, Rebirth, Spirit, Trickster*. Princeton: Princeton University Press.

1970b   *Mysterium Coniunctionis: An Inquiry into the Separation and Synthesis of Psychic Opposites in Alchemy*. 2nd edition. Princeton: Princeton University Press.

1976   *The Symbolic Life: Miscellaneous Writings*. Princeton: Princeton University Press.

JUVENAL

1983   *Sixteen Satires upon the Ancient Harlot*. Steven Robinson, tr. Manchester: Carcanet New Press.

KAHANE, REUBEN

1984   "Hypotheses on patronage and social change: comparative perspective." *Ethnology* 23 (January): 13-24.

KELLER, JOHN ESTEN

1949   *Motif-Index of Mediaeval Spanish Exempla*. Knoxville: University of Tennessee Press.

KENNEDY, JOHN S.

1961   "The lady in tears." *In A Woman Clothed with the Sun*. John J. Delaney, ed., pp. 89-112. Garden City, N.Y.: Doubleday.

KEYES, FRANCES P.

1941   *The Grace of Guadalupe*. New York: Julian Messner, Inc.

1961 "Bernadette and the beautiful lady." *In A Woman Clothed with the Sun*. John J. Delaney, ed., pp. 115-143. Garden City, N.Y.: Doubleday.

KIDD, B. J.

1922 *A History of the Church to A.D. 461*. Volume 1. Oxford: Clarendon.

KIRAY, MUBECCEL

1976 "The new role of mothers: changing intra-familial relationships in a small town in Turkey." *In Mediterranean Family Structures*. J. G. Peristiany, ed., pp. 261-271. Cambridge: Cambridge University Press.

KLASSEN, PETER J.

1979 *Europe in the Reformation*. Englewood Cliffs, N.J.: Prentice-Hall.

KRALJEVIĆ, SVETOZAR

1984 *The Apparitions of Our Lady of Medjugorje*. Michael Scanlon, ed. Chicago: Franciscan Herald Press.

KROLL, JEROME, and BERNARD BACHRACH

1982 "Visions and psychopathology in the middle ages." *Journal of Nervous and Mental Disease* 170 (January): 41-49.

KURTZ, DONALD V.

1982 "The Virgin of Guadalupe and the politics of becoming human." *Journal of Anthropological Research* 38 (Summer): 194-210.

LA BARRE, WESTON

1969 *The Peyote Cult*. Enlarged edition. New York: Schocken Books.

LAFAYE, JACQUES

1976 *Quetzalcoatl and Guadalupe: The Formation of Mexican National Consciousness*. Chicago: University of Chicago Press.

LAMBERT, M. D.

1977 *Medieval Hersey: Popular Movements from Bogomil to Hus*. London: Edward Arnold Publishers.

LASSERRE, HENRI

1872 *Our Lady of Lourdes*. New York: D. and J. Sadlier.
[1868]

LATOURETTE, KENNETH SCOTT

1937 *A History of the Expansion of Christianity*. Volume 1. *The First Five Centuries*. New York: Harper and Brothers.

LAURENTIN, RENÉ

1964 *Mary's Place in the Church*. London: Burns and Oates.

1965 *The Question of Mary*. New York: Holt, Rinehart, and Winston.

LEACH, EDMUND

1969 "Virgin birth." *In Genesis as Myth and Other Essays*. E. Leach, ed.,
[1966] pp. 85-122. London: Jonathan Cape.

LEFF, GORDON
  1967   *Heresy in the Later Middle Ages.* 2 volumes. New York: Barnes and
         Noble.
LEROI-GOURHAN, ANDRE
  1967   *Treasures of Prehistoric Art.* New York: Abrams.
LEWIS, OSCAR
  1959   *Five Families: Mexican Case Studies in the Culture of Poverty.* New
         York: Basic Books.
  1965   *La Vida.* New York: Random House.
LIPOWSKI, ZBIGNIEW
  1980   "Organic mental disorders: introduction and review of syn-
         dromes." *In Comprehensive Textbook of Psychiatry III.* H. Kaplan,
         A. Freedman, and B. Saddock, eds. 2: 1,359-1,392. Baltimore:
         Williams and Wilkins.
LIVY
  1940   *Livy.* Frank Gardner Moore, tr. 13 volumes. London: Heinemann.
LOWRIE, WALTER
  1947   *Art in the Early Church.* New York: Pantheon Books.
MACMULLEN, RAMSAY
  1974   *Roman Social Relations: 50 B.C. to A.D. 284.* New Haven: Yale Uni-
         versity Press.
  1981   *Paganism in the Roman Empire.* New Haven: Yale University Press.
MALHERBE, ABRAHAM J.
  1977   *Social Aspects of Early Christianity.* Baton Rouge: Louisiana State
         University Press.
MALINOWSKI, BRONISLAW
  1955   *Sex and Repression in Savage Society.* New York: New American Li-
  [1927] brary.
MALOY, ROBERT M.
  1961   "The Virgin of the Poor." *In A Woman Clothed with the Sun.* John J.
         Delaney, ed., pp. 215-267. Garden City, N.Y.: Doubleday.
MARASPINI, A. L.
  1968   *The Study of an Italian Village.* The Hague: Mouton.
MARGOLIS, ROBERT; D. MARGOLIS; and KIRK W. ELIFSON
  1979   "Typology of religious experience." *Journal for the Scientific Study of
         Religion* 18 (March): 61-67.
MARNHAM, PATRICK
  1981   *Lourdes: A Modern Pilgrimage.* New York: Coward, McCann and
         Geoghegan.
MARROU, HENRI
  1964   "The great persecution to the emergence of medieval Christianity."

In The First Six Hundred Years. Jean Danielou and Henri Marrou, eds., pp. 221-328. London: Longman and Todd.

MARTIAL
1920   *Epigrams.* 2 volumes. Walter C. A. Ker, tr. London: Heinemann.

MASON, JOHN (tr.)
1851   *Lucretius: On the Nature of Things.* London: Bohn.

MAY, HERBERT G., and BRUCE M. METZGER (eds.)
1973   *The New Oxford Annotated Bible.* Revised Standard Version. New York: Oxford University Press.

MCGRAITH, WILLIAM C., MSGR.
1961   "The Lady of the rosary." *In A Woman Clothed with the Sun.* John J. Delaney, ed., pp. 175-212. New York: Doubleday.

MEEKS, WAYNE
1983   *The First Urban Christians.* New Haven: Yale University Press.

MELLAART, JAMES
1975   *The Neolithic of the Near East.* London: Thames and Hudson.

MEYENDORF, JOHN
1962   *The Orthodox Church.* New York: Pantheon Books.

MICHELL, JOHN, and ROBERT J. M. RICKARD
1977   *Phenomena: A Book of Wonders.* London: Thames and Hudson.

MIEGGE, GIOVANNI
1955   *The Virgin Mary: The Roman Catholic Doctrine.* Philadelphia: Westminster Press.

MINN, LOUIS
1980   "Clinical manifestations of psychiatric disorders." *In Comprehensive Textbook of Psychiatry III.* H. Kaplan, A. Freedman, and B. Saddock, eds. 1: 990-1,034. Baltimore: Williams and Wilkins.

MOORE, BRIAN
1983   *Cold Heaven.* Toronto: McClelland and Stewart.

MOSS, LEONARD W., and STEPHEN C. CAPPANARI
1982   "In quest of the Black Virgin: she is black because she is black." *In Mother Worship.* James J. Preston, ed., pp. 53-74. Chapel Hill: University of North Carolina Press.

MOTOLINIA, FRAY TORIBO
1950   *History of the Indians of New Spain.* E. A. Foster, tr. and ed. Santa Fe, N.M.: Cortes Society.

MUNN, HENRY
1973   "The mushrooms of language." *In Hallucinogens and Shamanism.* Michael J. Harner, ed., pp. 86-122, New York: Oxford University Press.

MURDOCK, GEORGE P., and CATERINA PROVOST
  1973   "Measurement of cultural complexity." *Ethnology* 12 (October): 379-392.
MURDOCK, GEORGE P., and DOUGLAS R. WHITE
  1969   "Standard Cross Cultural Sample." *Ethnology* 8 (October): 329-369.
MURDOCK, GEORGE P., and SUZANNE WILSON
  1972   "Settlement patterns and community organization: cross cultural codes 3." *Ethnology* 11 (July): 254-295.
MURRAY, COLLIN
  1981   *Families Divided: The Impact of Migrant Labor in Lesotho.* Cambridge: Cambridge University Press.
NADELSON, LESLEE
  1981   "Pigs, women, and the men's house in Amazonia: an analysis of six Mundurucu myths." *In Sexual Meanings: the Cultural Construction of Gender and Sexuality*, S. Ortner and H. Whitehead, eds., pp. 240-272. Cambridge: Cambridge University Press.
NEAME, ALAN
  1967   *The Happening at Lourdes: The Sociology of the Grotto.* New York: Simon and Schuster.
NELSON, CYNTHIA
  1973   "The Virgin of Zeitoun." *Worldview* 16 (September): 5-11.
NEUMANN, ERICH
  1963   *The Great Mother: An Analysis of the Archetype.* Princeton: Princeton
  [1955] University Press.
NEWMAN, JOHN HENRY
  1967   *Apologia Pro Vita Sua.* Martin J. Svaglic, ed. Oxford: Clarendon.
  [1865]
NORTHCOTE, J. SPENCER, REV.
  1852   "Summary of his sermon." *The Times*, October 26, 1852, p. 3.
  1875   *Celebrated Sanctuaries of the Madonna.* Philadelphia: Peter F. Cunningham and Son.
O'CARROLL, MICHAEL
  1982   *Theotokos: A Theological Encyclopedia of the Blessed Virgin Mary.* Wilmington, Del.: Michael Glazier.
O'CONNELL, CHARLES C.
  1948   *Light over Fatima.* Westminster, Md.: Newman Bookshop.
O'KEEFE, DANIEL
  1949   *The Story of Knock.* Cork: Mercier Press.
O'NEIL, C.
  1967   "Devotion to the saints." *In New Catholic Encyclopedia.* 12: 962-963. New York: McGraw-Hill.

OVID
1947   *Hebroides* and *Amores*. Grant Showerman, tr. London: Heinemann.
1951   *Ovid's Fasti*. Sir James Frazer, tr. London: Heinemann.

OWENS, L. G.
1967   "Virgin birth." *In New Catholic Encyclopedia*. 14: 692-697. New York: McGraw-Hill.

PAIGE, JEFFERY M.
1974   "Kinship and polity in stateless societies." *American Journal of Sociology* 80 (September): 301-320.

PALMER, JEROME
1981   "Virgin Mary in Egypt." *In Miracles*. Martin Ebon, ed., pp. 118-126. New York: New American Library.

PARKER, SEYMOUR; JANET SMITH; and JOSEPH GINAT
1975   "Father absence and cross-sex identity: the puberty rites controversy revisited." *American Ethnologist* 2 (November): 687-706.

PARSONS, ANNE
1969   *Belief, Magic and Anomie: Essays in Psychological Anthropology*. New York: Free Press.

PASCAL, CECIL BENNET
1964   *The Cults of Cisalpine Gaul*. Latomus: Revue d'Etudes Latines 75: 1-222.

PATAI, RAPHAEL
1967   *The Hebrew Goddess*. New York: KTAV Publishing House.

PELLETIER, JOSEPH
1971   *Our Lady Comes to Garabandal*. Worcester, Mass: Assumption Publications.

PETERS, EDWARD
1980   *Heresy and Authority in Medieval Europe: Documents in Translation*. Philadelphia: University of Pennsylvania Press.

PETITOT, HENRI
1955   *Saint Bernadette*. Cork: Mercier Press.

PETTERSSON, OLOF
1967   *Mother Earth: An Analysis of the Mother Earth Concepts According to Albrecht Dieterich*. Berlin: Lund.

PIUS XII, POPE
1948   "Apostolic constitution on the sodality of Our Lady." *In On Sodalities of Our Lady* (pamphlet), pp. 1-14. El Paso, Tex.: Revista Catolica Press.

PORTELL, J.
1970   "Hallucinations in pre-adolescent schizophrenic children." *In Origin and Mechanisms of Hallucinations*. Wolfram Keup, ed., pp. 405-411. New York: Plenum Press.

PURCELL, MARY
1961 "Our Lady of silence." *In A Woman Clothed with the Sun*. John J. Delaney, ed., pp. 147-171. Garden City, N.Y.: Doubleday.

RABKIN, R.
1970 "Do you see things that aren't there: construct validity of the concept 'Hallucination,' " *In Origin and Mechanisms of Hallucinations*. E.W. Keup, ed., pp. 115-123. New York: Plenum Press.

RAHNER, KARL
1963 *Visions and Prophecies*. Freiburg: Herder and Herder.
1981 *Concern for the Church*. New York: Crossroad Publishing.

REHAGE, J. W.
1967 "Canon law of celibacy." *In New Catholic Encyclopedia*. 3: 366-369. New York: McGraw-Hill.

REIDER, NORMAN
1959 "Chess, Oedipus and the Mater Dolorosa." *International Journal of Psychoanalysis* 40 (516): 320-333.

RICE, PATRICIA C.
1981 "Prehistoric Venuses: symbols of motherhood or womanhood?" *Journal of Anthropological Research* 37 (Winter): 402-414.

RICHARD, ABBE M.
1971 *What Happened at Pontmain*. Washington, N.J.: Ave Maria Insti-
[1939] tute.

RINALDI, GIAN M.
1981 "A madonna's fierce 'armada.' " *In Miracles*. Martin Ebon, ed., pp. 53-63. New York: New American Library.

ROGERS, S. C.
1975 "Female forms of power and the myth of male dominance: a model of female/male interaction in peasant society." *American Ethnologist* 2 (November): 727-756.

ROGO, D. SCOTT
1983 *Miracles*. Chicago: Contemporary Press.

ROSE, H. J.
1928 *A Handbook of Greek Mythology*. London: Methuen.
1959 *Religion in Greece and Rome*. New York: Harper.

ROSTOVTZEFF, M.
1926 *The Social and Economic History of the Roman Empire*. Oxford: Clarendon.

RUSSELL, JEFFREY (ed.)
1971 *Religious Dissent in the Middle Ages*. New York: John Wiley and Sons.

RYAN, FINBAR, THE MOST REVEREND
1949 *Our Lady of Fatima*. Westminster, Md.: Newman Press.

SAHAGUN, BERNARDINO, FRAY

1959 *General History of the Things of New Spain: Book Nine, The Merchants.* C. Dibble and A. Anderson, trs. Santa Fe, N.M.: School of American Research and University of Utah.

1969 *General History of the Things of New Spain: Book Six, Rhetoric and Moral Philosophy.* C. Dibble and A. Anderson, trs. Santa Fe, N.M.: School of American Research and University of Utah.

1979 *General History of the Things of New Spain: Book Four, The Soothsayers, and Book Five, the Omens.* C. Dibble and A. Anderson, trs. Santa Fe, N.M.: School of American Research and University of Utah.

SALIBA, JOHN A., S.J.

1975 "The Virgin-birth debate in anthropological literature: a critical assessment." *Theological Studies* 36 (September): 428-454.

SANTOS, LUCIA

1976 *Fatima in Lucia's Own Words.* Fr. L. Kondor, ed. Fatima, Portugal:
[1935-   Postulation Centre.
1941]

SAUNDERS, GEORGE R.

1981 "Men and women in southern Europe: a review of some aspects of cultural complexity." *Journal of Psychoanalytical Anthropology* 4 (Fall): 435-466.

SCHAFF, PHILIP

1910 *History of the Christian Church.* Volume 2. *Ante-Nicene Christianity.* New York: Charles Scribner's Sons.

SCHILLER, GERTRUD

1972 *Iconography of Christian Art.* Volume 2. *The Passion of Jesus Christ.* Greenwich, Conn.: New York Graphic Society.

SCULLARD, H. H.

1982 *From the Gracchi to Nero: A History of Rome from 133 B.C. to A.D. 68.* 5th edition. London: Methuen.

SHARKEY, DON

1961a "The Virgin with the golden heart." *In A Woman Clothed with the Sun.* John J. Delaney, ed., pp. 215-238. Garden City, N.Y.: Doubleday.

1961b *The Woman Shall Conquer.* New York: All Saints Press.

SHOWERMAN, GRANT

1901 "The Great Mother of the Gods." *Bulletin of the University of Wisconsin, Philology and Literature* Series 1 (February): 221-333.

SIEGAL, RONALD, and MURRAY E. JARVIK

1975 "Drug induced hallucinations in animals and man." *In Hallucina-*

tions: Behavior, Experience and Theory. R. K. Siegal and L. J. West, eds., pp. 81-161. New York: John Wiley and Sons.

SINGH, PURUSHOTTAM

1974 *Neolithic Cultures of Western Asia.* London: Seminar Press.

SINNIGER, WILLIAM, and ARTHUR BOAK

1977 *A History of Rome to A.D. 565.* 6th edition. New York: Macmillan.

SLATER, PHILIP E.

1968 *The Glory of Hera.* Boston: Beacon Press.

SMITH, JODY BRANT

1983 *The Image of Guadalupe: Myth or Miracle?* Garden City, N.Y.: Doubleday.

SMITH, RAYMOND

1956 *The Negro Family in British Guiana.* London: Routledge and Kegan Paul.

SMITH, W. ROBERTSON

1894 *The Religion of the Semites.* London: A. and C. Black.

SMITH, WILLIAM B., REV.

1980 "The theology of the virginity *in partu* and its consequences for the Church's teaching on chastity." *Marian Studies* 31 (December): 99-110.

SOLOMON, PHILIP, and JACK MENDELSON

1962 "Hallucinatons in sensory deprivation." *In Hallucinations.* Louis J. West, ed., pp. 135-145. New York: Grune and Stratton.

SPINKA, MATHEW

1966 *John Hus' Concept of the Church.* Princeton: Princeton University Press.

SPIRO, MELFORD

1979 "What ever happened to the id?" *American Anthropologist* 81 (March): 5-13.

STACEY, JOHN

1964 *John Wyclife and Reform.* Philadelphia: Westminster Press.

STEPHENS, WILLIAM N.

1962 *The Oedipus Complex: Cross-Cultural Evidence.* New York: Free Press of Gencoe.

STERN, JEAN

1975 "La Salette: bibliographie." *Marian Library Studies* 7 (December): 3-302.

1980 *La Salette: documents authentiques.* Paris: Desclée de Brouwer.

STEVENSON, J.

1978 *The Catacombs: Rediscovered Monuments of Early Christianity.* London: Thames and Hudson.

STORR, ANTHONY

1973   *Jung*. London: Fontana/Collins.

STRAUS, ERWIN W.

1962   "Phenomenology of hallucinations." *In Hallucinations*. Louis J. West, ed., pp. 220-238. New York: Grune and Stratton.

SWAN, HENRY H.

1959   *My Work with Necedah*. Volume 4. Necedah, Wisc.: For My God and Country, Inc.

SWANSON, GUY

1967   *Religion and Regime: A Sociological Account of the Reformation*. Ann Arbor: University of Michigan Press.

1968   "To live in concord with society: two empirical studies of primary relations." *In Cooley and Sociological Analysis*. A. Reiss, ed., pp. 87-124. Ann Arbor: University of Michigan Press.

1973   "The search for a guardian spirit: a process of empowerment in simpler societies." *Ethnology* 12 (July): 359-378.

1974   "Descent and polity: the meaning of Paige's findings." *American Journal of Sociology* 80 (September): 321-328.

SWATOS, WILLIAM H.

1981   "Church-sect and cult: bringing mysticism back in." *Sociological Analysis* 42 (Spring): 17-26.

TENTORI, TULLIO

1982   "An Italian religious feast: the *fujenti* rites of the Madonna dell'Arco, Naples." *In Mother Worship*. James J. Preston, ed., 94-122. Chapel Hill: University of North Carolina Press.

THOMAS, L. EUGENE, and PAMELA E. COOPER

1978   "Measurement and incidence of mystical experiences: an exploratory study." *Journal for the Scientific Study of Religion* 17 (December): 433-437.

THOMPSON, SMITH

1955   *Motif-Index of Folk-Literature*. 6 volumes. Bloomington: Indiana
[1932-   University Press.
1936]

THURSTON, HERBERT

1908   "Celibacy of the clergy." *In The Catholic Encyclopedia*. 3: 481-488. New York: Robert Appleton.

1927   "The false visionaries of Lourdes." *The Month* 3 (October): 289-301.

1933   "Lourdes and La Salette: a contrast." *The Month* 162 (December): 526-537.

1934   *Beauraing and Other Apparitions: An Account of Some Borderline Cases in the Psychology of Mysticism.* London: Burns and Oates.

TUDEN, ARTHUR, and CATHERINE MARSHALL

1972   "Political organization: cross-cultural codes 4." *Ethnology* 11 (October): 436-464.

TURNER, VICTOR, and EDITH TURNER

1982   "Postindustrial Marian pilgrimage." *In Mother Worship.* James Preston, ed., pp. 145-173. Chapel Hill: University of North Carolina Press.

UCKO, PETER J., and ANDRÉE ROSENFELD

1972   "Anthropomorphic representations in palaeolithic art." *In Santander Symposium*, M. A. Basch and M. A. Garcia Guinea, eds., pp. 149-187. Madrid: Santander Press.

ULLATHORNE, WILLIAM, REV.

1942   *The Holy Mountain of La Salette.* Altamont, N.Y.: La Salette Press.
[1854]

VAILLANT, GEORGE C.

1962   *Aztecs of Mexico.* Revised by S. B. Vaillant. Harmondsworth: Penguin.

van der MEER, F.

1967   *Early Christian Art.* London: Faber and Faber.

VAN HOOF, MARY ANN

1971   *Revelations and Messages.* Necedah, Wisc.: For My God and Country, Inc.

VERMASEREN, MAARTEN J.

1966   *The Legend of Attis in Greek and Roman Art.* Leiden: Brill.

1977   *Cybele and Attis: The Myth and the Cult.* London: Thames and Hudson.

VERNON, JACK A., and THOMAS E. MCGILL

1962   "Sensory deprivation and hallucinations." *In Hallucinations.* Louis J. West, ed., pp. 146-152. New York: Grune and Stratton.

VESSELS, JANE

1980   "Fatima: beacon for Portugal's faithful." *National Geographic Magazine* 158 (December): 833-839.

von MATT, LEONARD, and FRANCIS TROCHU

1957   *St. Bernadette.* Chicago: Henry Regnery.

WALSH, MICHAEL

1955   *The Apparition at Knock: A Survey of Facts and Evidence.* Leinster: Leinster Leader.

1970   *The Glory of Knock.* Tuam, Ireland: Jarlath's College.

WALSH, WILLIAM J.

    1904a *The Apparitions and Shrines of Heaven's Bright Queen.* Volume 1. New York: Cary-Stafford.

    1904b *The Apparitions and Shrines of Heaven's Bright Queen.* Volume 2. New York: Cary-Stafford.

    1904c *The Apparitions and Shrines of Heaven's Bright Queen.* Volume 3. New York: Cary-Stafford.

    1904d *The Apparitions and Shrines of Heaven's Bright Queen.* Volume 4. New York: Cary-Stafford.

WALSH, WILLIAM THOMAS

    1954 *Our Lady of Fatima.* New York: Doubleday.

WARNER, MARINA

    1976 *Alone of All Her Sex.* New York: Alfred Knopf.

WEIGERT-VOWINKEL, EDITH

    1938 "The cult and mythology of the *Magna Mater* from the standpoint of psychoanalysis." *Psychiatry* 1 (August): 347-378.

WEINSTEIN, DONALD, and RUDOLPH M. BELL

    1982 *Saints and Society: The Two Worlds of Western Christendom, 1000-1700.* Chicago: University of Chicago Press.

WEINSTEIN, E. A.

    1970 "Relationships between delusions and hallucinations in brain disease." *In Origin and Mechanisms of Hallucinations.* Wolfram Keup, ed., pp. 53-57. New York: Plenum Press.

WHALE, JOHN (ed.)

    1980 *The Man Who Leads the Church.* San Francisco: Harper & Row.

WHYTE, MARTIN KING

    1978a *The Status of Women in Preindustrial Societies.* Princeton: Princeton University Press.

    1978b "Cross-cultural codes dealing with the relative status of women." *Ethnology* 17 (April): 211-237.

WILKINSON, L. P.

    1975 *The Roman Experience.* London: Paul Elek.

WILLIAMS, HAROLD L.; GARY O. MORRIS; and ARDIE LUBIN

    1962 "Illusions, hallucinations, and sleep loss." *In Hallucinations.* Louis J. West, ed., pp. 158-165. New York: Grune and Stratton.

WILSON, BRYAN

    1976 "Cult of Mary." *New Society* 36 (May 13): 367.

WITT, R. E.

    1971 *Isis in the Greco-Roman World.* London: Thames and Hudson.

WOLF, ERIC R.

1958 "The Virgin of Guadalupe: a Mexican national symbol." *Journal of American Folklore* 71 (January): 34-39.

1969 "Society and symbols in Latin Europe and in the Islamic Near East." *Anthropological Quarterly* 7 (July): 287-301.

YORBURG, BETTY

1983 *Families and Societies.* New York: Columbia University Press.

ZALECKI, MARIAN

1976 "Theology of a Marian shrine: Our Lady of Czestochowa." *Marian Library Studies,* New Series 8: 51-315.

ZERNOV, NICHOLAS

1961 *Eastern Christendom.* London: Weidenfeld and Nicolson.

ZUCKERMAN, M.

1970 "Reported sensations and hallucinations in sensory deprivation." *In Origin and Mechanisms of Hallucinations.* Wolfram Keup, ed., pp. 133-148. New York: Plenum Press.

INDEX

LIBRARY OF CONGRESS CATALOGING-IN-PUBLICATION DATA

CARROLL, MICHAEL P., 1944–
THE CULT OF THE VIRGIN MARY.

BIBLIOGRAPHY: P.   INCLUDES INDEX.
I. MARY, BLESSED VIRGIN, SAINT—CULT.   2. MARY, BLESSED VIRGIN, SAINT—
APPARITIONS AND MIRACLES.   I. TITLE.
BT645.C34 1986   232.91   85-43273
ISBN 0-691-09420-9 (ALK. PAPER)